Honey,
I'm Home!

Honey, I'm Home!

SITCOMS: SELLING THE AMERICAN DREAM

Gerard Jones

GROVE WEIDENFELD
New York

Published by Grove Weidenfeld
A division of Grove Press, Inc.
841 Broadway
New York, New York 10003–4793

Published in Canada by General Publishing Company, Ltd.

Photographs have been provided by kind permission of: Bettmann Archive; Archive Photos, NYC; and Columbia Pictures Television.

LIBRARY OF CONGRESS CATALOGING-IN-PUBLICATION DATA

Jones, Gerard.
Honey, I'm home! : sitcoms, selling the American dream / by Gerard Jones.—1st ed.
p.   cm.
Includes bibliographical references.
ISBN 0-8021-1308-7 (alk. paper)
1. Comedy programs—United States.   2. United States—Social conditions—1945–   3. Television broadcasting—Social aspects—United States.   I. Title.
PN1992.8.C66J65   1992
302.23′45′0973—dc20   91-19761
CIP

Manufactured in the United States of America

Printed on acid-free paper

Designed by Kathryn Parise

First Edition 1992

10   9   8   7   6   5   4   3   2   1

For LESLIE JONES, my mother,
who always let me watch TV but never
let me get away without
thinking about it

Acknowledgments

T hanks are due to the kindly librarians at the Museum of Broadcasting in New York and the UCLA Film Archives, to Jeanne McLellan of the Bettmann Archive for her sympathy and ingenuity, and to those who bore with me, let me expound, and gave their perspectives during this endless project: Jennie Kajiko, Joe Filice, Will Jacobs, Ray Jones, and others, to whom I will apologize after publication. This book might not have existed if not for the people at *TV Gold* magazine, who invited me to write the articles that formed the nucleus of the project, and Carol Mann, who saw a book where there were only fragments. It surely would not have been what it is without the attentions of Mark Polizzotti, my initial editor, and it would have suffered under a much duller title without his successor, Bryan Oettel.

Contents

All of us here in this room are rather like one big family and I think our family could be a lot happier if we were considerate and friendly toward one another. And as far as little boys and girls liking each other, well, you don't have to be silly about it, but I do think you should have mutual respect and learn to get along together. You know, if you do that, you'll be taking a big step toward becoming the kind of men and women we want you to be.

—*Miss Landers,* Leave It to Beaver

Edith—stifle yourself!

—*Archie Bunker,* All in the Family

Honey, I'm Home!

Introduction

Theo wants to buy an expensive designer shirt to impress a girl. His father, Cliff, who has his priorities straight, forbids him. Theo is resentful. His sister Denise, who fancies herself a fine seamstress, offers to sew him a duplicate of the designer shirt. The household is briefly united in anticipation of this simple solution to the problem. But when Denise finishes the shirt, it proves to be an asymmetrical grotesquerie. Theo is angry and depressed. His parents, however, having their priorities straight, shame him into wearing the shirt on his double date, for his sister's sake. Social disaster looms. Then, to Theo's surprise—and our reassured chuckles—his friends think his shirt is "cool." Theo impresses the girl. He forgives his sister. Cliff chortles knowingly, content that paternal wisdom has been upheld, youthful pretensions have been exposed as shams, sound priorities have been restored, and family discord has been healed. Cliff makes a joke to relieve the last remaining tension. Music plays; credits roll. A woman appears on our screen to sell us Weight Watchers frozen foods.

This little drama played on *The Cosby Show*, the most popular situation comedy of the 1980s, but it had played hundreds, thousands of times before—with different characters and different pretexts, but always the

3

same basic structure: Domestic harmony is threatened when a character develops a desire that runs counter to the group's welfare, or misunderstands a situation because of poor communication, or contacts a disruptive outside element. The voice of the group—usually the voice of the father or equivalent chief executive—tries to restore harmony but fails. The dissenter grabs at an easy, often unilateral solution. The solution fails, and the dissenter must surrender to the group for rescue. The problem turns out to be not very serious after all, once everyone remembers to communicate and surrender his or her selfish goals. The wisdom of the group and its executive is proved. Everyone, including the dissenter, is happier than at the outset.

It happened that way with Cliff and Theo, Mary and Murray, Rob and Laura, Lucy and Ricky, Jake and Molly. As predictable and reassuring as ritual drama. Except that its roots lie not in ritual but in commerce.

The sitcom is á corporate product. It is a mass consumption commodity, designed, like a sedan, to be constructed decade after decade on the same safe, reliable pattern, yet allowing enough surface variations to be resold as a new product every few years. On a less conscious level, it is an expression of the underlying assumptions of the corporate culture that has come to dominate American society. The ideals upheld by the sitcom are the ideals on which modern bureaucratic business and government are founded: The consensual solution is the best solution; ideology and self-interest only stand in the way of mutual benefit; the boss is the boss because he is more experienced at operating the systems of social life; the boss's wisdom must be respected, but only when he is responsive to the needs of his charges; disagreement is usually caused by bad communication; there is no real conflict between our various interests; we all benefit by compromising, not by standing on principle; there is no reason we all can't end up happy. The promises of bureaucratic democracy, managerial capitalism, secular humanism, and mass consumption are miniaturized, tested, and found true in the funny travails of TV families. The sitcom is the Miracle Play of consumer society.

The sitcom is more directly, of course, about families and workplaces than about society in the greater sense. But even the family has had to adapt to our times with many of the same tools that industry and government have used. Sex roles have blurred; economic rules have changed; generational conflicts have become steadily more complicated. Patriarchal authority is nearly dead, and tradition is weak. Negotiation, consensus, and compromise have become essential in managing the modern

4

family. No problems, of course, are ever solved as easily as on television. Perhaps, with such methods, no fundamental problems are ever fully solved at all. But sitcoms at least give us clues to how to patch up our difficulties well enough to laugh together and get through the evening. The sitcom is a primer on managing our private lives by the systems of our new mass society.

The sitcom is also a mirror. A foggy mirror, to be sure, that misses a lot of our blemishes and care lines, a mirror with a rosy glow and a limited range; but one of its functions has always been to show the American family to itself, to open an alternate family room within our own, to let us stop and check ourselves over before we step back outside into the winds of change. Some shows hold up models of what our culture thinks we should be like: the Cleavers, the Bradys, the Huxtables. Others enable us to dispel some anxiety by laughing affectionately at those who have even more trouble dealing with daily life than we do: the Kramdens, the Clampetts, the Bundys. Both types reassure us that there are others out there like us, that we will always work out a way to get by.

The sitcom is a daydream. In an age when the family is threatened and co-workers are opponents and neighbors are strangers, it's pleasant to have an imitation family to retreat into. Wouldn't it be nice to be able to go, as one theme song puts it, "where everybody knows your name, and they're always glad you came"? For a half hour a week the sitcom can make that possible.

The sitcom may even be a teacher. At times the producers of the programs have certainly treated it as though it were. Compared, of course, with what we learn about life from family, friends, co-workers, teachers, personal misadventures, and even the quasi reality of mass media news, what we gather from TV entertainment is inconsiderable. But I know that when I was little, I used to search domestic comedies for clues to how the grown-up world functioned outside what I could see in my own home; I believe I even thought that the shenanigans of Rob and Buddy and Sally might represent real relations in the workplace. And surely sitcoms teach something through reinforcement; they make us feel good briefly by reflecting and dramatically reconfirming that which we already wish to believe. They may not change our behavior, but they may strengthen our confidence in continuing as we are.

The sitcom is, finally, the quintessential TV entertainment. It's small; it's intimate; it's a friendly thing to invite into the home and a comforting thing to watch with the family. It benefits from regular viewing because

5

even its repetition is much of its charm. And because it creates feelings of warmth and security and positive regard for modern life, it's a perfect shill for a sponsor's products. The sitcom has been the tube's most dependably popular genre for forty years, accounting for more top-rated programs than any other type. It is more popular now than when it began. It is commercial broadcasting's perfect product.

It's a very conservative form, hewing to its basic structures as determinedly as the detective drama or the football game. Yet because it deals with the most familiar aspects of our lives, it must change with us if it is to survive. Often sitcoms try to duck away from external realities, using gimmicks to distract us, but if they fail to grapple at some level with the fears and desires of a significant number of Americans, they usually die fast. When a sitcom does grab for the spirit of the times, it can become enormously popular, even become a national craze, a part of the cultural common coin.

All entertainment has hidden meanings, revealing the nature of the culture that created it. Sometimes the sitcoms don't reveal their secrets easily, for no other form has ever striven so energetically to please all parties and offend none. Still, nothing is so innocuous that it can hide its worldview and its values completely. Often the very manner in which the sitcoms have sought mass acceptance reveals more about our culture than a bolder, more idiosyncratic, more aesthetically defensible vision might. Through sitcoms we can trace the hopes and concerns of the majority of Americans over the past forty-five years. We can trace the manner in which modern corporate culture has come to dominate our society and how we came from the confidence of World War II to our present confusion of national identity.

1

Out of the Ether

The sitcom is a product of American radio. And American radio—more than any of the other technologies that transformed the country in the first decades of this century—was a product of the power, the needs, the logic, the ideals of corporate culture.

Most of the new industries then reshaping America, like the automobile, were dominated by independent inventor-industrialists, creative patriarchs like Henry Ford. In its early, experimental days, radio followed the same pattern; all its essential patents were in the hands of Guglielmo Marconi by 1913. When the new medium proved its usefulness in the First World War, Woodrow Wilson considered nationalizing it, as the U.K. was doing. The conservative reaction that followed the war guaranteed that American radio would remain in private hands—though not the hands of Mr. Marconi. In 1919 General Electric, one of America's largest and most vigorous new public corporations, formed a new entity called the Radio Corporation of America and, with government approval, bought out Marconi's assets. RCA's board chairman was the forward-looking Owen D. Young, leader in the business community, eventual adviser to Herbert Hoover, friend to Franklin D. Roosevelt, proposed by influential Democrats for the New York governorship and the presidency. He was the

7

embodiment of a new, holistic spirit in managerial capitalism, in which rival businesses and government agencies planned in concert for their mutual good—and, ostensibly, for the good of the public.

Hopes ran high for the new medium in those years. In 1916 a Marconi employee named David Sarnoff dared envision the radio as "a household utility . . . to bring music into the home by wireless"—not to mention "lectures, events of national importance, and baseball scores." Five years later Herbert Hoover, then the secretary of commerce, was calling radio "an instrument of beauty and learning." Intellectuals saw it as a tool for the enlightenment of mankind.

By 1920 thousands of fascinated amateurs across the country were experimenting with sending and receiving messages. It was an inexpensive hobby, but a growing business for RCA. A "cat's whisker" receiving set could be bought for under four dollars. More expensive tube-operated sets were on their way. There wasn't much to hear yet except static, cross talk, and some scratchy Victrola music, but Americans in those years were in love with gadgetry.

A couple of other radio manufacturers, Westinghouse and AT&T, found themselves being left behind by RCA and sought a way to juice the market. They decided they could sell radios to more than just hobbyists if they gave the general public something worth listening to. In October 1920 Westinghouse secured a Commerce Department license for America's first government-approved radio station, KDKA in Pittsburgh, and a month later it launched its broadcasts with running coverage of Warren Harding's victory in the presidential race.

Radio sales in Pittsburgh did jump in response, but such opportunities for fast-breaking news didn't present themselves often to the infant medium, with its shoestring budgets and nearly nonexistent staffs. When programming had to resume on day two for KDKA, it was back to the scratchy Victrola music.

Radio stations began popping up across the country, mostly owned by Westinghouse, AT&T, or RCA, following the same safe pattern of recorded music and occasional news, attracting listeners mainly through novelty. Then, in 1922, the number of transmitters and interested listeners reached a critical mass. Radio exploded as a national craze. When the year began, there were 28 licensed stations in America. When it ended, there were 576. Within two more years there were more than 1,400.

Technology made huge leaps to keep up with demand. Early headphone sets were replaced by loudspeaker sets that made listening a family pastime. The radio was no longer a four-dollar gadget tossed into a closet but an imposing piece of wood furniture dominating the family room. By 1924 one-third of all the money spent on furniture in this country was spent on radios and radio parts.

Suddenly station programmers found themselves facing a ravenous public appetite for exciting new sounds in their living rooms; Victrolas were no longer enough. Stations began a desperate scramble to fill airtime. A New Jersey announcer was known to recite Rudyard Kipling's "Boots" five times a day. In New York City announcer Norman Brokenshire was once caught with five minutes of dead air: he threw open a window, stuck the microphone through it, and announced: "Ladies and gentlemen, we now bring you the sounds of New York City." It soon became clear that radio would have to create its own live programming. In January 1922 Westinghouse station WJZ in Newark, New Jersey, had begun transmitting church services; when God proved not enough, it turned to Ed Wynn. The February 19, 1922, broadcast of Wynn's vaudeville show *The Perfect Fool*, before a rounded-up studio audience of cleaning ladies, electricians, and switchboard operators, marked the beginning of American entertainment broadcasting.

Such programming was great for winning listeners, but it had a drawback: It cost money, more than could be justified by increased radio sales. AT&T found the solution. In the summer of 1922 it opened WEAF on Long Island, a station dedicated to testing the public's appetite for entertainment programming, with the finest technology available and an unprecedented twelve hours per day of solid broadcasting. To pay for this, AT&T experimented with selling time to sponsors at the rate of a hundred dollars per ten minutes. A local realtor took the bait, and commercial radio was born.

Within two years sponsorship had become common enough for Secretary Hoover to worry about its effect on the young medium: "If a speech by the President is to be used as the meat in a sandwich of two patent medicine advertisements, there will be no radio left." Hoover believed that American industry, acting in concert, should support broadcasting. Industry had other ideas. David Sarnoff of RCA, perceiving radio as a great cultural institution, thought it should be supported by foundation endowments, just like libraries and colleges. Martin P. Rice of General Electric dared advocate selling licenses to the public for radio ownership, such as those the British government used to pay for its BBC. But the foundations weren't taking radio very seriously, and few politicians, in those post-Progressive days of laissez-faire and leadership by business-men, wanted to flirt with nationalization. Stations and their owners were left to work out their own financing. Inevitably they turned to sponsorship.

If corporate ownership had limited experimentation in radio program-ming, sponsorship tightened the bounds even more. Sponsors wanted nothing from radio but positive images for their products. As Roy Durstine of the Batten, Barton, Durstine & Osborn ad agency wrote, the purpose of the sponsored program was simply to "create good will" between con-sumer and producer. Programming had to be cautious, accessible, time-tested, and, above all, inoffensive. Sponsors liked music, happy, pretty, generally acceptable music. The A&P Gypsies. The gag and song patter of the Happiness Candy Company's Happiness Boys. They didn't like straight comedy as much. For one thing, major vaudeville comics were too expensive, and the cheaper ones were rarely worth the trouble. For another, it became clear that audience, broadcasters, and sponsors alike appreciated regularity: Rosella Scheiner, ten-year-old violin prodigy, will play at seven fifty-five and eight-fifty every evening, and you can count on it. No comedian had enough material to deliver fresh daily.

But the audience wanted more. And gradually, in stations scattered across the country, programmers and sponsors and entertainers evolved a new form to satisfy the demand: the family serial. The origins of these nightly or weekly dramas-with-a-chuckle are obscure. Alice Goldfarb Marquis, after trying to trace their roots, concluded that they were "neither invented nor developed" but "appeared to spring full-blown out of the ether." Even their content is uncertain, since few shows of that time were ever recorded. The best known is *The Smith Family*, starring Jim and Marian Jordan, broadcast on Chicago's WENR; but some remember it as a daily show beginning in 1925, others as a weekly from 1927. It has been referred to as an "early situation comedy" and as an ancestor of the soap opera. It may have concerned an Irish-American couple trying to marry off their two daughters, or it may have followed the cute travails of mid-western WASPs. (The confusion springs partly from the fact that the Jordans were busy radio performers, sometimes acting in various shows at once; programs have been confused even in their own reminiscences.)

No doubt the greatest inspiration for these serials was the family comic strips, like *The Gumps* and *Gasoline Alley*, that began sweeping the nation's newspapers in 1919. Each daily installment of those strips contained a miniepisode, usually with a punch line, but all fitted together to form an unending narrative that kept bringing readers back for more.

The *Chicago Tribune* had struck gold with Sidney Smith's *The Gumps*, and in 1926 its management decided to try an adaptation of the strip on the radio station it owned, WGN ("World's Greatest Newspaper"). Station manager Henry Selinger asked a couple of resident voice comedians, Freeman Gosden and Charles Correll, to tackle it, but they preferred to create their own serial about a couple of lovable black bumpkins named Sam and Henry. They drew upon the comic strips for further inspiration, seeking a vocal equivalent to the tall-short contrast of Bud Fisher's *Mutt and Jeff*: Sam was small, young, and innocent; Henry was deep-voiced and domineering. Selinger found others to play the Gumps, but that series is barely remembered. *Sam 'n' Henry*, under a different name, soon went on to transform radio entertainment.

Whatever their origins, family serials met an emotional need of the radio audience. In the mid-'20s the United States was just coming out of a long period of internal conflict and ideological challenge. The Progressive movement, labor strife, the world war, and Wilson's internationalism had rubbed raw the American nerves. At the start of the decade millions of Americans pressed to turn back the social and political clock, to "return to normalcy." A Red Scare, Prohibition, and a resurgent Ku Klux Klan tried to throw a WASP blanket over our national troubles. But as the decade progressed, America's own children rebelled. Popular culture glamorized a new class of hooch-swilling, iconoclastic orgiasts. A new money fever gripped the populace, urban and rural, Menckenite and fundamentalist. Americans chased bubbles, let businessmen run the country, forced themselves to think positively, win friends, and influence people. Under it all lay a deep anxiety. The icon of the age was a huge electric sign over Columbus Circle in New York City, flashing on and off, on and off with its relentless message: "You should have $10,000 at the age of 30, $25,000 at the age of 40, $50,000 at 50."

In the face of all that, what could be sweeter than to click on the oaken box in the living room and listen to the folksy voices of the Smith family as they grappled with their daily troubles but survived?

Radio then had a mainly middle-class audience, and that audience liked the family serials. So did the sponsors. Radio was a more intimate medium than any before it; the invisible actors in the home seemed to be speaking directly to the listener, engaging his unguarded attention and winning his trust. If they could win that same trust for Pepsodent or Sal Hepatica, then surely everyone would be happy.

What humor could be found in the early radio serials was genteel indeed. But there was that other, very different strain of American comedy always flirting with the airwaves. Vaudeville was loud, urban, unrestrained, given to broad lampoons of American types and polite behavior. On the vaudeville stage the Irish and the Jews could step up and shout out jokes that relieved the tensions of being caught on the lip of the melting pot. Comedians could create characters that were often more contemptible than admirable—W.C. Fields's drunk, Jack Benny's skinflint, Gracie Allen's dizzy dame—and still win the love of a large audience. Where the serials invited their audience to care about characters that shared their most commonplace traits, vaudeville forced them to laugh at characters that personified their most grotesque foibles.

Vaudeville predated the corporate mentality and made no bones about it. It was confrontational, not conciliatory. It assumed, for one thing, that it was permissible to laugh at people of other ethnic groups. Most ethnic humor was performed by comedians who were themselves of the targeted group. For first- and second-generation immigrant Americans, laughter helped take the sting out of a painful alien status; at the same time, by pointing out the most glaringly foreign traits of the immigrants, comedians used negative examples to teach them how to assimilate. For mainstream Americans, "dialect" routines shored up commonly held views of foreigners, but they also made those foreigners seem amusing and lovable and consequently less threatening. Although not always benign, ethnic humor eased the assimilation process for both sides.

The blackface acts were a trickier case. Performed by members not of the targeted group but the oppressing majority, and lampooning the accents and concerns of a continuing subculture, not of one or two generations caught between old country and new, they found little support among black audiences and were vilified by some black critics. Yet even these acts, at least in the case of the popular northern blackface comics of the 1920s, represented more than just oppression and ridicule.

The American '20s was a period of conflicting emotions held in painful tension; that tension was never greater than in white northerners' feelings about blacks. In the wake of the war thousands of blacks had poured from the South into cities like Chicago and New York, seeking new freedom and opportunities. They forged a new urban subculture and found a huge white audience for its creations. The black middle class grew, as more and more blacks dared to open their own businesses, dared even to win economic independence of whites. Northern whites, who'd rarely had to deal with blacks except as domestics, reacted with excitement, curiosity, bafflement, and fear. Race riots erupted in several cities in 1919; the one in Chicago killed 15 whites and 23 blacks. Chicago nightlife swirled around black music, yet the Ku Klux Klan scored huge successes in the Midwest, recruiting 250,000 in Indiana and capturing that state's government in the 1924 elections. Blacks responded with flamboyant, militant figures like New York's Marcus Garvey and Chicago's Elijah Muhammad.

By the late 1920s such movements were quieting, but individual blacks and whites were still caught in painful cultural conflicts. The new northern blacks felt tensions not unlike those that European immigrants had before them, trapped between their rural southern heritage and this bustling young urban culture in which they desperately hoped to succeed. Whites were trapped between fond old stereotypes and a need to comprehend this unsettling ethnic upheaval. Only in the '20s could a *New York Times* film critic have praised King Vidor's *Hallelujah* for its sensitive portrayal of black life, then noted that it most effectively captured the "peculiar religious hysteria of the darkies and their gullibility."

Blackface vaudeville thrived on this tension, endeavoring to capture some of the richness of black subculture while reducing it to clownish and sentimental clichés that relieved white fears.

Gosden and Correll brought a new dimension to blackface (or "blackvoice") with the serial structure of *Sam 'n' Henry*. Beginning with the first episode, in which their two rustics ambled into Chicago from Alabama in a mule wagon, they developed characters more complex and human than any encountered on the vaudeville stage: Sam and Henry were naïfs in the exploitative big city, stereotyped "dumb darkies" in a sense, yet always played sympathetically as good-hearted victims of modern greed.

Sam 'n' Henry elicited only mild audience interest, but Gosden and Correll's luck began to change in early 1928, when they moved to station WMAQ and revamped the show. They performed for six nights a week at eleven, fifteen minutes per night. Their popularity grew, and they soon moved to 7:00 P.M., prime listening time. Within a year Chicago had gone crazy over this new show, called *Amos 'n' Andy*.

The protagonists were Amos Jones and Andy Brown. A step beyond Sam and Henry in urban assimilation, they were owners of the Fresh Air Taxi Company (so named because their only cab didn't have a windshield). They were members of the Mystic Knights of the Sea Lodge, a gimcrack outfit run by a blowhard called the Kingfish. Although he acted the role of the smooth operator, Kingfish was in fact the victim of his overbearing wife, Sapphire. Amos and Andy's world was a burlesque vision of the new black urban society, with its shoestring businesses, its hustlers, its fraternal societies and sex role conflicts.

Gosden and Correll played their characters with traditional minstrel show accents. Lines like "I'se regusted" and "Now ain't that sumpin'?" were always good for a patronizing chuckle; they reassured white listeners that under their middle-class affectations, the new urban blacks were just the same old harmless coons. (They were great as catchphrases, too, keeping the show on the public's lips and minds.) Yet the comedians also displayed an uncommon awareness of the nuances and pretenses of contemporary city life. The tension between the married, more stable Amos and the lazy, wildcatting Andy was a classic '20s conflict, not just a stereotypically black one. The Kingfish, with his pseudoeducated affectations and clumsy hustling, was a familiar figure to Americans in the Age of Getting Ahead. Most important, Gosden and Correll were able to develop their characters with enough genuine warmth and wit to make listeners care about them. When, in a long, suspenseful serial, Andy almost married the grasping Madame Queen, thousands of people wrote and called with their heartfelt reactions.

The black community was never united in its opinion of *Amos 'n' Andy*. A study published in *Sociology and Social Research* in 1932 found that black students and leaders (nearly all middle-class) reacted to the show with everything from affection to "marked resentment." Novelist Raymond Andrews recalled the split within his own black community: "Besides the Joe Louis fights, perhaps Daddy's, and the community's, favorite radio show was 'Amos 'n Andy.' . . . Mama wasn't an Amos 'n Andy fan. She said the show made fun of colored folks. When Daddy disagreed, Mama said that the day they put on radio a 'serious' show about coloreds, depicting a colored doctor or lawyer like they did for whites, then she would listen to Amos 'n Andy. Mama never got around to listening to Amos 'n Andy." The program's sponsor, Pepsodent, claimed that surveys and fan mail showed a large black audience (as well as a large black buyership for its product).

Gosden and Correll sent contradictory messages to their listeners, which surely worked to their benefit. White bigots could chuckle at the darkies crying, "Oo wah, oo wah, oo wah!" Struggling urban blacks could feel a pang of sympathy when Andy got stung by another get-rich-quick scheme. The fact that fans couldn't see the actors helped; although most listeners probably knew that Gosden and Correll were white, their voices inevitably conjured black faces to mind, which softened the bite of the blackface routine. This ability to send dual messages has worked well for mass media comedy, as TV was to discover with *The Beverly Hillbillies* and *All in the Family.* Only one message had always to be unambivalent: good will toward the sponsor. Gosden and Correll never made fun of white teeth.

Amos 'n' Andy created the tension between sentimentality and laughter that became the driving force of the situation comedy. Drawing upon vaudeville traditions and radio innovations, it gave listeners characters that they could simultaneously care about and laugh at. Although still a daily serial, complete with cliff-hangers, it pointed the way to the sitcom.

Other ethnic serials inevitably followed in the wake of Gosden and Correll's success. The first and best was *The Rise of the Goldbergs*, a New York program detailing the daily travails of an immigrant Jewish woman named Molly Goldberg. Her husband, Jake, struggled to run a small clothing company. Their two children were a pair of budding Americans who often had to be taught respect for tradition and motherly wisdom. They lived in an overcrowded Jewish neighborhood, through which tromped a large cast of neighbors and relatives, an intimate and believable slice of American life.

The Goldbergs reveals a couple of tendencies that persisted on radio and early television: New York produced tonier, thinkier programs than the rougher cities to the west, and Jews were portrayed with greater warmth and sentimentality than any other ethnic group. These were no *goyische* comedians doing corny dialect. The show was created, written, directed, and produced by the indefatigable Jewish actress Gertrude Berg, who also played Molly. She based the character on her own mother and grandmother, whose difficulties with English inspired many of Molly's malapropisms and Yiddishisms: "In the pot, put the chicken," "Give me a swallow the glass," and "It's late, Jake—time to expire." Like Amos and Andy's manglings of English, such lines supplied laughs and memorable catchphrases. But Berg presented her protagonist in an unwaveringly positive light, and as she pointed out repeatedly, she never did a "Jewish accent." Molly's language troubles were all in the structure.

The stories were low-key and seriously presented; if not for Molly's lines, many would have worked on straight family serials. Unlike *Amos 'n'*

Andy, the show carried a clear message, which Molly imparted with varying degrees of implication and explication: The family is paramount in human life and is the foundation of a good society.

All such serials—ethnic and white bread, caustic and mild—soothed the fears of a patchwork nation in turbulent times. All of them exploited radio perfectly and sold household products faithfully. The most effective of them won the allegiance of Americans for decades to come. In the beginning, however, they were all local phenomena. By the late 1920s radio was just beginning to draw Americans into a mass popular culture.

The experimental and amateur stage of broadcasting was then well past. Radio was an ongoing, profitable corporate concern, and following the classic pattern of corporate culture, it was time to centralize and rationalize the business. Secretary Hoover did his part, supervising the formation of the Federal Radio Commission in 1927. The FRC devoted itself mainly to reducing interference on the airwaves by restricting the number and wattage of broadcasters. It occasionally made noise about advertising or programming but never took real action; Hoover described the government's role as that of a "neutral broker" between commercial concerns.

It was the corporate visionary Owen D. Young who took the lead in organizing radio. He conceived the idea of a network, to be called the National Broadcasting Company. It would own some stations outright and sign exclusive programming deals with others. Its public shares were divided among RCA, GE, and their competitor Westinghouse. It got a running start with forty stations in major markets and a telephonic linkup, through a deal with another competitor, AT&T. Its capital would come from sponsorship, and its airtime would be affordable only by large national companies. As a publicly owned, scientifically planned union of diverse capital interests, it was the very model of a modern major corporation. On November 15, 1926, NBC gave out its first offering: a four-and-a-half-hour variety show, sponsored by Dodge.

With forty markets suddenly available to a single program, the amount of money sponsors were willing to spend on those programs jumped astronomically. In 1929 Fleischmann's Yeast dished out a tidy sum to hire popular crooner Rudy Vallee for a weekly variety show. This *Fleischmann Hour* featured a dazzling variety of acts and features and paved the way for much radio programming in the 1930s, including original comedy sketches written for prominent vaudeville comics.

The network idea worked. NBC even formed a second one, its Blue

Network, with different programs and sponsors, to double-penetrate the bigger markets. In 1927 the Columbia Phonograph Company, having realized years before that radio airplay significantly boosted record sales, put together a sixteen-station network. With its limited programming it faltered early, but the idea intrigued the son of one of its sponsors, twenty-six-year-old cigar heir William Paley. With investments from his father and some friends, Paley arranged to buy the Columbia Broadcasting System from its parent company and made himself its president.

Paley was bold and crafty and scored an early coup. Thanks to the advent of talkies (using mostly RCA and GE technology), the American people were suddenly fascinated with the voices of movie stars. Paley cut a deal with Paramount Pictures to use its stars in radio broadcasts. Inspired by Rudy Vallee's success, he then snagged a number of vaudeville headliners to host comedy-variety shows, including Eddie Cantor, Jack Benny, Fred Allen, and George Burns and Gracie Allen. All but Cantor were soon stolen away by NBC, but CBS was nonetheless able to threaten its rival in some major markets.

By the start of the 1930s radio had essentially become a two-network enterprise. Dozens of independents later grouped together for self-preservation into the Mutual Broadcasting System, and still later the federal government forced NBC to divest itself of the Blue Network in an antimonopoly action. Still, no one would seriously challenge NBC or CBS, and the two networks eventually controlled the early days of television. The apparatus was in place to pour mass entertainment simultaneously into nearly every living room in America.

The dominant force in the whole system was sponsorship. This was a boom time in radio advertising. By the beginning of 1929 over one-third of all American homes had radio; that meant a market of over forty million listeners. One survey showed that 80 percent of radio owners listened on a daily basis. And the numbers kept going up. In 1928 NBC had only 39 sponsoring companies. In 1931 it had 343. The amount of money spent on radio advertising more than quadrupled from 1928 to 1934. During the same years newspaper advertising dropped by 30 percent, and 246 daily papers folded.

Sponsors never hesitated to use their power over the young medium. Shows were usually named after them, not their characters or stars: *The Jell-O Program* (starring Jack Benny), *The Chase and Sanborn Hour* (starring Eddie Cantor), *The Linit Bath Club Revue* (starring Fred Allen). Nor did their influence end with the titles. As Allen, one of radio's

17

harshest internal critics, noted, "It was inevitable that the sponsors would soon consider themselves authorities on the tastes of the general public. . . . Men who ran oil companies, drug, food, and tobacco corporations were attending auditions, engaging talent."

The networks raised no objections. NBC president Merlin H. Aylesworth believed that the "good will" generated by a program for its sponsor circled around to help radio itself. An effective advertisement, he wrote, "creates such a friendly feeling in the listener that when he has occasion to buy, he is very likely to remember favorably the industry that has provided him with good entertainment." Roy Durstine of the BBDO ad agency described his image of the typical radio listener: "A very tired, bored, middle-aged man and woman whose lives are empty and who have exhausted their outside sources of amusement when they have taken a quick look at the evening paper." For Durstine, the sponsor's mission was a noble one, a sort of Corporate Man's burden: "Radio provides a vast source of delight and entertainment for the barren lives of the millions."

This is the essential equation of sponsored arts. As the critic Kenneth Hey defined it, "The whole ritual was honest and forthright; the corporate society provided entertainment for its customers, much as the paternalists at the turn of the century 'took care' of their employees." The commercials reminded listeners that this entertainment came to them "thanks to the graciousness of some large corporate entity and that gratitude could be shown through an appropriate store purchase." The modern roles of consumer and corporate provider were being defined.

Some network programming (especially the unsponsored shows that filled less desirable airtimes) was bold and a bit highbrow. But most of it was pressed into a safe and generic mold by the sponsors' prime directive: that no one's sensibilities ever be offended by their programming. Real jazz might agitate a dairyman in Sauk Centre, serious classical music might bore a housewife in Baltimore, but a "jazzy" version of "Sweet Sue" or a young tenor warbling "Danny Boy" could be pleasant background music for anybody.

Nonetheless, one group was very offended: intellectuals. Merrill Dennison, in *Harper's* magazine, wrote of the spread of sponsorship: "To radio's attitude that it was an industry was added the advertising agency's theory that it was a midway." This had created "an era of factory production of entertainment." In the *Atlantic Monthly*, William Orton went a step further, fearing that when mass culture "dominates and colors all activity, civilization itself may be in peril. The redemption of the mass cannot come except from minorities." But the mass apparently didn't want to be redeemed. It wanted to listen to *Amos 'n' Andy* and brush its teeth with Pepsodent. And in the United States the mass was very much in control.

There was no question that radio had become important to the American people. When *Amos 'n' Andy* burst from the confines of WMAQ and hit the NBC network in August 1929, it became a national sensation. It commanded two-thirds of the radio audience by the early 1930s. Stores across the country played it over loudspeakers so that customers needn't end their shopping early to rush home and listen. Movie theaters altered their schedules so that features would end by 7:00 P.M.; they then played the show for their customers before going on to the next feature. Witnesses from the period speak of walking down the street and following the whole program, hearing it blaring from one open window after another.

To some extent *Amos 'n' Andy*'s popularity was no doubt due to excitement over this new national experience. For the first time Americans could all enjoy the same event at the same moment. It was the surest sign that we had truly entered a new world. Gosden and Correll were in the right place at the right time to herald it. Even so, the public did feel a genuine connection to the characters. One episode ended with Amos and Andy in desperate need of a typewriter; nearly two thousand typewriters were immediately sent in by listeners. Audience response grew increasingly fervent through the '30s. NBC reported two million fan letters for its various shows in 1928. It got five and a half million in 1936 and then nearly equaled that in just the first half of 1937.

NBC quickly put other funny serials on the air: *The Goldbergs*, *The Smackouts*, *Easy Aces*, and *Vic and Sade*. But something had changed since the first wave of family serials. Except for *The Goldbergs*, these all evinced an acerbic, absurdist attitude toward American life. *The Smackouts* (starring Jim and Marian Jordan, who had been *The Smith Family*) regaled us with the humorously pointless tales of a small-time grocer. *Easy Aces* made a scatterbrained, word-mangling dope of an American wife. And Paul Rhymer's sly, dry *Vic and Sade* mocked the smallness and trivia of Middle America with its plotless dramas and ingeniously looping conversations.

It wasn't surprising that America's taste in humor had undergone a shift in the first years of the 1930s. The stock market had crashed, banks were collapsing, thousands of people were being thrown out of work, families were being shattered by economic stress, the president was a laughingstock, the army was firing upon veterans in the shadow of the White House, and whispers of class warfare were in the air. The world had been turned upside down. The inevitable humorous response was a manic affirmation of chaos, laced with a knowing cynicism about the vanity and hypocrisy of human endeavors. This was the time of movies like *Twentieth Century* and *Duck Soup*, of comic strips like E. C. Segar's *Popeye*. Radio comedy could never go quite so far in lampooning the times, not under the watchful eyes of sponsors. Yet some comedians did create forms that allowed them to cut through the mist of "good will" and speak to their listeners' disillusionment.

Series with repeating characters and situations were by then well established as ideal for commercial broadcasting: low-risk; easy to sell; easy to sustain with replacement personnel. Variety shows may have been more popular, but their long-term value was threatened by their tendency to devour their own comedic resources; Carroll Carroll, who wrote for Edgar Bergen, Burns and Allen, Rudy Vallee, and many others, admitted that he and his fellow writers had to assemble scripts from files of old gags because "radio needs too much material too often. It eats up copy too fast." Writers, producers, and comedians cast about for techniques to keep the material fresh. The best solution was found by Jack Benny and his staff for their Canada Dry/Chevrolet/Jell-O program, who reshaped the variety show along the lines of the family serial.

Benny's formula made him the likable but ridiculous focal point for plots and gags. Surrounding him were Mary Livingstone, Benny's off-mike wife but an undefined "foil" on the show, trading wisecracks with the star; Don Wilson, the announcer, who took abuse from Benny about his weight and wove humorous commercials into the program; the bandleader Phil Harris, playing a loud, hard-drinking southerner; and the vocalist, first Kenny Baker and then Dennis Day, played as a naive, dim-witted mama's boy. Other characters—most notably Benny's rebellious black valet, Rochester—made frequent appearances.

Within these familial confines, Benny and his writers unleashed a tempest of funny insults, unresolvable hostilities, and noisily tumbling class barriers. Benny laid down what would become the standard sitcom structure—the weekly half hour, the live audience, the company of funny characters delivering gag lines—but he never used that structure to demonstrate consensual solutions or tug the heartstrings or present an ideal of life. He never even asked listeners to suspend their disbelief, instead he invited them to join in on the joke within a joke by making references to his audience, his writers, his script, his role as a hired clown.

Benny also displayed a refreshing honesty toward the nature of sponsorship. In his first show for Canada Dry he mocked his role as a huckster by peppering his monologues with painfully self-conscious puns on the sponsor's name ("Her father very often partakes of the forbidden beverage. In fact, he drank everything in the United States and then went north to drink Canada dry"). Finally he delivered a straight commercial but followed it with "Gee, I thought I did that pretty swell for a new salesman, eh? I suppose nobody will drink it now."

Fred Allen followed Benny's lead and took it further, starting many a conflict with his acid remarks about sponsors and networks (an ad agency vice-president, he said, "is a man who comes into the office at nine o'clock in the morning to find a molehill on his desk. It's his job to make a mountain out of it by five o'clock"). He was cut off the air in mid-program more than once, but that only gave him more ammunition and more attention. "Our program has been cut off so many times," he once said on the air, "the last page of our script is a Band-Aid."

This was the sharp edge of vaudeville, carried over to radio; it was also an expression of the public's attitude toward its commercial leaders. In the '20s Americans had allowed themselves to believe that big business, if left to its own devices, would create a paradise on earth. Now they were paying for their naiveté with a depression, while the companies that had deceived them were going on shilling their products. Comics like Benny and Allen understood. As Benny said to open his first show, "This is my professional debut on radio. That means I'm finally getting paid." Every American knew that getting paid was the whole point. If that meant pushing a product, then the entertainer would push it. But he could also place himself in the ranks of the common man by smart-assing about it.

Sponsors may have been unhappy with this attitude, but those that endured it found themselves with popular programs and rising sales. When General Foods became Benny's sponsor in an effort to sell a failing product called Jell-O, he demanded a free hand not only with the show but with the commercials. "I warned them that I wouldn't make ridiculous claims about Jell-O," he recalled. "I intended to make fun of it and predicted I would sell a lot of Jell-O. . . . Everybody loved it. Except the sponsor—at first. From a rating of 22.9 we climbed to 35.3 in a few months. Jell-O was the talk of the country. . . . The mountains of unsold

Jell-O disappeared." Americans like a good sport, and companies that participated in the mocking of corporate rituals won a great deal of that precious "good will." Forgiving conflicting attitudes and ideologies in the interests of income is a key to modern corporate life.

The Benny show was well written and superbly performed. It became an enormous popular hit and inspired nearly all the other variety shows to follow its lead. The ridiculous hero, the foil, the pompous announcer, the wild bandleader, and assorted supporting screwballs became stock figures. Nearly all used the half hour structure, the self-referential humor, the loose plots built around the stars' ostensible failings, the formulaic needling that allowed gags to be recycled endlessly to good effect.

Their combined success impelled a geographic shift with big implications: They moved the center of entertainment broadcasting away from New York, where the executives were, to Hollywood, where the big-name talent was. Benny moved west in 1935, and Burns and Allen shortly followed. Of the big variety stars only Fred Allen clung to New York. With the move came an influx of Hollywood writers and Hollywood sensibilities, which brought slicker production and broader humor to radio; those sensibilities later took over television.

These shows created a new form with the content of vaudeville and the shape of the serial. A new series came from the other direction in 1935, pouring the content of the family serial into this new comedy-variety form. In the process it created radio's most effective humorous comment on the American family.

When Don Quinn, producer-writer of *The Smackouts*, learned that the Johnson Wax people wanted a new weekly show to sponsor, he sold them a concept for a half hour comedy about the preposterous characters in the hick midwestern town of Wistful Vista. Jim and Marian Jordan starred as the stubborn, garrulous Fibber McGee—given to wild boasts and domestic incompetence—and his long-suffering wife, Molly. Their supporting cast was a bestiary of caricatured small-town cranks, bores, and Babbitts.

Like the Benny show, *The Johnson Wax Program with Fibber McGee and Molly* never presumed to suspend the cynical listener's disbelief but acknowledged itself constantly as artifice. Plots were loose, giving way to comedy bits and musical numbers. Sponsorship was cleverly lampooned. In the middle of the story announcer Harlow Wilcox would saunter over to the McGees', strike up some small talk, and then slyly, annoyingly bend the conversation around to the virtues of Johnson's Wax.

Fibber took to calling him Waxy and warning him not to try to slip in a commercial.

Even so, its characters took on a "regular folks" believability that struck deeper chords in the average listener than celebrity clowns like Benny and Allen. Its most famous running gag was the prolonged clamor of falling junk that ensued every time Fibber opened his overfilled closet. After the last tinkling sound had died, he'd always remark, "Gotta straighten out that closet one of these days." On one level this was a celebration of the sound effects man's art, and every listener appreciated it as such. On another, it was a touch of mundane satire that reminded many Americans of their own never-finished chores. Here the tension between compassion and comedy that *Amos 'n' Andy* had pioneered was brought to a new level of complexity and self-awareness.

By the late 1930s Americans were in the mood to listen to families on radio. *McGee* started soft in the ratings but moved steadily upward until in 1939 it reached fourth place, right behind Jack Benny. Other family-oriented programs were enjoying similar fortune. A weekly serial drama, *One Man's Family*—"dedicated to the mothers and fathers of the younger generation and to their bewildering offspring"—appeared on a San Francisco station in 1932 and gradually became a network success. It was a popular favorite by that evening in 1938 when its central character delivered his credo: "It's my opinion that the family is the source from whence comes the moral strength of the nation. And disintegration of any nation begins with the disintegration of the family," to which one of his bewildering offspring replied, "There's a rising tide of sentiment growing throughout the world, fostered by people who are sick of the way things are going. Perhaps it's the answer we've all been looking for."

Perhaps it was, indeed. A new spirit began to infuse America as the fears of the early depression were battered back by the Roosevelt administration. Even when it became clear that hard times weren't going to be swept away by the New Deal, most Americans felt a renewed connection to the American system and were again prepared to trust it to create a better tomorrow. Roosevelt preached cooperation in the management of the nation, just as Owen Young and Herbert Hoover and other power brokers had before him. But the latter had spoken for a managerial aristocracy that limited government power and excluded most of the public. Roosevelt's message of cooperation was more profound. He saw the salvation of the United States in a union of labor and management, government and capital, consumer and producer, a union with its nexus in the White House. The idea didn't take at first, as the bloody labor conflicts of 1937 and 1938 showed. But it began to burrow into the hearts and minds of the citizenry.

Comedy took a sudden swing away from conflict and cynicism, toward sentiment and reconciliation. With the huge success of Frank Capra's *It Happened One Night* in 1934 Hollywood began churning out dozens of "screwball" comedies, whose most constant feature was a bringing together of conflicting groups, usually a rich girl and a working-class boy or vice versa. A new cycle of movies, the most popular of which were the *Andy Hardy* series, followed in the late '30s. These created ideal small towns in the American heartland, where traditional security and strong parental figures mixed painlessly with the slangy, swinging world of modern teens. For conservative middle-class audiences battered by unwelcome change, these movies provided a seductive fictional retreat, a place such citizens could believe they had once lived in and might create again if nation and family could be held together. As war enveloped Europe and Asia and threatened to cross the oceans, such nostalgic retreats played a larger and larger role in popular culture.

Broadway got into the act quickly. *Life with Father*, a bit of light domestic nostalgia, set box-office records beginning in 1939. The year before, playwright Clifford Goldsmith had enjoyed a solid success with *What a Life*, about a slightly goofy but very ordinary family named Aldrich. It had been promptly adapted into a serial on Rudy Vallee's radio show and was well received. Then, in 1939, *The Aldrich Family* premiered as a half hour NBC series.

When devotees of old radio remember their favorite shows, *The Aldrich Family* rarely makes the list. Listening to it with contemporary ears, it seems far less funny and charming than *Fibber McGee* or the Benny show or even *Amos 'n' Andy*. The plots were trivial (son Henry gets a new pair of pants, father Sam has trouble with pigeons) but lacked the whimsy of *Vic and Sade*. It certainly didn't rely on star power; in a little over a decade on the air, five different actors played Henry, three played his father, three his mother, and seven his sister. Yet in its first year it soared to sixth place in the ratings. It remained stunningly popular through the '40s and inspired an entire genre of imitators.

The Aldrich Family's elements spark associations with a hundred later radio and TV shows. Dad was a slightly bumbling and self-important chap, but his concern was for his family. Henry was a naive and restless teen, liable to get himself in trouble through his own good intentions. His sister was a cute nuisance. His friend Homer was a little more selfish, a little more goofy, but got his gentle comeuppance when appropriate. They all lived in Centerville, state unknown, an insular town of midwestern sensibilities but mild weather.

Henry's mother wouldn't be as familiar to the modern sitcom watcher. She was domestic, yes, but also hard-edged, rather humorless, concerned with old proprieties. She didn't sound like a pretty woman. There was righteous indignation in her voice when she yelled out the opening catchphrase of every show: "Hen-ry! Henry Aldrich!" And there was real fear in Henry's croaked "Coming, Mother!" She was no June Cleaver or Donna Stone. Dad, too, despite his occasional humorous blundering, was of a tougher, earlier order. He expected to be obeyed, and Henry knew it; although occasionally embarrassed, Sam never had to apologize to his children or reason them into accepting his viewpoint. The Aldriches were a cutesy image of the traditional middle-class family, with parental and societal authority intact. At times they even made reference to going to church, something that was to be heard of very rarely in the relentlessly secular world of postwar sitcoms.

The show never made an issue of its traditionality, never even seemed conscious of it. There were no messages in the plots, only pleasant chuckles. The dialogue contained far more cornball gags than it did statements of values. The show merely offered up—in unthreateningly, uncritically humorous form—a nostalgic family image that pleased Americans on the eve of World War II.

The Aldrich Family was a natural union of forms. It took its shape and its gag-heavy dialogue from Jack Benny, Fibber McGee, and the rest. It took its concerns from the family serials and *Andy Hardy* movies. It had no ongoing, serial plots, just as it had no announcers tromping through the scenes, no commercials woven into dialogue, no musical breaks. It was self-contained, domestic, mildly funny, reassuring. It was the first true situation comedy.

Other sitcoms followed, varying the theme. *Blondie* shifted the spotlight from dizzy but lovable son to dizzy but lovable mom. *The Life of Riley* defined bumbling-dad humor. *The Great Gildersleeve*, about a pompous fool who inherits custody of his orphaned niece and nephew, was the first of the "bachelor father" comedies. *Abie's Irish Rose* put an ethnic spin on the form, with its melting pot comedy of a Jewish-Irish marriage; *Beulah* did the same, centering on a black maid (played by a white actor). *Duffy's Tavern* reflected the social dislocation of the big city at the end of the depression by moving the sitcom elements out of the home and into a bar, with a "family" made up of employees, regular patrons, and guest stars. Each had its gimmick, but each faithfully followed the basic pattern: *Gildersleeve* and *Beulah* were both *Fibber McGee* spin-offs, but each abandoned its parent show's reality-warping nature in favor of pure sitcom suspension of disbelief. Each began as a solid success and became increasingly popular as the war finally caught up with the United States.

Nostalgia, family, home, and small towns were important entertainment themes during those fearful years. But there were other dynamics at work in these sitcoms. While none of them truly satirized the family, none of them quite idealized it either. Each one sought out an area of conflict—sexual, generational, ethnic—and milked quiet laughs out of it.

Americans chortled at the weekly humiliations of Chester A. Riley and Throckmorton P. Gildersleeve because real dads were losing their traditional power. Modern consumer society had been steadily equalizing the roles of men and women. Rapid social and technological change made each generation of kids seem savvier, each generation of parents seem dumber. Corporations and government reached deeper and deeper into private life; the old ideal of the independent breadwinner—farmer, craftsman, professional, laborer—was being replaced by that of the "company man." Male autonomy was threatened by bosses, regulations, even unions. Comparing themselves with their own ideals of masculinity, men came easily to feel like weaklings and bumblers. Many a man must have said to himself what Riley said on the air: "What a revoltin' development this is!"

The new sitcoms took some of the sting out of these conflicts. Vaudeville had tackled many of the same issues decades earlier, but in a caustic and confrontational way. In the sitcoms inept dads could be lovable. Kids rebelled, and wives knew better than their husbands, but it was all just cute and funny. It was okay to be powerless as long as you were loved. The sitcoms reassured nervous fathers, helped wives embrace their husbands' failings, flattered restive kids. A pat on the head for everyone.

The sudden success of the sitcoms pressed the vaudeville series to follow their example. For its first several years George Burns and Gracie Allen's program had been a simple extension of their vaudeville act. Burns played the long-suffering straight man and Allen the dingbat whose half-witted worldview created its own "illogical logic" ("You know, my niece has three feet." "Your niece has three feet?" "That's right. My sister says I wouldn't recognize her since she grew another foot"). Burns recalls: "Our original format was a variation of the flirtation routines we did in vaudeville. Gracie and I were both supposed to be single, and she was being pursued or was pursuing either me or the orchestra leader or the announcer or one of our guests." This despite the fact that all their fans knew they were married in real life. But ratings began dropping in the early 1940s. "The show had been in the top ten since we'd started," Burns says, "but we were gradually losing our audience. Finally the answer came to me . . . our jokes were too young for us. . . . From that moment on we were going to be married on the show. Our ratings immediately began to improve."

George and Gracie weren't becoming the Aldrich family. The plots of their marital misadventures turned around celebrity guest stars and were pure show biz: Gracie asks Lana Turner's help in getting George elected to the Beverly Hills City Council; Gracie wants to adopt Mickey Rooney to give him a proper education; Gracie wants Frank Sinatra to persuade George to give up singing. Nonetheless, marriage and homelife were becoming nearly universal elements of radio comedy.

NBC continued to dominate the ratings during the war, with nearly all the big vaudeville stars and most of the new sitcoms. Then, in 1944, CBS scored a major success in an unexpected quarter: a mild bandleader and his mild singer-wife from the wacky Red Skelton program. They had been minor foils for Skelton, playing up their recent marriage for some cute couple comedy. But when they took over as Skelton's summer replacements, they found themselves with a huge, affectionate audience. Ozzie and Harriet Nelson, sold as "America's Favorite Young Couple," were promptly given their own show.

The Adventures of Ozzie and Harriet formed a bridge between the show biz comedies and the family sitcoms. It had musical breaks and celebrity guest stars, but it portrayed Ozzie and Harriet themselves as normal spouses and parents, living a wholesome life outside the spotlight. Unlike Burns and Allen and other celebrity couples, the Nelsons featured their children on the show (played by child actors until their own kids, David and Ricky, were old enough to take the parts). If the Aldriches were a product of '30s nostalgia for a fading America, the Nelsons were the model of the postwar couple. They demonstrated that a snazzy modern life-style was compatible with a solid family.

That was a message young Americans wanted to hear as the war wound down. They'd had enough fear, change, and dislocation and by late 1944 were already looking ahead to a life of greater prosperity and stability. They wanted to settle down and raise the next generation. But for the young and the fertile—the boys who'd seen Paree, the girls who'd gone to work in factories—there was no going back to Centerville. Their lives, they were told, would include prefab housing, television, more affordable cars, and countless laborsaving devices. They wanted it all, traditional and futuristic. Ozzie and Harriet were the first entertainers to show them, even indirectly, that they could have it. Their mixture of show biz glamour and folksy parenthood would serve television well in the decade to come.

The ideal of national oneness that the New Deal and its cultural allies had promoted now was virtually institutionalized as a societal goal. The war had pulled Americans apart physically but drawn them together in imagination. By the end of 1945 they were drawing together physically again, making babies and planning a future. Sponsors and networks were looking to that future, trying to guess what its entertainment would be like. Some of them knew that sitcoms would be a big part of it. They also knew that radio would not.

2

Cheese, Baseball, and Music

There never really was much doubt that the radio networks would dominate television broadcasting. RCA, General Electric, and Westinghouse, the parents of NBC, had funded all the important research for the new technology and held all the important patents. GE's station W2XCW in Schenectady became, in 1928, the first regular TV broadcaster in the world. Later that year RCA's W2XBS in New York became the first to start up under an FRC license. Their only rival in the early years was CBS, which opened its station W2XAB in New York in 1931.

TV didn't take off the way radio had. In 1923 RCA's David Sarnoff was predicting that very shortly "television will make it possible for those at home to see, as well as hear, what is going on at the broadcast station." But technological setbacks and the depression slowed things. Twelve years later Sarnoff, then president of the company, was saying, "As a system of sight transmission and reception, comparable in coverage and service to the present nationwide system of sound broadcasting, television is *not* here, nor around the corner." Much of the problem was that TV receivers couldn't be made so cheaply that a customer might buy one on a whim, as had been the case with early radios. Anyone who wanted to watch the local broadcast of the opening of the New York World's Fair in 1939 would have to pay between two hundred and a thousand dollars to watch a nine-inch-wide white-streaked image of something he or she could see a few weeks later in a newsreel for a quarter. That was a high price to pay for immediacy. Obviously TV broadcasters would have to invest a great deal in programming before their audience was big enough to pay back the cost. Only the two big networks and their backers had the equipment and the capital to develop such a complex, expensive new system. Whereas the radio stations had popped up like mushrooms around the country, television stations were to spread slowly outward from New York City.

Others tried. An electronics manufacturer named Allen B. Du Mont set up an independent research corporation in 1931 and within a few years had decided to form his own national network to fuel the sales of his TV sets. He needed capital to do it; that came in 1938, when he sold 40 percent of his stock to Paramount Pictures. Movie moguls had been frustrated at radio's threat to their box office, and they wanted to head off a similar problem with TV by getting a piece of the action. But neither they nor Du Mont had any experience with broadcasting, daily programming, or sponsorship. When the competition got hot, they were going to lose.

Television broadcasting was purely experimental and noncommercial for nearly twenty years. NBC steadily lobbied the Federal Communications (né Radio) Commission to allow commercial broadcasting, arguing that that was the only way to fund its independent development into a mass medium. The New Dealers in the FCC had their doubts, but corporate logic finally won. On July 1, 1941, NBC's WNBT New York flickered onto the air. Game shows and news readings filled its schedule. Its first commercial showed only a Bulova watch ticking away for sixty seconds. It was a quiet start, but TV seemed to be on its way.

Then, five months later, the Japanese bombed Pearl Harbor, and another round of reversals began for the new medium. Wartime economy measures virtually halted broadcasting. NBC had to worry about the government-ordered sale of its Blue Network (which became the American Broadcasting Company in 1944). A musicians' union ban on TV appearances from 1946 to 1948 retarded entertainment broadcasting. Sales of television sets continued to be sluggish; in 1946 there were only ten thousand sets in the country, more than half of them in New York.

TV programming was a bad bet for sponsors. Not only was the audience far smaller than radio's, but TV shows were far more expensive to produce. The biggest ratings hit of 1946 was a nonmusical variety show called *Hour Glass*; its sponsor, Standard Brands, noted virtually no effect on sales and calculated that it had lost money. *NBC Television Theatre*, the network's most prestigious offering, went unsponsored for more than three years.

There were no sitcoms on infant television. Most of radio's weekly serial factories had left New York for Hollywood. Regular companies of comedy writers and actors would have been difficult to assemble on TV budgets. Early entertainment programming depended mainly on young talents from the legitimate theater: They were creative; they were eager for jobs; their work garnered praise from critics and from the well-to-do easterners who owned most of the TV sets. Thus early television, when it wasn't showing boxing or wrestling, tended to be serious and tony.

Rather unexpectedly it was serious televised drama that finally made sponsorship profitable. The executives of Kraft Foods, certain that TV would eventually be an advertising boon, tried a targeted campaign in May 1947 to test the new medium's audience. They sponsored their ad agency, J. Walter Thompson, to produce a classy drama series for NBC. Between acts of *Kraft Television Theatre*, a pretty spokeswoman pushed a new product, Imperial cheese, that had been flopping in the stores. Three weeks after the program's premiere, Imperial cheese had sold out of New York City groceries. Other sponsors soon rushed in. *Chevrolet Tele-Theatre*, *Philco Playhouse*, *Fireside Theatre*, and *Ford Theatre* were dominating the late-evening hours within a couple of years.

Five months after *Kraft*'s premiere the joint network broadcast of the World Series proved that TV was becoming a mass phenomenon, thanks to the installation of sets in bars all over the urban Northeast. Nearly four million people saw Tommy Henrich's RBI single win it for the Yankees, almost 90 percent of them in taverns. Finally, in May 1948, the musicians' union settled with the networks. Variety shows began to flood the airwaves. Cheese, baseball, and music had gotten television under way at last. As TV writer Max Wilk put it, "The sleeping pygmy began to stir."

The American public was primed for TV. An NBC newspaper ad crowed: "1947 marked the end of television's interim period. 1948 marks TV's appearance as a major force. The greatest means of mass communication in the world is with us." All it needed was a good push.

Something akin to a sitcom had just made its first tentative appearance. In late 1947 the DuMont Network got Anacin to subsidize *Mary Kay and Johnny*, a frothy fifteen minutes of "young couple" chitchat of a sort

31

that had become quite popular on daytime radio. It performed well enough for NBC to steal it away the next year, but the big network had little luck with it. Something had happened between the young couple's debut and their trip to NBC, something that was to bury the sitcom for years beneath an avalanche of vaudevillian comedy.

The something appeared as one of a series of rotating hosts on *Texaco Star Theater*, a splashy variety show featuring every East Coast performer who'd never quite made it big on radio. It's doubtful that anyone expected much of that homely, mugging borscht belt burlesquer with a reputation for stealing jokes and a propensity for appearing in drag. But Milton Berle clicked. He became television's first sensation, seemingly bigger even than Amos and Andy had been twenty years before.

Within months his *Texaco Star Theater* was the top-rated show in the country. By 1949 75 percent of the TV audience was watching him. Legends spread of shopkeepers closing up Tuesday nights with the notice "Gone home to watch Uncle Miltie." TV sales skyrocketed as his popularity grew. There were about half a million sets in America when he came on the air in June 1948. That number doubled within a year. In 1950 over six million sets were sold. Berle didn't mind taking credit for those sales, although he did it with a joke: "Since I've been on television, they've sold a lot of sets. My uncle sold his, my father sold his. . . ."

At first glance Berle's popularity is baffling. He had been kicking around vaudeville, movies, and radio for years with no sign that he was what Americans had been hungering for. Certainly much of his newfound popularity was due to the fact that he understood both the limits and uses of primitive television. His show was visually striking and always surprising but never subtle; his outlandish costumes, whether an evening gown or a Superman suit, showed up clearly even on a snowy seven-inch RCA. And he was in the right place at the right time, a flashy figure who charged into view just when millions of Americans were looking for an excuse to buy televisions.

It appeared that America's TV taste was running counter to its quieter radio taste. But in fact, Milton Berle was not to all America's taste. His popularity was a regional phenomenon. In 1949 only twenty-four cities got network broadcasts, most of them in the Northeast. Of the million TV sets in use, 42 percent were in New York City. The FCC contributed to the situation when, in the fall of 1948, it became nervous over the boom in TV sales and clamped a freeze on new station licenses; originally intended to last only a few months, while the government sorted out its feelings about the young medium, the freeze dragged on for nearly four years.

Well over half of Berle's viewers were thus in East Coast cities. A lot of them watched in working-class bars; even in 1950 only 9 percent of American homes had television. Berle was a sensation with the people who had always favored his kind of comedy: working- and lower-middle-class New Yorkers, gathered in bars and friends' houses, enjoying a party atmosphere. As TV became a home appliance nationwide, his ratings fell quickly and far.

For the time being, though, his success inspired a rush for comedy-variety programs: *Colgate Theatre*, *Fireball Fun-for-All*, *Cavalcade of Stars*, *Arthur Godfrey*, *Ed Sullivan*. This wasn't where most TV executives saw the future of programming, but it was what economics demanded. Milton Berle was selling TVs, selling NBC, and, most important of all, selling Texaco. During the Berle boom, sponsors took firm control of the infant medium. Even in radio the networks had been willing to carry some unsponsored airtime. But by the beginning of the 1948–49 season every hour on the network schedule had a sponsor.

Advertisers had had to fumble around radio for a few years to learn how to use the medium, but they entered television with their broadcast skills sharply honed. Critics who'd been disappointed by American radio's commercial course had good reason to be pessimistic about TV. This was clearly a powerful medium, threatening to change the very nature of our perception of the world. As Daniel Boorstin wrote, "Just as the printing press five centuries before had begun to democratize learning, now the television would democratize experience." To put such a tool in the hands of manufacturers and advertising agencies seemed to many a very frightening prospect.

Control by sponsors proved to be even tighter on television than on radio. The high cost of TV production made it imperative for advertisers to protect their investments. They sought to do so by applying to TV shows the same methods they used in industrial production; they demanded a steady, middle level of quality that permitted very few great programs but risked few utter failures. Although projects like *Kraft Television Theatre* were noble-sounding, their dramatic range was restricted by the need to support the sponsor's calculated image. The *Kraft* dramas were well produced, well acted, well directed, and well written but always had to endorse basic American values and social structures. As Kenneth Hey summarized them, they "tended to depict a wholesome society, occasionally misguided by commonly felt desires, peopled with morally delicate but psychologically normal characters. . . . Most were forgiven their transgressions." They fitted the pattern of what Martin Gottfried has called "right-wing theater," the worldview of which includes "a belief in God, a respect for law, a love of country, a need for order, a sense of family, a concern with appearance, a willingness to be organized, a recognition of the good in social responsibility . . . marriage, social systems, maturity." No searing critiques, no Beckett or Pinter, would ever be tested on the cheese-buying public.

Comedy, bearing less prestige and allowing for less artistic strutting, would be controlled even more tightly by the sponsors' requirements. Among hundreds of pharisaic rules imposed on comedy writers was this gem handed down by the Sherwin-Williams Paint Company, sponsoring *The Ray Bolger Show*: "Do-it-yourself activity around the home by the husband or wife should never be ridiculed or made to appear difficult." The paint people no doubt felt that the loss of a few standard domestic comedy springboards was nothing against the loss of a few customers who might be softheaded enough to let *The Ray Bolger Show* affect their judgment.

There was precious little sponsor mocking on television such as Fred Allen and Jack Benny had once indulged in. The sponsors' position was clearly stated in the editorial for the first issue of *Sponsor* magazine, launched in 1946 for the would-be television advertiser: "Censorship is integral to the central purpose of creating good will." (Even when sponsors didn't mind, comedians seemed loath to ridicule an institution so venerable as a consumer product manufacturer, with American humor in its tamer, more conservative postwar mood.)

Commercial programming operated on one dubious assumption: that the American audience, rural or urban, northern or southern, has uniform taste. As early as 1928 NBC commissioned a study by an MIT professor to support this very point, mainly in order to reassure sponsors. Nearly thirty years later Robert Kintner, the president of ABC, said: "I think the taste of America is almost identical from Maine to California."

Patterns of book, record, and ticket sales seemed to argue against this, so programmers conceived the philosophy that's become known as dead centerism. No program, said this wisdom, should offend the values or beliefs of any group in any region of the country. All entertainment should be held in colloidal suspension at the dead center of the American melting pot.

For the young playwrights and directors working on NBC's sound stages, it was a painful system to accept. There was still optimism about the medium's artistic potential in 1948, when the Authors League called a New York meeting to discuss the future of writers on television. Among the attendees were many bright lights, both literary and popular: Lillian Hellman, John Hersey, Elmer Rice, Oscar Hammerstein II, Moss Hart. Hart addressed the group with high hopes: "If we can retain control of our material, if television is handled properly—by creative minds—it could become the most exciting medium we've ever had." But he also voiced the fears that underlay the meeting: "Whatever form the medium takes, we writers must get together on common ground. My friends, there's that box standing in the living room with its glass eye staring out at us, and unless we build our ark now, what comes out of it will wash us all away."

The flood began as television became more democratic and sponsors developed a clearer idea of the medium's nature. Max Wilk, who wrote a great deal for early television, including the sitcom *Mama*, before dropping out to write novels and plays, reflected bitterly on "the remorseless waves of giveaway shows, old movies, game shows, staged quizzes, commercials, interviews, taped situation comedies, and all the rest of that living wallpaper." Writer Reginald Rose said: "What television has done, and has learned, is the same thing that food manufacturers have learned to do, and that is to make everything plastic, and to make people need and enjoy and demand plastic." His plastic food metaphor is especially pointed. Rose was a prominent writer for *Kraft Television Theatre*. Fred Allen used the harshest words: "Television is a triumph of equipment over people, and the minds that control it are so small that you could put them in the navel of a flea and still have room beside them for a network vice-president's heart. . . . They call television a medium because nothing on it is ever well done."

Contrary to Allen's remark, however, the controlling minds were not always small. In 1949 David Sarnoff hired a remarkable man named Sylvester ("Pat") Weaver as his head of new television operations. Weaver was a sponsorship man through and through. He'd been an advertising manager for American Tobacco and vice-president in charge of radio and television for Young & Rubicam advertising. He was also an articulate visionary, viewed by many who worked with him as a brilliant mind. Jack

Paar, the talk show host who became known for his battles with networks and sponsors, called him "one of the most creative executives in television."

Weaver was certainly one of the most important, setting the tone for NBC television during its period of greatest supremacy. He called his programming strategy Operation Frontal Lobes. As he described the network's purpose, "Your mission would not be just to make money, and it is not just to entertain people and it's not just to sell goods, and it's not just to have social influence, and it's not just to elect people to political office. . . . The real thing here is a power greater than print, which can change society and shape it for the better, and it isn't even going to be hard to do it."

The heart of Weaver's social philosophy was communication. "I believe totally in the fact that communications are the way we're going to bring about a mutation in the human condition, and make us from tribal idiots, certainly preadult fools, eventually into the first civilized adult society." This, of course, is an essential assumption of modern corporate culture. As William H. Whyte pointed out in *The Organization Man*, corporate structures interpret problems as the result of communications breakdowns. Without this conviction, without this denial of the possibility of irreparable conflicts of interest, the system cannot function. As Whyte observes, the modern social ethic maintains that man, "of himself, is isolated, meaningless; only as he collaborates with others does he become worthwhile, for by sublimating himself in the group, he helps to create a whole that is greater than the sum of its parts."

For Pat Weaver, the first step in getting people to communicate was getting them to listen to his message. "We used comedy at eight P.M., practically every night, in order to dominate the audience. We put on people like Berle, Bob Hope, Dean Martin and Jerry Lewis—and then, at nine, we'd let the audience flow on to shows with more substance. . . . In that grand design, entertainment was used to get people to watch the medium and to get caught by it, but the end would be that we would . . . liberate them from tribal primitive belief patterns."

Weaver valued the artist as part of the team. "You got your creative people in and you talked about something that was to be an exciting new step for mankind . . . you really *did* get them excited, because all people, and particularly creative people, really do want to have a better world. . . . Therefore you can get to them and you can make them work harder, work better, really outperform their talents."

Weaver created a philosophical underpinning for what was already corporate practice: manufacturers, advertisers, networks, and artists, working in concert to shape "cybernetic civilization." This was the ideal of America's rising leadership class in the aftermath of World War II. That the system worked to the economic benefit of sponsoring corporations was all to the good. The betterment of the sponsors meant the betterment of the managerial capitalist system, which meant the betterment of America and the world. The betterment of the network meant the betterment of communication, which meant the betterment of global civilization and bureaucratic democracy. With proper communications all people would see that they were only co-workers in one great organization. This would become the principal message of the sitcom.

3

Without Sanka, No Marriage

No one quite knew what America was in 1948. During the war most citizens had looked forward to a bountiful future, to new families, to endless peace. But peace had brought inflation, housing shortages, the cold war, accusations of Reds in our midst, nuclear terror. Some of those troubles, said the authorities, would prove transient. Others, like the cold war, seemed unsolvable except by greater horror. The new world did unquestionably bring one nifty new invention: television. But except for Uncle Miltie, no one knew quite what it was either.

Still, there were signposts to the future. The marriage rate was double its prewar levels. Nearly three and a half million babies were born in 1946, an astounding 20 percent jump over the year before. Births in 1947 soared 12 percent higher still, and 1948 showed only the slightest decline.

The business world could not have been happier. *Time* magazine chortled that 1947 had brought "3,800,000 new consumers" into the world. Industry had stagnated briefly after the war, when government orders slackened. Now it could throw its heightened productivity into the making of clothes, toys, household appliances, even prefab homes. A realtor-industrialist named William J. Levitt was starting to build suburban houses on assembly lines. *Fortune* crowed: "We need not worry too much about a post-armament depression. A civilian market growing by the size of Iowa every year ought to be able to absorb whatever production the military will eventually turn loose." American businessmen were already banking on the baby boom. William Paley was banking on sit-coms.

In 1946 Paley left his wartime assignment as director of the government's Psychological Warfare department and retook the helm of CBS. His network was still trailing NBC in the ratings, but not hopelessly. Paley's guidance had made CBS News the most prestigious and popular news source of the war. Now he wanted to challenge NBC in its two strongest areas: prime-time entertainment and television. Convinced that TV would never hit the big time until color broadcasting was possible, CBS executives had put most of their time and capital into developing a color system, at the expense of programming. CBS's color was unquestionably ahead of NBC's, but both were years from practicability, and the public didn't want to wait. As CBS producer Worthington Miner noted, the popularity of the 1947 World Series "forced CBS to abandon its insistence on color and to recognize that public demand for television was going to make it essential for the company to get into the picture—and fast."

Paley looked at his entertainment options and decided that CBS needed a "feel" of its own, something it could offer that NBC could not. Sitcoms, he felt, were his best bet. They were easy to maintain week after week, they encouraged regular viewing, and they suited America's domestic mood. Paley realized that many families, even if they did nothing else as a group, would be watching TV together regularly. If the people inside the box were a family reflecting the people outside the box, so much the better. Even after Berle had exploded onto the tube, Paley maintained that sitcoms would prove stabler and more exploitable in the long run.

The success of *Ozzie and Harriet* boded well. By 1948 Paley had followed with several more radio sitcoms, all cute, all wholesome, all slickly written and well acted, with distinct gimmicks. *My Friend Irma*, with Marie Wilson, was a classic "dumb blonde" vehicle. *Our Miss Brooks* featured Eve Arden as a wry, reluctantly unmarried schoolteacher. *Life with Luigi* brought a new group of heartwarming ethnics, Italians, into the sitcom realm. *My Favorite Husband*, starring an ambitious comedienne named Lucille Ball, followed the misadventures of a cute pair of "young marrieds." They were all solid radio successes, cutting in on NBC ratings. (NBC even felt compelled to respond with a cute family sitcom of its own in 1949, a bland "bumbling dad" vehicle called *Father Knows Best*.)

Then, in September 1948, Paley scored his biggest coup of all. With the aid of some creative accounting he showed Freeman Gosden and Charles Correll that they could slash their taxes by two-thirds by selling *Amos 'n' Andy* to CBS and signing on as hired entertainers. Paley had stuck in his thumb and taken NBC's plum. NBC's other headliners immediately asked their network to cut them similar deals, but NBC's brass played cautiously, as overdogs so often do; fearing that Paley's maneuver might be found illegal, they refused. Within weeks CBS had Jack Benny, Burns and Allen, Groucho Marx, Red Skelton, and Edgar Bergen under contract. The industry press called it "Paley's Comet."

Paley left his new hit shows on radio for the moment, but he was thinking ahead: "I was not only thinking of radio. . . . I wanted people who I thought would be able to transfer from radio to television." A few months later CBS announced its plans to put *Amos 'n' Andy* on television. Immediately, apprehensive rumblings were heard from the black intelligentsia. Paley assured them that this version of *Amos 'n' Andy* would not be a blackface show but would star only the finest black actors, to be selected in a nationwide talent search. Paley was willing to take his time developing this one. It would be, he believed, the medium's first huge sitcom hit, the beginning of the CBS television dynasty.

In the meantime, CBS had to move quickly to get a few quality programs on line. The network installed a manager of program development in the spring of '48, giving the job to one of those bright young New Yorkers, Worthington Miner. "I started in the theater, and I had only had a brief and unhappy spell with motion pictures," Miner said. His assignment was to create one drama anthology, one variety show, one kids' show, and one sitcom. He approached them all with a theatrical slant: "In my directors I was looking for a theatrical set of standards, a respect for the literate word and the provocative idea. . . . Going into television was nothing to me but an opportunity to do all the things I couldn't have done in the theater, and also to reach an audience so much more vast than any audience we'd ever reached." The results were impressive. For his first three projects Miner came up with *Studio One*, Ed Sullivan's *Toast of the Town*, and *Mr. I Magination*, all critically acclaimed and popular.

For his sitcom, Miner wanted a known quantity, something with an established radio audience. Technology, unfortunately, prevented him from using any of radio's big Hollywood-based stars. Radio had found several solutions to the difficulty of broadcasting across the three-hour time difference from California to the East. Some programs were simply broadcast early in California and transmitted live by phone wire across the country. Some were actually performed live twice. Eventually recording technology became sophisticated enough to lift that burden: A program was broadcast live for eastern listeners, simultaneously recorded, and then played from the recording for the West. TV didn't have those options.

Phone cables weren't complex enough to carry video broadcasts, so programs could be sent only by special coaxial cables, which hadn't yet been laid across country. The only cost-effective alternative was to shoot cheap, blurry films, called kinescopes, straight off a TV monitor and ship them east. "Watching a kinescope," as Max Wilk said, "was like looking at a bowl of gray pea soup. Here and there you could barely make out the croutons." The networks had been content to dump kinescopes on their smaller western audience, so long as the East got the real live thing. They were not inclined to let kinescopes from Hollywood compete against live programming in the huge eastern market. So Miner took what he could from New York radio: the respected but fading *Goldbergs*.

During its heyday Gertrude Berg had parlayed her creation into a Broadway play, a couple of books, and a comic strip. But as the immigrant generation of Jews receded into memory, her type of humor began to decline. NBC had already dropped it from its national schedule by the time Miner picked it up, but on January 10, 1949, the TV *Goldbergs* premiered to good reviews and solid ratings, the first successful sitcom on television.

Although converted from a serial to a weekly half hour with self-contained episodes, the program was essentially the same as it had been on radio. Gertrude Berg still wrote, directed, and starred in it, though she now left production to Miner. Jake still ran his clothing business; Molly still sought to find the "perfect match" for her teenaged kids, still mangled the language, still meddled and gossiped but ultimately helped her family find the right solution to every problem. The TV show placed a greater emphasis on Molly's live-in uncle David than the radio version had. David was a scholarly, thoughtful old man, rarely used for laughs, often for a message. Perhaps the events of the 1940s had made Berg feel a need to present a less quaint, more substantial view of Jewish tradition.

Plots continued to revolve around the conflict of tradition and newness, Jewish ways and mainstream American ways. In one show fourteen-year-old Rosalie has discovered the pop Freudian psychology then invading popular culture. Her mother is giving her "inhibitions," she says. She's giving her "emotional scars." So she announces her intentions to cut her hair and wear lipstick. She goes off to a baby-sitting job without taking her homework, and soon her parents discover that she's arranged for a boy to meet her there. Jake is furious. He has ordered Rosalie to abandon these wild ideas, but she has ignored him. "I am the father in the home, or what am I? If I am, I want to know!" Molly is troubled but philosophical. "The world is different now," she says. Her greatest allegiance is not to social codes but to the happiness of her flesh and blood.

Ultimately, of course, the situation works itself out. Nothing happens with the boy, and Rosalie even loses her courage when the time comes to cut her hair. Jake is grateful, and at Molly's urging he compromises: Rosalie can get her hair trimmed but not chopped. Fade-out on a close shot of Rosalie's hair clippings wafting to the floor.

This is clearly recognizable as a sitcom structure, but the specific conflict seems strangely archaic. Mainstream America went through these battles—haircuts, makeup, underage smooching, adolescent psychobabble—in the 1920s. This "Rosalie Bobs Her Hair" plot could have impact only to an audience acquainted with the conservatism of recent immigrants. Yet even for Jewish New Yorkers in 1949, this could scarcely have had much immediacy. Molly's generation was fading. It was Rosalie's generation that was now raising teenagers. And getting coiffures. And misquoting Freud.

Solutions always came very easily for Molly. No real crisis ever occurred in this matter of the haircut. Rosalie's own good-girlness saved the day for everyone. A sitcom dealing with more pressing conflicts would probably have had to put someone through the wringer: Jake puts his foot down, alienates Rosalie, and has to learn the hard way to understand youth. Or Rosalie gets a friend to cut her hair, but it's a horrible hatchet job, and she rues the day she ever disobeyed her papa. Molly's easy outs could have been satisfying only to viewers who knew that such conflicts were already safely in the past. *The Goldbergs* was set in the present, but it was nostalgia, to soothe the nerves of adult, urban easterners who had once loved and battled Mollys of their own in their struggles to become Americans.

She was perfect for her function. Once every show she would lean out her window, speaking confidentially to us just as if she were gossiping with her ubiquitous but never-seen neighbor Mrs. Bloom. And she would say something like "Without his Sanka decaffeinated coffee, Mr. Goldberg would be grouchy as a bear. I tell you, I tell you truly, really, and I would not lie to you because if I did, would you ever believe me? If Mr. Goldberg did not drink Sanka decaffeinated coffee, I don't know what I would do, I . . . I don't even know if we'd still have a marriage, I mean it, I really do. . . ." If the eternal mother herself could not soothe her viewers' nerves, then she could tell them where to turn. General Foods calculated that Sanka sales rose by 57 percent among television owners during Molly's brief tenure as its spokeswoman.

Only six months after Molly first leaned out of her televised window, another ethnic matriarch premiered on CBS. We saw her first in a photo album, as a woman's hand turned the pages. The woman's voice-over drew us into her nostalgic mood: "I remember the big white house on Elm Street, and my little sister, Dagmar, and my big brother, Nels, and, of course, Papa. But most of all, I remember Mama." We entered the home of the Hansen family, Norwegian immigrants in San Francisco at the turn of the century. The center of their universe was a simple living room in a stately house, with a coffeepot placed prominently at its axis.

As the story begins, Papa Hansen wishes he were an American citizen. There is a school nearby that will teach him what he needs to know in order to pass the citizenship test, but Papa is a proud man. He is an adult, educated in Norway. He cannot bear the embarrassment of returning to school, studying again "like a child." Mama thinks his pride is foolish, but she knows too well that she would only hurt him by challenging it. She goes to the school herself, learns everything a citizen must know. But Mama isn't interested in becoming an American citizen. That's for the menfolk. She uses what she learned to tutor Papa at home. Finally he takes the test and becomes an American.

The Hansens were created in a semiautobiographical novel by Kathryn Forbes called *Mama's Bank Account*, a female Norwegian equivalent of Clarence Day's *Life with Father*. Broadway producers seized upon it, hoping for another ethnic-nostalgic hit like *Father*, and called it *I Remember Mama*. It did well enough to inspire RKO to make a movie of it in 1948. Meanwhile, General Foods, pleased with its success with *The Goldbergs*, wanted a second series to push its Maxwell House coffee. The Hansens looked like a fine companion set to the Goldbergs.

Mama, as the TV show was called, was quieter and tonier than *The Goldbergs*. Mama had an accent—more of a lilt, really—but no laughs were milked from her syntax. The cast was theater-based: Broadway star

Peggy Wood as Mama, Judson Laire as Papa, Dickie Van Patten as Nels, Rosemary Rice as Katrin, and as Dagmar a bright little kid named Robin Morgan, who later became a prominent feminist activist. They performed live with no commercial breaks for the show's seven-year run (the commercials ran only at the beginning and the end, but the cast did use that coffeepot in the living room an awful lot). More than any other program *Mama* evinced the tendency of early TV to marry the themes and contents of theater to the programmatic structure of radio.

Mama's director, Ralph Nelson, had previously acted on and written for Broadway. Later he made a name for himself in thoughtful, theatrical movies: *Lilies of the Field*, *Requiem for a Heavyweight*. He and the show's principal writer, Frank Gabrielson, both were of Scandinavian extraction and approached the Hansens with understanding. The producer, Carol Irwin, told prospective new writers: "We never go in for quick plots, with contrived twists and turns, and easy solutions. What happens here is that we're dealing with honest characters, and our audience knows them and identifies with them. We keep playing off their actual experiences, and that's why, I think, we're keeping our audience."

Mama's pacing was often excruciatingly slow and overly verbal. It resembled soap operas and dramas like *One Man's Family* more than it did other comedies, which was perfect for appealing to the housewives whom General Foods had targeted as its Maxwell House buyers. Max Wilk, who wrote occasionally for the show, reported that General Foods valued the Hansens highly as representatives and protected their stories from network interference.

Apart from pace and tone, however, *Mama* and *The Goldbergs* were much alike. Both were nostalgic looks at a vanished transitional age in American social history; *Mama* was simply more overt about it, being set forty years in the past and framed by Katrin's photo album. Both featured craftsman fathers (Papa Hansen was a carpenter) who tried vainly to lay down the old-world law to their budding American children; both used a mother as a loving familiar center to bring the opposing forces into harmony.

Generational and sexual conflicts were at the heart of many of *Mama*'s plots. In one, Papa learns that Katrin is reading a controversial romance novel and forbids her "to read a book that people say is bad." Katrin protests that Papa can't condemn a book that he hasn't read, but Papa is firm. Mama decides to check the book out for herself. She loves it. Now Papa's virility is threatened. A friend tells him that "women read such things when they are restless—and need romance . . . you know, when their husbands are getting older . . . and . . ." Mama reassures him that she loves him as much as ever, as "the father of my children. My friend. My companion that I have never been away from—in thousands and thousands of days and nights." The rifts are healed. As a final chuckle, to relieve the tension, Papa comments on Mama's sudden, unaccustomed eloquence. "I guess it must have been this book I have been reading," she says, and they fade to the Maxwell House ad.

In another installment Papa is offered a foreman's position at a construction company, but he turns it down because he doesn't feel it's proper for him to command other men. His kids—restless little Americans with their eyes on the future—complain that they need the extra money. Papa takes the job, but a day later he announces he's lost it. The kids decide he's a failure, he doesn't know how to get ahead in the world. But Mama learns the truth: Papa lost his foremanship because he couldn't bring himself to fire a man. The kids see the light. They're proud of their father for his gentleness.

The Hansens' problems were usually harder to solve than the Goldbergs' and carried a bit more bite, but both families were enacting the same drama: a nostalgic recapitulation of America's assimilation of European immigrants in the first part of the twentieth century. It was the drama of the death of traditional culture, the creation of a universal national culture. No medium could have been better for that drama than television. This was Pat Weaver's "communications," his "transcendence of tribalism" in its most accessible form.

The patterns of *The Goldbergs* and *Mama* have held true for ethnic-oriented sitcoms ever since, down to 1989's *Famous Teddy Z*. The older generation struggles under its traditional culture as the younger one apes American values. The old ones can be cantankerous but are sentimental deep inside. There are a few older fringe characters, neighbors or relatives, whose traditionality makes them foolish; they remind us that the old ways are not the best ways. Balancing them are American acquaintances whose extreme selfishness, ambition, or materialism causes complications and reminds us that the new ways aren't always the best ways either. The best ways, say these shows, are the consensual ways, the group-oriented ways. In recent shows the moderating force has generally been the young man of the family, whereas in these older ones it was usually the mother, but the basic message is the same.

The Goldbergs and *Mama* looked backward and forward: a fond farewell to a pluralistic past and models for the creation of the new homogeneous system to which postwar America was committing itself. Although other ethnic comedies followed—most notoriously *Amos 'n' Andy*—they marked the end of a stage of national popular culture. It would be up to the contemporary, pointedly nonethnic Nelsons and Andersons and Cleavers to play out America's family comedies over the years to come.

The Hansens came to a dignified end as their audience slowly shrank below the cancellation threshold in 1956. The Goldbergs weren't so lucky. Despite all their efforts to resist the present, the present finally caught up to them. In June 1950 they had just finished their second season to solid ratings, at one point placing seventh overall. The staff was taking a summer break, looking forward to season number three, when a nasty, anonymous little book called *Red Channels* began to circulate through the offices of the broadcasting industry. It listed people who worked in radio and television who were supposedly Communist, or pro-Communist, or had some distant affiliation to some "Communist front" organization. One of those listed was Philip Loeb, who played Jake Goldberg.

General Foods wanted Loeb dismissed. Maybe executives were afraid that viewers would suspect him of fluorinating their Sanka. Gertrude Berg rushed to his defense and for nearly a year kept him on the show. But *Red Channels* continued to draw more publicity. General Foods announced it was pulling out of the program. Berg refused to budge. CBS sided with the sponsor. NBC offered to pick the show up, which might have been a good chance for it to pay Paley back for his "comet," but no sponsor would touch it. Finally Berg offered to pay Loeb two years' salary, conditional upon his resignation.

Berg brought *The Goldbergs* back, seemingly by sheer strength of will. Harold J. Stone and then Robert H. Harris took Loeb's place. But it had lost precious months; it had lost the familiar Jake; it had lost its audience. Maybe it had lost its era as well. It bounced from NBC down to DuMont, then into syndication on local stations, then into extinction in 1955, the same year Philip Loeb died of an overdose of sleeping pills.

There's an ugly appropriateness in the fact that a Red Scare killed the Goldbergs. They were the product of a troubled, patchwork prewar America. Loeb's leftist affiliations (which were never specified) most likely dated to the depression, when it was common for thoughtful urban Americans—including a large number of Jews—to look leftward for solutions to the crisis. In the late '40s America was pulling together, clinging to a centrist, procorporate position, transforming itself almost overnight into a world power. By the millions Americans were becoming William H. Whyte's "organization men," purging themselves of depression extremism, downplaying ethnicity, many denying their own pasts. At its best the new mood brought a spirit of cooperation, consensus, assimilation, egalitarianism. At its worst it turned Americans against anyone who reminded them of dissent, who might have made them doubt the ideal of consensus. Like Philip Loeb. Even, in a sense, like the Goldbergs.

4

Normal Lives in Normal Surroundings

The success of *The Goldbergs* demonstrated that radio shows could move effectively to television, good news for everyone involved in producing programs, since transferring an established property was easier and safer than creating something new.

General Foods quickly sought another heartwarming family to go with its Goldbergs and Hansens, and this time it was NBC that offered a property: *The Aldrich Family*. Typically cautious, however, the network insisted upon a new cast for the TV show, while keeping the regular cast on the radio version. (Even the TV version suffered an unwelcome cast change after its first season: Jean Muir, who played Mrs. Aldrich, showed up in *Red Channels* right along with Philip Loeb. With no Gertrude Berg to fight for her, however, the sponsor managed a quick and discreet dismissal.) The show started fairly well in the ratings, against weak competition, but its old-fashioned appeal didn't hold viewers of the new medium, and it quickly faded.

NBC's caution doomed its other radio spin-off, *The Life of Riley*, from the start. The show's strongest point had always been William Bendix's vocal characterization of Riley. The substitution of a young, unknown Jackie Gleason didn't click with audiences, and it died in less than six months. It did, however, mark a technical advance: It was the first sitcom shot on film.

Many producers saw the future of television in film. With a little extra time and money a TV program could be shot like a movie, allowing for fancier staging and a slicker veneer than live TV. A filmed program could be shot anytime, shown anytime, and even shown more than once if the audience demanded it. The only obstacle was that extra time and money. NBC tried to keep costs down on *Riley*, making it a dreary one-camera affair, but even so, the cost of filming was enough to make its weak ratings doubly painful. The following year the network took another ill-fated stab at filmed sitcoms with *The Hank McCune Show*, a slapstick vehicle about a lovable bumbler. Ratings weren't terrible, but production costs drove away its sponsor after what was then the minimum life span for a series, thirteen weeks. (It did, however, win a place in cultural history as the first TV show to use a laugh track.)

ABC—then still the struggling fourth network, trailing even DuMont—had the only successful filmed series of those early years with *The Lone Ranger*. But when that network tried the same method with a comedy—*Life with the Erwins*, another bland bumbling dad opus starring a minor movie actor named Stu Erwin—it didn't do nearly as well. ABC tried changing the name of the show to *The Trouble with Father* (perhaps hoping that through some trick of residual memory viewers would think of it as *Life with Father* and tune in by accident), then *The Stu Erwin Show*, then *The New Stu Erwin Show* but was never able to make it more than a borderline success.

ABC also tried a Hollywood-based kinescoped sitcom, *The Ruggles*. Landing a popular movie character actor like Charlie Ruggles for a weekly series was quite a coup for the little network, and all the pieces seemed in place for a successful cutesy "befuddled father" comedy, but technology was against it. Its ratings were solid in the West, where it played live, but dismal in kinescope country. After trying it in twelve different time slots in three years, ABC let it go.

William Paley wasn't going to let CBS squander its energies on character actors, cheap filming, and old shows with new casts. He was playing for high stakes, and he wanted his radio headliners on the tube. The first, in 1949, was Ed Wynn; the first major performer to try radio became the first radio star to try TV. With the next season came Jack Benny and George Burns and Gracie Allen.

Benny was then sitting on top of the radio world and consented to do only four TV broadcasts in that first season, while keeping his radio series running unbroken. Burns, on the other hand, looked at his softer radio ratings and decided to take the leap; he and Gracie sharply curtailed their radio work and even moved temporarily back to New York in order to make a biweekly TV series. Benny stuck with radio until 1954, and even after moving to television, he retained his comedy-variety format, opening his shows with a monologue in front of a stage curtain. Burns and Allen also retained the spirit of their radio show (Burns recalled: "I met with . . . Bill Paley at the Brown Derby restaurant in Los Angeles to outline the format we would use. We agreed that Gracie would play Gracie . . . and I would play the guy who stood next to her"). But they continued their drift toward comedic domesticity by performing mainly in a living-room set, the quintessential sitcom milieu.

Benny's shows were popular but few. Burns and Allen's showed promise, but they hadn't cracked the top twenty-five in the ratings. *The Goldbergs* and *Mama* both were solidly popular, but neither could challenge NBC's comedy-variety giants. Paley was still looking forward to his big sitcom hit, still convinced it would be *Amos 'n' Andy*. Gosden and Correll's radio show was still very popular after twenty years, and CBS planned to produce and promote the TV version to the hilt.

It would be shot on film at the Hal Roach Studios with an unheard-of per episode budget of forty thousand dollars to guarantee a Hollywood sleekness; this would not be *The Life of Riley*. It would be directed by Charles Barton, whose résumé included Universal's popular Abbott and Costello movies. He was no auteur, but he was a better journeyman than nearly anyone in TV at the time; he set the pattern for the rhythmic alternation of two-shots and medium-close shots that became a sitcom standard.

The highly publicized talent search of 1949 and 1950, which involved eight hundred auditions and fifty screen tests, brought good results. Spencer Williams—a veteran of black-produced movies since the '30s and the writer, director, and star of his own movie, *Go Down Death*— landed the Scarlett O'Hara role of the series, Andy Brown. Broadway comedian Alvin Childress was to be Amos, and Tim Moore, a vaudevillian who once toured with Mantan Moreland, would be the Kingfish. One of Hollywood's most popular black character actors, Willie Best, got the job of the lazy janitor, Lightnin'. Ernestine Wade carried over from the radio show, as Sapphire. Freeman Gosden and Charles Correll were to remain as the old overseers of the show. The scripts would be handled mainly by Bob Mosher and Joe Connelly, who'd proved themselves the best character writers on the radio show staff. CBS wanted to show that it would preserve the heart of the old series while adapting it to the new medium and new times. Network executives expected to hear a buzz of anticipation. Instead, they heard a hiss of objection.

In retrospect it's clear that CBS's timing could not have been much worse. The aftermath of World War II found the power, vocality, and political sensitivity of American blacks hitting a new crest. The black bourgeoisie had been growing for decades in number and strength and pride. Now it was making itself felt. NAACP membership increased ten times over during the 1940s. By 1948 black leaders were making waves in American journalism and entertainment. The Democratic party courted them in the election. President Truman appointed a Civil Rights Commission and declared 1949 a "Year of Rededication" to the principles of racial equality. Hollywood began a series of "message movies" in 1949—*Pinky, Home of the Brave, Lost Boundaries*—and the message was that racial discrimination must end. The liberal concept of full integration— gradual, painless, nonviolent, but inevitable—captured the American conscience.

Radio was not to be left behind. NBC hired a public relations firm to work toward "a more realistic treatment of the Negro on the air and the hiring of more Negro personnel." CBS broadcast Katherine Dunham's *The Story of a Drum*, and ABC *The Jackie Robinson Show*. WDAS in Philadelphia was broadening the horizons of black entertainment broadcasting with *The Bon Bon Show*. And WMAQ in Chicago, where Amos and Andy had gotten their start, tackled major issues with *Destination Freedom*.

TV programmers dragged their heels on all provocative issues; they avoided even using blacks as characters and entertainers. But black hopes were high for the new medium. As far back as 1939 Julius Adams of the *Amsterdam News* had been calling television "our new hope." By the beginning of the 1950s *Ebony* magazine was calling TV "an amazing new weapon which can be all-powerful in blasting America's bigots. . . . Television has supplied ten-league boots to the Negro in his fight to win what the constitution of this country guarantees." The mainstream entertainment industry newspaper *Variety* ran a headline in 1950 celebrating the prospects for easy social change: NEGRO TALENT COMING INTO OWN ON TV

WITHOUT USING STEREOTYPES—A SURE SIGN THAT TELEVISION IS FREE OF RACIAL BARRIERS. Blacks were even ready to conquer TV on its own terms, sponsorship terms. *Ebony* published a study showing that blacks outpurchased whites, per capita, in consumer goods.

This was all part of what Walter White of the National Association for the Advancement of Colored People (NAACP) called the "rising wind" of a new era. Surely, thought middle-class black leaders, no one would be stupid enough to spit against that wind. Especially not CBS, which had distinguished itself as the most liberal of the networks. Bill Paley, after all, had worked closely with Roosevelt during the war. And the CBS News team—Edward R. Murrow, William Shirer, Eric Sevareid, and others— had a decidedly northeastern liberal slant.

Yet there it was, in the black and white of CBS's programming announcements. As the historian Thomas Cripps has written, "Into this world of newly felt, newly flexed black middle-class consciousness, activism, and wealth descended *Amos 'n' Andy*, complete with baggy pants, plug hats, foul cigars, pushy wives, misfired schemes, and mangled grammar." Black leaders felt shocked, betrayed, and angry.

The NAACP protested to the press and CBS that *Amos 'n' Andy* "depicts the Negro in a stereotyped and degrading manner. . . . It strengthens the conclusion among uninformed or prejudiced people that Negroes and other minorities are inferior, lazy, dumb, and dishonest." Walter White particularly deplored the characters' use of "street slang." The black lodge members and independent businessmen of *Amos 'n' Andy*, he thought, were portrayed as "quacks and thieves, slippery cowards ignorant of their professions." He made clear that he found the program insulting, not only to black Americans in general but to the black bourgeoisie in particular.

CBS executives had clearly misread the mood of black America. They'd been accustomed to getting a little heat on the *Amos 'n' Andy* radio show, but for every black objection there had always seemed to be a word of praise. But the times were different, the medium was different. Even in 1939, when writing of the "new hope," Julius Adams had issued a warning about *Amos 'n' Andy*; although blacks endured the stereotyped voices on radio, he said "it would be suicide to put a show like this on television." Ten years later feelings were running much hotter.

CBS, however, wasn't totally blind. Producers and promoters worked quickly to create the impression that a progressive attitude governed *Amos 'n' Andy*. They hired a "Consultant on Racial Matters," Flournoy

Miller, with pristine credentials as a socially conscious black entertainer: Fisk 1917, veteran of the Cotton Club, largely responsible for discovering Josephine Baker and Lena Horne, performed in Hollywood's all-black *Stormy Weather*, collaborated with Eubie Blake and Noble Sissle in creating *Shuffle Along*, the musical that in 1920 had "put the Negro back on Broadway." CBS publicized his background and his new position, along with the credentials of the all-black cast.

The head writers, Mosher and Connelly, promised a new, more sensitive approach to the characters and their milieu. Gosden and Correll were subtly distanced from the project, and more authority was placed in the hands of racially sensitive director Charles Barton. Black entertainers began to speak out in favor of the show as an opportunity for work and visibility. Network heads hoped that all this would quiet the storm. But as production plans proceeded, the resistance grew stiffer.

More unexpected trouble came in finding a sponsor, enough to delay the debut by a full season. Finally Schenley Distilleries, makers of Blatz beer, was lined up, and the schedule was set. *Amos 'n' Andy* was to premiere in June 1951, during the summer season, when the big competing comedy-variety stars were on vacation. CBS wanted nothing to hurt its prize project.

At stake for CBS was a valuable property, an expensive and widely hyped project, a shot at prime-time dominance. But at stake for organized blacks, as Thomas Cripps wrote, "was the right to a nationwide monopoly of broadcasting facilities through which the image of Afro-Americans was to be presented to an enormous American audience." The NAACP had a coordinated protest ready to roll. The morning after the premiere, thousands of angry letters, phone calls, and telegrams were racing off to CBS. And even more letters went straight to the almighty sponsors, announcing a black boycott of Blatz beer.

Variety gave the protest front-page headlines. Inside, its editorials joined the fray, calling for an end to *Amos 'n' Andy*'s stereotyping, bristling especially at Willie Best's portrayal of "the molasses-tempered janitor who is a throwback to the Stepin Fetchit era." Sympathetic groups offered support. The American Jewish Committee even nominated a team of consultants, including such prominent black intellectuals as political scientist Robert MacIver and psychologist Kenneth Clark, to create a substitute sitcom that would be found "unobjectionable," that would present blacks along the lines of those "loveable, admirable" Goldbergs. Regrettably no one acted on the suggestion; it would be difficult to imagine a more curious social document than a sitcom devised by an academic committee.

The powers behind *Amos 'n' Andy*—CBS, Gosden and Correll, Schenley Distilleries—avoided commenting on the controversy. But voices did begin to rise in defense of the show, voices from the black community itself. Columnist Billy Rowe of the *Pittsburgh Courier* wrote that the interests of the race were greatly served merely by the ability of blacks "to look at people of their own color, performing for people of every color." *Amos 'n' Andy*, he declared, was "the greatest television show on earth." As for the NAACP, they were just a lot of "pinks."

Black performers, seeing the NAACP's actions as injurious to the future prospects of blacks on television, rushed to the show's defense. Cast member Ernestine Wade noted that "agitation from officials of Negro organizations in the past jeopardized the progress of Negro shows." The Coordinating Council of Negro Performers threatened a picket of NAACP offices. The respected black actor and screenwriter Clarence Muse went so far as to call *Amos 'n' Andy* an "artistic triumph" and announced that he was switching to Blatz beer. The NAACP made no answer to these challenges, other than to keep hammering at the show.

Looking back on this hue and cry decades later, one can only wonder if anyone was really watching the show. Surely it was no "artistic triumph." Yet by the same token it seems scarcely insulting enough to justify such a ferocious assault.

The characters and their milieu were essentially the same as on radio, but with ethnic characteristics toned down and admirable aspects heightened. Amos was the respectable straight man; with his wife and daughter he was the very model of middle-class sitcom propriety. Andy was still the comic fool, answering the phone, "Fresh Air Taxi Cab Company, Incorpulated," still the girl chaser and financial schemer. But his speech was pointedly less dialect-driven than on radio, his stupidity less specific to an ethnic stereotype. If not for his color and some grammatical lapses, he'd have been just another in the legion of funny dopes who populated cornball Hollywood comedies.

There were some stereotyped holdover characters: Lightnin', the pushy Sapphire Stevens, the incompetent lawyer Algonquin J. Calhoun. But the people who made up the show's milieu—the shopkeepers, cops, landlords, neighbors, passersby who got sucked into Amos and Andy's misadventures—were always black and nearly always positively portrayed. They spoke like urbane northerners and were clearly not "slippery cowards ignorant of their professions." As Alvin Childress ("Amos") said later, "What its detractors fail to mention is that it was the very first time we saw a few blacks playing professionals—judges, lawyers, doctors." A few episodes did feature hard-core criminals as adversaries. They were always white.

Amos and Andy's physical environs were clean and ordinary and almost suffocatingly middle-class. Exteriors had that half L.A., half small-town look that was to distinguish sitcoms for the next twenty years. The Kingfish had a print of Frans Hals's *Laughing Cavalier* on the wall that his wife might have picked up at the same sale in which June Cleaver bought her *Blue Boy*.

The one very wrong note in this bourgeois idyll was George Stevens, the Kingfish. Lying, fleecing, strutting, mugging, wringing dues out of brothers in the preposterous Mystic Knights of the Sea Lodge, nostrils always open for a new scheme to get through life without working, he was still very much the coon. And he stole the show. Tim Moore turned in an expressive, energetic performance that brought to life the tritest plots and flattest lines. As Amos and Andy became duller and more respectable, he became the only sure source of laughs on the show. Since the show's creators had a greater stake in being funny than in being socially correct, he naturally began to carry most of the plots.

In one episode Kingfish discovers that Andy owns a valuable old coin and immediately begins to scheme. His wife, Sapphire, snaps, "You ain't thinkin' 'bout gyppin' him outa that coin, is you?" Kingfish widens his eyes. "Who, me? Innocent Stevens?" Then a baritone laugh: "I'll say I is!" Kingfish tries to trick Andy into giving him the nickel, but his scheme, as always, backfires; the coin is dropped into a pay phone, Andy and King-fish try to break the coin box open, and they're arrested (by a black cop). Kingfish hires lawyer Calhoun, who humiliates himself before the judge (also black). Kingfish finally has to swallow his pride and make a clean breast of the whole thing in order to get them off the hook.

Kingfish's countless schemes to cheat Andy often played specifically off the icons of middle-class propriety. One show finds Sapphire buying a house trailer on credit, planning to pay it off with four hundred dollars she's been saving. Kingfish, not knowing her plans, has already blown the money on his own fun. He has to get the money back before she finds out, so he contrives to use the trailer to bilk Andy out of the four hundred dollars: he sells him a cross-country tour, blindfolds him, and drives him around Central Park in the trailer. At each stop he sets up semiliterate signs identifying the place ("North Dakota, the State to Unlax In"). In the end, of course, Kingfish's wife and mother-in-law happen upon the scene and the schemer gets his comeuppance.

It was all fairly stupid stuff, but it served to delineate conflicting values for the characters: Sapphire's idea of fun was the family vacation, the house trailer, all mainstream Americana; even Andy, in his stupid way, shared the postwar middle-class dream to "see the U.S.A." It was Kingfish alone who stood for instant gratification, for being "nigger rich." And he was always the one to be defeated and humiliated.

This was *Amos 'n' Andy*'s solution to the problem of the Kingfish. As the series matured, he was used more and more as a negative foil, exemplifying improper behavior and suffering the consequences. In contrast with him, Amos and Andy themselves seemed increasingly responsible. They moved to the center of the modern social consensus; Kingfish was the disruptive outsider.

But it emerged quickly that the Kingfish was not to be reviled or even merely to be laughed at heartlessly. He was to be pitied. And in this lay one of the keys of contemporary social thinking: People who don't fit aren't evil but dysfunctional. They are too dangerous to be allowed to run unfettered, but to destroy them would undermine the very concept of consensus. They must be pitied and cared for, drawn by teaching or example or therapy into the happy group.

Kingfish gets himself in trouble on one show by lying to his family in rural Georgia about his great success in the urban world. After his humiliating exposure, he drags himself dejectedly away. Viewers might have laughed at his hammy exit, but they had to feel for him as well. Amos then struck at their feelings with a message of condescending tolerance: "I feel kinda sorry for the Kingfish. But you know, you can't much blame the Kingfish for wantin' the folks down in Marietta to think he's a big shot up here. It's just human nature for everybody to want somebody to think they is important. I guess that's what keeps a lot of us going in life."

Bob Mosher and Joe Connelly became masters of this theme: The loser puts on airs, bites off more than he can chew, is humiliated; his aspirations are understandable but irresponsible; his defeat is funny but touching; and the other characters tell us how to react, with the superior understanding of those who are living life properly. (They were to refine the theme further in a very different context—*Leave It to Beaver*—but with a character oddly similar to the Kingfish: Eddie Haskell.) Here was one of the keynotes of '50s TV being sounded tentatively in the offices of the Fresh Air Taxi Cab Company, Incorpulated.

The ultimate taming of the Kingfish occurred in an episode called "Happy Stevens." We open to find Kingfish and Sapphire fighting, as always. But whereas this has always been accepted as normal (by them) and funny (by us), now it's viewed as a problem; they've been listening to a pair of white marriage counselors on the radio called the Happy Harringtons. Suddenly this is no longer simply the stereotypically violent black marriage but a marriage gone bad, in need of outside help. They go on the Harringtons' talk show. They fight on the show, of course, but also break through to a few of their real problems. By the end of the show they're billing and cooing. Communication has saved their marriage. The Harringtons try to offer ridiculous "expert advice," but they need none of it. As a final little joke, the head of the radio station announces that he'd like to fire the Harringtons and replace them with the "Happy Stevenses."

This is a complex little plot. It involves ridicule of "experts," yet it is the apparatus and venue of the experts—structured communication, the talk show—that makes the reconciliation possible. It pokes a little fun at the broadcast media, but it is the media's entry into the private sphere of the marriage that first points out the problem as such. And in the end Kingfish and Sapphire become a superior version of the very white, very middle-class representatives of the perfect marriage. At heart this story is a model of the corporate society at work. Races, classes, and sexes are united through communication, not only personal husband-wife communication but the broader communication of the airwaves. All conflicts are illusory, and the proper system can solve them to the benefit of all. For one half hour at least the Kingfish joined the great new universal society. (The next week, of course, he was again trying to fleece Andy out of a few bucks, but such is formula comedy.)

Most *Amos 'n' Andy* plots defy any such analysis. If they aren't just more Kingfish schemes, then they are most likely by-the-numbers mix-ups such as all the Hollywood sitcoms used. Through it all, however, the creators show a drive to dignify and humanize their material. The results are often limpid or mawkish, but they leave little doubt of their basic prosocial position.

The most critically acclaimed of the episodes was the annually repeated Christmas show. Its action centers on Arabella, Amos's very sweet and very uncomical daughter (her original name on the radio show, revealingly, was Arbadella; the change of a couple of letters turned it from a burlesque of unusual black names into an evocation of class and culture). Seeing her sharing seasonal sentiment with her parents, "Uncle Andy" wants to do something special for her: He wants to buy her a talking black doll, even though it's too expensive for his means. This time he steers clear of the Kingfish and his schemes. He's going to find a job and work for the money. He even has to forgo buying the Kingfish a present in order to afford the doll, for which Kingfish—as the negative example—assails him. By Christmas Eve he is finally able to afford the doll and pays a very proper call on the Joneses to present it to the thrilled Arabella. Then she notices the snow falling. Without a trace of irony she says, "Wouldn't it be wonderful to have a white Christmas?" And Uncle Andy says, "Them's the best kind." Amos is moved by all this to tell Arabella a little story based on the Lord's Prayer, with an unobtrusively Christian message. And we fade out on the falling snow.

The Christmas show seemed almost calculated to quiet *Amos 'n' Andy*'s critics. Here was stupid old Andy converted by Christmas into the model middle-class citizen: choosing a child's interests above his own; choosing work over a get-rich-quick scheme; resisting Kingfish's anti-social criticism. Even his Christmas sacrifice was properly modern, quite satisfactory to corporate America: He bought an expensive, high-tech plastic doll in a department store. The series had moved its black subjects squarely into the middle of mainstream American society.

Variety promptly praised the "great value of showing a Negro family living normal lives in normal surroundings sharing the emotional and religious experience of all people." Spencer Williams ("Andy") said, "Now there's a situation that could happen in any home with any race of people, isn't that right?" But the critics would not be silenced. The NAACP protest hung on.

The protesters consistently focused on the characters' stereotyped dialects and mannerisms. For many, Andy's verbal crimes—"Poverty is rebarrassin' "—seemed to have overshadowed the sentimentality and determined conventionality of the Christmas episode. As Thomas Cripps has pointed out, what appeared to disturb NAACP leadership more than anything was the use of lower-class black cultural baggage in a middle-class context. The lumping of all blacks into a single cultural type was a particular sore spot with the black leaders who were trying to lead their people into integration with white society.

Unfortunately this sent a negative impression to blacks who weren't so bourgeois in their outlook; many NAACP statements on *Amos 'n' Andy* almost seemed to imply that the show was accurate in the portrayal of black rabble, that its only sin was in applying that portrayal to the owners of taxicab companies and the leaders of fraternal orders. Some NAACP opinions hinted at a general embarrassment toward black comic performers; talented though he might be, the black comedian often held up an image of his people—freewheeling, clownish, lower-class—which the educated bourgeoisie preferred to disown. This raised the specter of classism in the integration movement. As TV historian John E. O'Connor later commented, the controversy "opened fissures in the black leadership community that had significance far beyond the question of what would or would not get on TV."

The class question crystallizes when we consider the almost total lack of attention paid to ABC's *Beulah* during the same period. With CBS's publicity building on *Amos 'n' Andy*, ABC took its own funny-black radio show, filmed it in Hollywood with prominent black actors (Ethel Waters, Butterfly McQueen), and rushed it onto the air in October 1950—eight months before *Amos*. Beulah herself was pure Mammy, a big, loud "queen of the kitchen." She had a shiftless man in her life and a childlike girlfriend. "Somebody bawl fo' Beulah?" she'd roar when the white folks got themselves in another jam and needed the great black mother to rescue them. She was a stereotype. But she was also just a domestic servant. No one much bothered about her—certainly the NAACP didn't— and she died quietly of weak ratings.

For whatever reason, black opinion split early and angrily on *Amos 'n' Andy*. The NAACP was never able to mount a fully successful protest or boycott. Only one station took the program off the air during its first run. The Blatz people released a poll showing that 77 percent of the black people in New York liked the show. Even allowing for the distortions that occur in privately sponsored polls, that was an impressive number. By the time the second season began, the protest was beginning to break up.

But *Amos 'n' Andy* was encountering a more formidable opponent than protesters: ratings. It placed thirteenth in the Nielsens in its first season, a solid showing but not quite what CBS had hoped for. The next year it dropped to twenty-fifth, despite all the free publicity. At forty thousand dollars per episode, it quickly became hard to justify. And it had certainly turned into a huge public relations headache. In 1953 Schenley Distilleries had a chance to pick up sponsorship of the prestigious *Four Star Playhouse*. Believing that it would do its image some good and spare it a great deal of hostility, it dropped *Amos* and moved on to the new show. CBS chose to let *Amos* die rather than go through another round of trouble in looking for a new sponsor.

❑

Amos's demise marked the end of a cycle in American television. It was the death of the ethnic sitcoms. Even as *Amos* waned, NBC's revival of *The Goldbergs* was flopping, *Mama* was slowly fading, *Beulah* was dying, CBS's attempt to bring *Life with Luigi* over from radio brought only heated criticism and sponsor problems, and a couple of other efforts at cute-Italian shows, *Bonino* and *Papa Cellini*, were bombs.

More seriously, it marked the general disappearance of blacks from TV series. Not only would there be no more black sitcoms for fifteen years, but for a decade there would hardly be any black supporting characters or guest stars on TV. After all the fuss about *Amos 'n' Andy*, the white creators of American TV seemed to feel the safest course was simply to act as if blacks—and all other non-WASPs—simply did not exist.

As Cripps points out, it was a dubious victory for the NAACP. Despite the tangled mess of circumstances surrounding *Amos*'s demise, the legend grew that it had been killed by the NAACP protest. Within a few years black magazines were running articles with titles like "Requiem for the Kingfish" and "The Tragedy of Amos 'n' Andy." The NAACP was blamed for alienating a sympathetic network, ruining the careers of numerous black performers, and frightening sponsors out of supporting any more black-oriented programming.

The NAACP itself seemed to withdraw from the TV mainstream, preferring to work with black-oriented independent stations and study the broadcasting marketplace. It ignored the absence of blacks on network programming.

In any case, all the conflicts surrounding *Amos 'n' Andy* were soon to become irrelevant. The moderate-liberal dream of painless integration was shattered by the upheavals of the civil rights movement from 1955 on. The hopes, the powers, and the self-images of blacks would be so radically redefined over the next decade that neither Kingfish's mugging nor Amos's mainstream stability could have seemed relevant to much of anything. *Amos 'n' Andy*, like *The Goldbergs*, was the product of a brief but crucial passage in American history.

Ultimately what *Amos 'n' Andy* contributed to ethnic portrayals was far less significant than what it gave to the all-white sitcoms in its wake. Its characters and situations appeared again and again in safely nonethnic contexts during the 1950s; the Kingfish lived on in both Sergeant Bilko and Eddie Haskell.

Whatever its inflections, Americans seemed to have lost interest in watching this particular ethnic drama played out. By the beginning of the 1950s the assimilation of ethnic groups appeared to most Americans as a done deed; rightly or wrongly, the ideal of homogenization was being accepted as fact. The sitcom, accordingly, turned its attention away from the travails of broad social groups and toward the inner politics of the family.

5

Why Love Lucy?

Nineteen fifty-one is often pointed to as the year television grew up. In March of that year America joined in its first prolonged national television "event," the traveling investigations of the Senate Special Committee on Organized Crime. All four networks devoted their dead daytime hours to the committee's interrogations of colorful figures like Joe Adonis and Frank Costello, and ratings soared as high as twenty times their normal daytime level. Committee Chairman Estes Kefauver became such a celebrity that he took a run at the presidency the following year. Committee Counsel Rudolph Halley earned a gig as host of a CBS cop show, *Crime Syndicated*, and from there was elected president of the New York City Council.

A few months after the hearings ended TV finally became a truly national medium. The coast-to-coast coaxial cable was initiated on September 4 with Harry Truman's address to the Japanese Peace Treaty Conference in San Francisco. Nearly 90 percent of America's TV stations carried the same image at the same moment.

Although the FCC still kept a freeze on the licensing of new stations, TV sales were increasing sharply. The six million sets sold in 1950 doubled the sales of the entire preceding decade and multiplied total TV households sixfold in the span of a year. The numbers soared still higher in 1951, with nearly sixteen million sales. The percentage of households with television jumped from under 3 in 1949 to nearly 24 in 1951. Even with the government applying the brakes, television was clearly moving toward being a universal American experience.

The structure of TV broadcasting was still essentially the same as in the late '40s. The networks were in command. NBC was clearly king, with CBS a strong second. DuMont was third, but struggling. ABC was fourth, but with a few strong entries. Sponsors still owned entire programs and called nearly all the shots. Everything important still happened in New York, even after the connecting of the coaxial cable. TV was still the child of radio, theater, and vaudeville.

The movie community remained largely aloof. The big studios, frightened of the young medium, tried to avoid all intercourse with it, often even barring their contractees from appearing on it. Only a few small studios, like Hal Roach, made themselves available for TV production. Even performers who were free of studio prohibitions shied away from TV work. Hal Kanter, who wrote CBS's *Ed Wynn Show* for TV, found that "film people looked down on TV as a sort of freak child of show business. . . . They were mostly concerned with what they would look like on television. And they were absolutely right. The lighting was appalling, particularly treacherous for ladies." When that show's producer tried to exploit Wynn's Hollywood connections for guest stars, he was only able to bring in the likes of Buster Keaton, Joe E. Brown, and the Three Stooges, popular once but forgotten or fading then.

An exception, says Kanter, was that longtime almost star named Lucille Ball. She and her bandleader husband, Desi Arnaz, had appeared on *The Ed Wynn Show* at their first opportunity, in 1949. "She wanted to come on television to find out what this medium was all about," Kanter says. Ball said she found it "so frightening, but so wonderful. I'd never been in such a hurried, chaotic setting with these monstrous cameras all over the stage and not enough rehearsal. But it was great fun." It was good that she found it so. She had recently started a radio sitcom for CBS called *My Favorite Husband*, which rose quickly in popularity. In 1950 the network asked her and her radio producer, Jess Oppenheimer, to develop the show for television.

Ball had been visible in RKO and MGM movies since the '30s, playing a variety of comic and serious roles, often stealing scenes (*Stage Door*), sometimes winning a major lead (*Du Barry Was a Lady*), but never quite making the big time. In 1940 she married her Cuban singer-bandleader; he took an unsuccessful stab at the movies but for the most part spent the next decade touring with his dance band and the USO. The Ball-Arnaz marriage suffered badly from the long separations. "We'd been married for ten years," Ball said, "and together for maybe a year and two months in that time."

Ball wanted to find a regular gig for her husband in order to keep their household together. She talked Bob Hope into hiring Desi for his radio show, but radio was no longer the medium for long-term stability. From the moment CBS approached her with the idea of a *My Favorite Husband* TV show, she knew one thing: She wouldn't be doing it with her costar Richard Denning. Her husband on the show would be Desi.

According to Ball, CBS execs were incredulous. "They said, '*Desi*? Nobody'd believe *that*!' I said, 'What do you mean, nobody'd believe? He *is* my husband!' They said, 'Yeah, but . . . *American* domestic comedy.' " William S. Paley himself tried to intervene on behalf of sanity: "He's a bandleader, Lucy. He can't act. What'll we do with him?"

Certainly plugging Desi directly into *My Favorite Husband* would have been ridiculous. That show concerned the misadventures of George and Liz Cooper, a genial banker and his dizzy wife in Minneapolis. The plots were basic wife-gets-into-scrapes stuff: Liz becomes fascinated by fortune-telling and organizes a silly séance; Liz tries to play matchmaker for a couple of friends and almost ruins things for them; George tries to put Liz on a schedule, but she overdoes it to teach him a lesson. They were all played out against a background of middle-class midwestern gentility. In such a context Arnaz's broad, loud, Cuban-accented delivery would have been more than a bit bizarre.

Ball and Arnaz realized that a new concept would be needed, but CBS was convinced no concept could sell Desi to the public. The couple decided to prove that the network was wrong. They formed their own company, Desilu Productions, and in the summer of 1950 went on the road with a vaudeville show about the wacky adventures of a Latin bandleader and his movie star wife. The bit was scripted by Madelyn Pugh and Bob Carroll, Jr., writers of *My Favorite Husband*, and turned on Lucille's desperate efforts to break into Desi's act. The audiences were large and enthusiastic. The reviews were good. The Arnazes returned to Hollywood in triumph. CBS still wanted nothing to do with the Cuban.

Ball and Arnaz wouldn't be beaten. They began commissioning their own scripts, preparing to produce a sitcom on their own. When NBC started sniffing around, Paley's gang finally knew it had to give in. The number two network, banking on sitcoms, couldn't afford to lose a comedienne of Ball's talent and renown. Ball, Arnaz, Oppenheimer, Pugh, and Carroll were hired to create an "audition" kinescope in 1951. Ralph Levy, who had launched *Burns and Allen* only a few months before, was to direct it.

The script was cobbled together from the Ball-Arnaz vaudeville tour. Arnaz played bandleader Larry Lopez; Ball played his wife, Lucy, desperate to break into Larry's act. The plot was thin, stringing together burlesque bits, guest star appearances, songs, and dance numbers. Ball, however, did not want this to be a "real-life" star vehicle like *Burns and Allen*. Larry Lopez was a hardworking middle-class entertainer with a New York apartment; Lucy was a housewife, not an actress. "So far as I could see," said Ball, "a Hollywood couple has no problems in the eyes of the audience. If they have a big house, a car, a swimming pool, and live in California, tell me—what's their problem?" This show was aimed at Everyman. And Larry surely spoke for millions of men in postwar America when he denied Lucy a spot in his show and said, "I want a wife who's just a wife."

Everyone who saw the audition kinescope loved it, except the ones who really counted: advertisers. General Foods, which had sponsored *My Favorite Husband* and had had good luck with TV sitcoms (*The Goldbergs, Mama, The Aldrich Family*), chose not to back this one. Its ad agency, Young & Rubicam, didn't pitch it anywhere else. Ball's agent, Don Sharpe, headed for New York to show the kinescope personally to ad agencies. He got nowhere. CBS placed hard-sell, almost desperate-sounding ads in the trade papers. Finally, an ad agency head named Milton H. Biow thought he saw something in the show. He insisted that the vaudeville and musical numbers be reduced in favor of regular sitcom plots. He bargained the budget down. He demanded a weekly frequency instead of the biweekly that Ball and Arnaz wanted. When all conditions were met, he sold the show to Philip Morris, the cigarette people.

But the struggles still weren't over. Lucille Ball was pregnant; having miscarried once before, she was being especially careful to avoid undue stresses and difficulties. Arnaz was building a new nursery onto their house. Everyone was getting ready to gear up for local production when Milton Biow casually asked Jess Oppenheimer, "By the way—when are you and the Arnazes moving to New York?" The cast and crew were shocked. Biow and the Philip Morris people were equally shocked to hear that the Arnazes expected their show to be broadcast live from L.A. and kinescoped for the East.

The sponsor wouldn't budge: There would be no live broadcasting from Hollywood. Ball wouldn't budge either: She and her husband would not move. But she did suggest a solution: film. That solved the location problem, solved the picture quality problem, but added a major new problem. The costs would be huge. Arnaz, who had a stake in the show, was very doubtful, but Ball changed his mind. "Look, we'll do it for a year or so," she told him, "and if it bombs, then at least we'll have something like home movies to show our kids."

To sell the increased cost to the sponsors, the Arnazes agreed to a sizable salary cut—in exchange for full ownership of the show. Now it was all their gamble and all their responsibility. Over the course of one summer they taught themselves how to make a TV show. "We didn't know what we were doing, where we were going," said Ball, "we were experimenting on everything . . . except our writers."

Ball drew on her Hollywood contacts for one important bit of experimenting. She wanted a live audience, to preserve the immediacy of radio and vaudeville but not the static, single-camera look of a filmed stage play. She needed someone to develop a system of three-camera, simultaneous live filming; she turned to her cinematographer from *Du Barry Was a Lady*, Karl Freund. Freund had recently retired from cinematography with a remarkable résumé dating back to 1907. He'd invented the process shot and founded the Photo Research Corporation, had worked with Fritz Lang and F. W. Murnau in Germany, then shot some of Hollywood's most beautiful movies of the 1930s; he had conceived the "butterfly ending" of *All Quiet on the Western Front*. Yet there he was, as a favor to Lucy Ball, working at rock-bottom union scale to create a system for filming sitcoms. And it worked, too. The "three-headed monster," as Freund called it, is still the model for situation comedy shooting, although videotape has replaced film.

There were other production nightmares to come, but as if by sheer force of will, the comedienne and her bandleader pounded through them and made their show. On Monday, October 15, 1951, right after *Arthur Godfrey's Talent Scouts*, right across from NBC's *Lights Out* and ABC's *Curtain Up, I Love Lucy* made its debut. Ratings were high. Reviews were glowing. Word of mouth was even better. While CBS was still fretting over the letdowns of *Amos 'n' Andy* and *Burns and Allen*, Lucille Ball had

sneaked up and handed the network the sitcom hit it had been hungering for.

The first episode introduces us to Ricky Ricardo, a moderately successful Cuban bandleader with a regular gig in a New York club, and his
restive, scheming wife, Lucy. Their older neighbors, Fred and Ethel Mertz,
are about to celebrate their eighteenth wedding anniversary and want to
include the Ricardos. Trouble starts when the sexes split on how best to
celebrate: Lucy and Ethel want to go to a nightclub, Ricky and Fred to a
boxing match. The wives get huffy and announce that they'll go to a
nightclub *without* the men, and they may even take dates of their own.
Ricky and Fred, desperate to avoid being outmaneuvered, decide to show
up at the same club with other women. Ricky gets a female friend to agree
to line up a couple of girls and send them to the Ricardo apartment.
Sisterhood, however, is powerful: Ricky's friend blabs to Lucy.

Lucy and Ethel now attempt their coup de grace, dressing up as
revolting burlesques of hillbilly women and foisting themselves on the
boys. Ricky and Fred don't recognize their disguised wives, of course
(although we do). They are frozen with horror as Lucy and Ethel go
through their vaudeville hillbilly routine. Then Lucy betrays herself, dig-
ging up a pack of cigarettes where only she could have known they'd be.
The lights go on in Ricky's eyes. "Lucy!" he says ominously. She curls her
upper lip in chagrin. She is beaten, but Ricky forgives her and Fred
forgives Ethel. The couples kiss. We cut away to a commercial, and when
we return, we see just how complete Lucy's defeat has been: All four are at
the fights, Ricky and Fred cheering lustily, Ethel and Lucy doing their best
to endure.

In this little drama is the essential dynamic of all the early *I Love Lucy*
shows. The boys and girls come to a screeching impasse. Both parties are
being too bullheaded, but it's the girls who overreact with the first extravagant scheme to gain the upper hand. The boys try to outmaneuver them,
fail, and are nearly beaten. Then Lucy's hubris catches up to her. She
comes crashing down in a humiliating exposure (thanks, conveniently, to
the sponsor's product, a pack of cigarettes). Domestic harmony is restored, but not in compromise. The patriarch's will is done. His one
concession is a kiss of forgiveness for the little woman.

What can't be captured in a plot summary is the vitality and intensity of
the conflict. Ricky is no bland, smugly knowing sitcom husband but a
mercurial mass of cockiness, anger, self-delight, and stubborn authority,

all made grotesquely funny by Arnaz's accent and awkward delivery. Fred Mertz is a sour old man, a dig-in-the-heels survivor with scarcely any redeeming feature except his aura of having been abused by life. Ethel is a frustrated frump, a woman who clearly settled for less in life (and a husband) than she thought she should have had, who can regain her girlish enthusiasm for living only by plunging into Lucy's lunatic schemes against her own better judgment.

And Lucy is a force unto herself, a housewife who has put herself under her husband's command because she assumes that's the thing to do but who rebels against him constantly with every erg of her misdirected energy and every leap of her distorted imagination. If she had any kind of agenda, she could be a revolutionary. But she hasn't, and that's the key to her: Lucy has nothing but the sense that she isn't getting enough out of life, and if she could just get around Ricky's prejudices and restrictions *this* time, she could open new vistas of excitement and . . . something. Something she never articulates. She always claims to want to be in show business, and she goes to great lengths to break in, but when, in the sixth episode, she actually gets a chance to act on TV, she turns it down. A few episodes later, of course, she's right back at it.

Lucy Ricardo is the embodiment of female energy with no valid outlet. She is the mid-century American woman with no job, no power, no reinforcement for her aspirations, no kids, not even much housework (this being the age of the laborsaving device), yet with a mind and spirit excited by the possibilities of the twentieth century. She is a comic demon called forth from the boredom and frustration of an entire generation of housewives. She is what happens when a woman is allowed to go to college, tantalized with career possibilities, asked to give her all to warwork, and then told to retreat to the kitchen because that's what good girls are supposed to do.

Ball summed up the Arnazes rather simply: "The man would be the master of the house, and she would be a scatterbrain, but wily enough to get her own way in a comedic sort of fashion." But that's too simple. For one thing, Lucy isn't just a scatterbrain with a wily streak but a chameleon, a trickster, a self-defeating lunatic. For another, she almost *never* gets her own way. There is the one episode in which Lucy thinks Ricky has bought her a fur coat for their anniversary, only to discover he hasn't; after she exacts a bizarre vengeance, he feels guilty enough to buy her a moderately priced dress and hat. But that's about as close as she ever gets to winning a dispute.

Ball once reported feeling a peculiar affinity for housewife roles: "Of all the thirty or forty films I had made up to that time, I could find only three or four scenes in those pictures that I cared anything about. When I put them all together, I discovered they were all domestic scenes, where I played a housewife." With her desire to keep her marriage together, work with her husband, stay in L.A., and try to provide a home for her new daughter, Ball displayed a definite yearning for a "normal" life. Yet at the same time she was an extraordinarily ambitious, daring, and hardworking actress, who had never hesitated to stand her ground—against networks, sponsors, and her husband—in the fight to make *I Love Lucy* as she thought it should be. From the tension between those housewifely yearnings and that fierce professional drive she created an astonishingly vital and relevant comic figure.

The audience responded. *Lucy* started as the highest-rated sitcom on the air, mainly because it followed CBS's popular *Arthur Godfrey*, and from that strong start it just kept going up, passing Jack Benny, Sid Caesar, Martin and Lewis, Red Skelton, and finally even Godfrey and Berle. By March *Lucy* had become the highest-rated show on TV. On April 7 it became the first show ever to reach ten million households at once. It reached well over eleven million by season's end, which meant that about thirty-two million Americans were watching the Ricardos battle every week.

The reasons for its popularity aren't hard to find. First of all, it was funny. In terms of the number and force of its gags it was the first sitcom to rival the comedy-variety shows. Ball's timing and shticks were always at least equal to Berle's and Skelton's. Yet this comedy was presented within a sitcom structure, with constant and likable characters, which the variety shows lacked. In some respects *I Love Lucy* was a complete synthesis of TV comedy up to that time: It had the music and burlesque of Berle, the plot strength and slickness of *Amos 'n' Andy*, the behind-the-scenes charm of *Burns and Allen*, the naturalism of *The Goldbergs*. Even technically it was a synthesis, blending the rapidity and intensity of live TV with the editing and sleekness and shifts of angle associated with Hollywood movies. *Lucy* seemed to have achieved what all prior programs had only been groping toward.

To have had such a huge impact, though, and to have stayed so popular in rerun for forty years, it had to have communicated very strongly with the American family experience. Ball gave an interesting perspective on this when she tried to explain the enduring popularity of Lucy Ricardo:

"It must be that people have always identified with her. I kept the charac-ter the same because I liked her, and I knew her, and I dug her. . . . I always played straight, and let the others in the show get the laughs." That seems like a peculiar statement because in any given show most of the laughs were Lucy's. But in a sense Lucy was the most serious character on the show, the one least likely to be aware of the absurdity of a situation, the one least likely to make a conscious joke. She was, like many of her viewers, a hapless victim of modern tensions.

I Love Lucy came along at the moment when Americans were finally putting the depression and the war behind them and trying to shift back into "normalcy," which for women meant domesticity. The men were home and free, the economy was opening up, housing was becoming available, babies were being popped out by the million, and the house-wife was again a feminine ideal. As Mrs. Dale Carnegie wrote in *Better Homes and Gardens*, "The two big steps that women must take are to help their husbands decide where they are going and use their pretty heads to get them there. . . . Split levels may be fine and exciting when you're planning your house. But there is simply no room for split level thinking—or doing—when Mr. and Mrs. set their sights on a happy home, a host of friends and a bright future through success in HIS job."

The big catch, of course, which every woman knew but few had the nerve to say, was that housewifery got boring. Not only that, but it was never as neat and modern and efficient as *Better Homes and Gardens* tried to make it seem. Most Americans still lived in the cities, in apart-ments, in older buildings. Things went wrong; things got messy; lives turned ugly. *I Love Lucy* gleefully confronted us with that day-to-day ugliness. *Lucy* was never soothing, but it was liberating.

The '40s had fostered the "bumbling dad" sitcom on radio. Dad had been seeing his power erode, and now he was reasserting it. There had been plenty of "dizzy wife" comedies during the same years, but those wives had been well intentioned, ineffectual, exasperating, but not threat-ening. Lucy was a selfish explosion of elemental force.

Having unleashed the genie of the mad housewife, however, the show had to find a way to contain it. Because *Lucy*, as Ball's formula for the Ricardos' relations makes clear, would never have been subversive. It would allow the modern woman's frustrations to be played out, but it would never endorse them. Ricky always won, thanks to Lucy's own inability to grasp the workings of the real world. Her worldview was that of the naive housewife's idle daydreams, the worldview that a condescending husband might imagine his wife to have. Only humiliation can result from trying to actualize such dreams. Thus *I Love Lucy* simultaneously legitimized the yearnings of women for fuller lives and assured them that they would be better off keeping their dreams in their heads.

Ending each episode on female humiliation and male victory wouldn't, however, have endeared the show to very many viewers. A unifying, resolving element was needed, to create at least the semblance of a happy ending. That element is captured in the title. Whatever battles the Ricardos may wage, whatever disasters may afflict their home and friends, they are made all right by Ricky's love for Lucy—not by Lucy's love for Ricky, nor even by their mutual affection, but by Ricky's paternal, lordly conferring of forgiveness and acceptance. He knows Lucy's a nut, but as long as she's learned her lesson, he'll take her back and treat her well. It's said best by the final image of so many episodes: Lucy in embarrassment and chagrin, Ricky embracing her, and then the both of them closed in and covered up by a picture of a satin heart.

Ricky's love was the solution to another common problem in the early episodes, Lucy's sexual jealousy. The powerlessness of a housewife is never so apparent as when she's stuck at home while her husband, protected by the mysteries of the workplace and male camaraderie, is off having affairs. Other sitcoms had played with wives having silly suspicions about their loving husbands, but when Lucy convinced herself (as she often did) that Ricky was fooling around with some new show girl or singer, she whipped herself into delusionary intensity in order to expose and punish him. She was always wrong, of course. The "Ann, Mary, Helen, Cynthia, and Alice" he'd been talking about turned out to be members of a dog act. But Ricky's love was her only protection, and it wasn't enough to keep her fears from recurring again and again. (These episodes are a bit disturbing when viewed now, after Desi's constant infidelity during the *Lucy* years has become well known.)

I Love Lucy never favored the "corporate" resolutions of most sitcoms: discussion; quiet realization; the surrender of disruptive urges; consensus for everyone's "own good." It was a theater of battle. As such it reflected the combative, independent performers who had forced it into existence. It also reflected—or at least was well in tune with—the nervous, feisty energy of Americans at the beginning of the '50s. That was an energy that corporate-controlled television carefully avoided for the rest of the decade. Only one other sitcom, *The Honeymooners*, another creation of a willful comedian, would dare to play with such emotional forces. Perhaps it was more than doubts about Desi that caused sponsors to be so leery of the show.

To speak of realism with respect to *I Love Lucy* seems peculiar. No other TV show had plots as wacky: Lucy thinks Ricky is homesick for Cuba, so she makes up the living room to look like a Caribbean village, complete with chickens and mule; Lucy thinks Ricky is trying to murder her, so she charges down to his nightclub with a gun; Lucy gets into occultism and puts on a séance in which she contacts a dead cocker spaniel. Yet it had a strange integrity, a downplayed honesty about the facts of ordinary life. Lucy and Ricky slept in the same bed (that would have been forbidden under TV censorship codes except for the fact that the two actors were married in real life), and we saw them there reasonably often. Even the frequent sight of Lucy smoking (which may have been a concession to the sponsor) added to the sense of watching a real woman.

(In a quirky way the show even dealt with ethnic issues more effectively than the bland integrationist sitcoms that made those issues their focus. Ricky talked funny; others had difficulty understanding him; Lucy openly ridiculed him. He had old-world values and exotic tastes. His foreignness was both a handicap and his ticket to success. Although these issues rarely took center stage and were never resolved, they were presented with a refreshingly nonpatronizing humanity. Long after the *Amos 'n' Andy* debacle Desi was keeping a non-WASP presence alive on the home screen.)

The series really got to strut its frankness, however, when Lucille Ball discovered that she was pregnant in May 1952. Rather than dance around the issue, the Arnazes and Oppenheimer decided to go ahead and make Lucy Ricardo equally pregnant. Several episodes would deal with pregnancy, leading up to a "birth" show that would more or less coincide with the birth of the actual child (as it turned out, thanks to cesarean section, it coincided to the very day). CBS and the sponsor were nervous; TV didn't deal with such delicate subjects. But compared with the prospect of losing Lucille Ball from prime time for a few months, a few accusations of bad taste didn't seem so bad.

Supported by a battery of doctors and mainstream religious elders whose function was to safeguard against impropriety, Lucy went ahead and waddled and complained her way through a series of unabashed episodes about pregnancy. In the process she forged a bond with her viewers that no TV figure had yet enjoyed. The day before the birth episode, Dwight Eisenhower was inaugurated as president, the first inauguration since TV had become a common household item. He drew an impressive twenty-nine million viewers. The next night, the birth of Ricky Ricardo, Jr., drew forty-four million. Seventy-one percent of all TVs in use that night were tuned to *I Love Lucy*. CBS topped NBC for the week's ratings, a very rare event. Over a million letters, telegrams, and phone calls poured in, along with thousands of gifts for the Arnaz baby. The twin births made headlines worldwide.

I Love Lucy's popularity coincided with, and probably sped, television's growth into a universal American experience. When *Lucy* debuted, less than 24 percent of American households had television. By 1956, the last year of its domination, that percentage had soared to 72. In July 1952, between *Lucy*'s first and second seasons, the FCC finally lifted its ban on new station licenses; the number of stations more than tripled during the next two years. Lucy's enormous ratings were scored in a much broader demographic group than Berle's had been a few years earlier. She had to please West Coast viewers, suburban viewers, even some rural viewers. As her star rose, Berle's fell.

Lucy's new motherhood had completed her connection to the American public and made her show enormously successful. It also changed the spirit of her adventures. Ricky became much more solicitous of his wife now that she was the mother of his baby. He gave in to more of her whims and seemed far less eager to "teach her a lesson." For her part, Lucy became less rebellious, her schemes less frequent and bizarre. The show's philosophy hadn't changed, but its fires were dimming. Lucy, like America, was being domesticated. The struggles of postwar adjustment were being supplanted by the business of raising a family. Genial old Ike had replaced spunky old Harry. Ricky and Fred were playing golf.

Ratings slipped as the Ricardos' battles quieted. In the 1952–53 season *Lucy* had been watched, on average, by 67 percent of all TVs in use. The following year it was pulling in less than 59 percent, and the year after that less than 50. Yet even then it was the top-rated show of all.

Television was transformed during the *Lucy* years. It had finally been proved as a major American business, a growing income source that appeared to be inflation-proof and recession-proof. Advertising rates soared astronomically, yet sponsors kept paying and paying to ensure themselves precious time. For the networks this was a chance to regain control of programming; since few sponsors could afford to pay for an entire TV show by the mid-'50s, the networks were able to package their own shows and sell commercial spots to a number of different advertisers. The *Lucy* crew had had to battle its sole sponsor for important concessions; that would happen very rarely to future sitcoms.

Lucy also conclusively proved the value and workability of film in TV programming. Producers and networks scurried to produce dozens of filmed Hollywood-based sitcoms in the wake of *Lucy*'s success. Film had one clear advantage over live broadcasting: It could be played again and sold again. At first no one was sure the audience would want to see a show more than once (ABC had had good luck with *Lone Ranger* reruns, but they were perceived as having a kids-only audience). *I Love Lucy* certainly proved the rerun value of sitcoms.

The switch to film moved television production from New York to L.A., brought the movie business into the new medium, and hastened the shift of power from sponsors to networks. Robert Kintner, then the president of ABC and an early champion of film, summed up the change with a sad ambivalence: "The real reason why live programming ended is that we found out that the medium *sold* so well. . . . The medium got away from itself by its ability to *sell*."

I Love Lucy marked the end of the New York-based, vaudeville-derived era of TV entertainment. Ralph Levy played a role in that, by producing *Lucy*'s pilot, and later he was to score with more successful pilots, including *The Beverly Hillbillies* and *Green Acres*. But he, too, lamented the change, saying that those experiences "were not the same as working with Ed Wynn or George and Gracie or Jack Benny. These people were from another era of show business, one in which you took literally years to build your comedic character."

The end of the narrow demographics day of early TV drew some lamentations as well. CBS's Worthington Miner noted that "our total audience was then about twenty per cent of today's audience. . . . There's a law of diminishing returns when you increase an audience. That twenty per cent is now the expendable part of the audience, and that is why almost everybody who was an ardent viewer in the early days no longer looks at television."

Lucille Ball had fought and gambled and broken through network-think and sponsor-think to get the show she wanted on the air. It was just what the American public wanted to watch. It marked the coming of age of the medium. It gave CBS the boost it needed to pass NBC, ensured that the sitcom would be a TV staple, secured Hollywood's place as the capital of TV production, and proved that TV entertainment could be a nearly universal American experience. *I Love Lucy* was the first show to seize the national mood, not through the superficial topicality of the variety shows or the "problem plays" of the drama anthologies but through a vibrant caricature of American life. Its legacy, unfortunately, is not nearly so impressive.

6

The Sitcom Factory

In August 1951, as the *I Love Lucy* crew was rushing toward production, NBC took a whirl on a live-from-New-York sitcom called *Young Mr. Bobbin*, a quiet little thing about an ambitious teenager coming of age. It fared badly. As *Lucy* climbed relentlessly in the ratings, it became clearer and clearer that filmed sitcoms from L.A. would be the course of the future. A vapid Hollywood series about a beleaguered dentist, *Doc Corkle*, was readied to fill the demand. In the meantime, a summer replacement was needed for *Bobbin*.

NBC execs had had their eyes on a mild young comedian named Wally Cox and had featured him successfully on several variety shows. Cox, along with George Gobel and Steve Allen, epitomized a new postwar, postburlesque style of nightclub comedy: quiet, cool; brainy; appealing to America's growing number of young, college-educated, middle-class sophisticates. Fred Coe, producer of NBC's *Philco Playhouse*, was assigned to develop an eight-week sitcom vehicle for Cox. He hired two veteran New York television writers (by 1952 there were a few who could claim to be veterans), David Swift and Jim Fritzell. They developed a quiet but very witty little half hour about a bachelor science teacher at Jefferson High School, named Robinson Peepers. Not much happened in Mr.

Peepers's life. No séances, no outlandish costumes, no goats in the living room. He just dealt with the challenges and annoyances of students, timidly pursued an attractive young fellow teacher, and treated us to eccentric Coxian monologues on what he ate for breakfast and why. But the characters were quirkily appealing, and the level of verbal humor was high. *Mr. Peepers* immediately built a modest-size but passionate following. According to Jim Fritzell, NBC received almost two thousand telephoned complaints when *Doc Corkle* replaced it in the fall.

Perhaps the passion for *Mr. Peepers* explains why *Doc Corkle* was so savagely blasted by both critics and viewers. To modern eyes it comes off as just another bland *Lucy* follow-up, with Billie Burke as a dippy old spinster causing trouble for her bumbling brother-in-law. But the negative reviews, calls, and letters were so heated that the sponsor, Reynolds Metals, ordered the show yanked after its third week. Fred Coe and his team scrambled instantly to put *Mr. Peepers* back on the air. For the three years it ran, *Peepers* was the Indian Summer of the live sitcom, the last gasp of the quieter, smarter New York orientation.

As in all live TV, the *Peepers* crew was small, close, energetic, and overworked. A third writer, Everett Greenbaum, was added to help Fritzell and Swift (it was a great break for Greenbaum; he had just lost his job selling toy frogs at Macy's, a strangely fitting summer job for a sitcom writer). He has said, "In those days, nobody ever thought that you might have several teams writing one situation comedy series. They might have been doing that out in Hollywood, but in New York they hadn't heard about anything so efficient." He remembered the *Peepers* writing staff once going eight months without one day off.

The result was a show with a quiet surface but a witty heart. Peepers himself was a self-effacing, uncertain little man with a strong set of values and an impressive serenity in the face of comic misfortune. He spoke well to a generation of young professionals and quasi professionals trying to make their way in a new, booming America that no one quite understood. It was easy to imagine his having been drafted during the war, surviving the army in quiet befuddlement, going to college on the GI Bill, and now trying to build a new life without too much fuss. He was a new kind of Everyman, for an America still in transition.

The show's creative energies sagged a little during the second season. To boost them, the writers heated up the flirtation of Mr. Peepers and his romantic object, the school nurse, Miss Remington. In June 1954, as a season capper, the two were married. The wedding show was a big event, the first effort to recapture the sort of "landmark" quality of Lucy Ricardo's baby. A story circulated that Milton Berle, his own TV reign being ended by the rise of the sitcom, brought a noisy party to a halt by turning on *Mr. Peepers* and insisting that everyone be quiet while he watched it.

The ratings for the wedding were high, although nothing like those that Lucy's birth episodes had drawn. And they didn't carry over. Viewership declined during the third season, as the emphasis shifted to the cute marital difficulties of the newlywed Peepers. At the end of the season NBC and Reynolds, having determined that live shows were no longer as easy or as profitable as filmed ones, decided to cancel *Mr. Peepers*. Everett Greenbaum maintained thereafter that the marriage killed the show by making it more typical. Jim Fritzell felt that it enabled an already fading program to hang on for one more year. It doesn't really matter who was right. As Fritzell said, "We were destroyed by technology."

Lucy made film an inescapable fact of sitcom production. And film meant Hollywood. The fall of 1952 saw seventeen new sitcom entries, more than doubling the number of sitcoms on the air. The year 1953 brought fifteen more, and the following season nineteen. Nearly every one was filmed in L.A.

This was bad news for the critics and broadcasters who liked shows like *Peepers*. Even before television, many thought that L.A.-based radio had been falling prey to the superficial glitz and interior hollowness of the movie biz. Certainly there were plenty of writers and performers gliding between radio and the movies. And no sooner had television started moving west than the third-string directors, writers, and comedians crawled out of the woodwork, creating shows like *Hank McCune* and *Stu Erwin*.

TV producers in California very quickly picked up the method of staffing, which was used to write many Hollywood radio series. By this method there would be be no dominant writer or team of writers on a series, no Gertrude Berg or Greenbaum and Fritzell. Instead, a premise would be developed by committee, after which a writer or a team with a good résumé (preferably including some movie work) would be brought in to develop it into a pilot script. That script would be heavily reworked by more committees, which might include the producer, network reps, stars, and, of course, the sponsor and its ad agency. Once the series was launched, at least thirteen advance scripts would be commissioned— sometimes by as many different writers. A "story editor" would be hired (sometimes, but not always, the writer of the pilot script) to watch over the scripts and keep them as uniform as possible. To make uniformity easier to achieve, the show had to be kept as generic and unsubtle as possible.

The California sitcom emphasized plot over character. Characters had to be developed and learned; plots could be pulled intact from one show and laid over the characters of another with a little fine tuning. There was the plot where Stu Erwin tries to prove to his wife that he can fix the plumbing by himself and sends the household into wacky confusion. And the plot where Hank McCune attends a sales convention, only to confuse the hotel reservations clerk and throw a meeting of a silly fraternal order into chaos. Such dizzy doings were familiar from *Blondie* movies, radio sitcoms, even Three Stooges shorts. Inspired execution, of course, can make ancient plots funny, but these were slow, by-the-numbers jobs, tired before they were born, saying little about their times. None of them sought the energy or risk of a live audience, preferring the loyalty of a laugh track. Sadly, the success of *Lucy* pumped hardly any new life or verve into them; it only caused them to multiply.

Eyeing *Lucy*, producers concocted innumerable shows featuring women, especially cute but dizzy women: *I Married Joan*, *My Friend Irma*, *My Little Margie*, *Heaven for Betsy*, *A Date with Judy*, *Meet Millie*, *Life with Elizabeth*, *Honestly Celeste*, *Dear Phoebe*, and on and on. There were single career gals in *Private Secretary*, *Boss Lady*, and *Our Miss Brooks*; pairs of gals in *The Whiting Girls* and *So This Is Hollywood*; even an older gal in *December Bride*.

Most of these shows turned on wacky women causing funny troubles for their menfolk. Almost never did they involve women battling men, as Lucy did Ricky. Perhaps producers and writers were afraid to attempt the delicate, potentially explosive tension of *I Love Lucy*. Or perhaps they just missed the point, as imitators so often do. Nearly every one of these new sitcom women caused trouble only inadvertently in trying to safeguard her male superior's best interests. Susie McNamara of *Private Secretary* tended to meddle in her beloved boss's personal life; the teenage daughter on *My Little Margie* caused countless mix-ups in trying to protect her widowed father from scheming older women.

These sitcoms thus backed away from the sexual conflict that so energized *Lucy*, retreating instead to the level of wish fulfillment, comforting to female viewers who wanted to see themselves as helpful handmaidens and male viewers who wanted to view their women as exasperating but never threatening. If, in their approaches to resolving conflict, *Amos 'n' Andy* was corporate and *I Love Lucy* was authoritarian, these were just plain evasive. They created formulaic fantasy worlds in which conflict and resolution were purely formal exercises.

Many of the new sitcoms were transfers from radio: *Ozzie and Harriet*, *December Bride*, *Father Knows Best*, *My Friend Irma*, *Duffy's Tavern*, *Life with Luigi*, *Ethel and Albert*, a new attempt at *Life of Riley*, and a Ball-less version of *My Favorite Husband*. By 1954 nearly every successful sitcom had left radio for the new medium. TV had clearly conquered broadcasting.

It was conquering the movie industry's resistance as well. In the early going the big movie studios had tried a two-pronged strategy of resisting television while trying to buy their way into it. Paramount Pictures, not long after buying into the DuMont Network, purchased a major Los Angeles TV station, KTLA. In the late '40s the studio tried to subsidize a couple of ill-fated alternatives to network TV: "theater television," in which tickets would be sold to watch large-screen television in a movielike setting, and "subscription television," an ancestor of cable TV. About the same time 20th Century-Fox bought a subscription TV company.

The networks fought the movie people off. As early as 1948 a young producer named Jerry Fairbanks concocted the idea of syndication, in which he would produce filmed TV series for sale to individual stations. He needed support from the stations in order to convince the movie studios that he had a market. But network executives pressured their stations into rejecting the Fairbanks plan, even threatening to cut off network news broadcasts if they bought a syndicated program. Fairbanks came up empty-handed.

As the '40s became the '50s, the studios were facing hard times. A postwar box-office slump had been followed by government anti-monopoly actions that separated the production halves of the studios from their theater-owning halves. United Paramount, now a huge theater chain with no studio to feed it, tried to crash television by merging with ABC in 1951, but the FCC held up the merger for two years. Many smaller studios sold their film backlogs to television for quick cash. Some, like Hal Roach, rented their facilities for TV production.

The major studios still tried to ignore television into nonexistence, barring their people from appearing on it, convincing themselves that it couldn't last. Harry Cohn of Columbia phrased the studio attitude most succinctly in a conversation with ABC's Kintner: "You dumb young son of a bitch, you won't get any of my stars, you won't get any people—*you* can't make films! People want the companionship of the theater, they want the idea of going out of the house, they want their movies the way they *are*!"

Finally, however, TV simply proved itself too lucrative and too promising, and Columbia was the first to deal with the devil: In 1951 Cohn formed a subsidiary, Screen Gems, initially for the purpose of selling his films to TV stations, but ultimately to produce TV shows of his own. Any lingering doubts about TV's potential were dispelled in October of that year when that ex-RKO and ex-MGM contract player named Ball became the most popular performer in America.

How could other movie veterans not follow? In 1952 it was Ann Sothern (*Private Secretary*), Bob Cummings (*My Hero*), Marie Wilson (*My Friend Irma*), Eddie Albert and Ed Begley (*Leave It to Larry*). Perhaps most significantly, Bud Abbott and Lou Costello suspended their successful movie series in favor of a syndicated sitcom. Over the next two years the stars got bigger: Ray Milland (*Meet Mr. McNulty*), Donald O'Connor (*Here Comes Donald*), Ray Bolger (*Where's Raymond?*), Ronald Colman (*The Halls of Ivy*), Mickey Rooney (*Hey Mulligan*), and more. In many cases they brought their writers and their formulas with them. In the case of *Topper*, with Leo G. Carroll, an actual movie series was adapted to television.

Lucy marked her own victory during her fourth season, in late 1954. Ricky's nightclub act, in one episode, has attracted some important attention; MGM is looking for a fresh Latin face to star in its forthcoming movie *Don Juan*, and Ricky gets the offer. He promptly packs up Lucy and the Mertzes and heads for Hollywood in a subplot that was to run through the rest of the season and well into the fifth. MGM, the biggest and richest of the old studios, once fiercely opposed to cooperation with television, now let its name and personnel be freely used. William Holden, John Wayne, Richard Widmark, and Harpo Marx guest-starred, as did producer Dore Schary and gossip columnist Hedda Hopper.

Much was made in these episodes of Lucy being star-struck, of the gang singing "California, Here I Come," of Ricky being terrified of offending his producer. Yet the real message is clear: TV had grown huge and swallowed Hollywood, making the movies' glamour its own. (The Arnazes punctuated the point still further in real life; in 1956 Desilu bought the studio lot of Ball's former boss, RKO.)

Show biz settings became stock-in-trade for the new sitcoms. *I Love*

Lucy, after all, had shown how character conflict could be combined with the excitement of nightclubs. *Make Room for Daddy*, a Desilu production, starred Danny Thomas as nightclub singer Danny Williams. *The Duke* was about a nightclub owner. Abbott and Costello played a couple of unemployed actors. Ray Bolger and Donald O'Connor played singer-dancers, Mickey Rooney a TV page, and Ezio Pinza, on *Bonino*, an opera singer. *So This Is Hollywood* grabbed hold of a couple of trends, following the adventures of a pair of cute gals in filmland.

The shows were, unquestionably, more slickly produced, more lively in execution, more interesting in conception than nearly all the pre-*Lucy* sitcoms. Hollywood had its strengths. They were popular, too; none challenged *Lucy* or even the big comedy-variety shows, but in 1953 they accounted for five of the twenty-five top-rated programs. For CBS they were nothing but good news: *Our Miss Brooks, Private Secretary, December Bride,* and *Topper* all were CBS hits. NBC's only solid winner was *The Life of Riley* (this time *with* William Bendix). By the end of the 1952–53 season Bill Paley had finally achieved his goal: CBS had overtaken NBC in season-long ratings. The sitcom strategy had paid off.

❏

The new shows had proved themselves as commercial products. But there was a sterility at the heart of them, a contrivance of conflict and an avoidance of real emotion that had distinguished Hollywood comedy since World War II. During the depression comedy had attracted movieland's best and brightest, and the results were a cycle of intelligent, complex, and challenging films. But as the '40s dragged on, those gave way to bland romantic farces and a series of *Maisie* and *Blondie* movies that turned "screwball" comedy into a sleepwalking exercise. It was that tired tradition that flooded into television in the early and mid-'50s.

TV in general was becoming blander and safer during those years. The FCC's thaw on new station licenses provoked national debates on suitable television content. The House Interstate Commerce Committee even conducted inquiries into television morality in 1952. In March of that year the National Association of Broadcasters adopted a stiff self-censorship code. Hollywood influence only sped the process. As one L.A. TV producer said at the time, "Most of us are from the motion picture business, where we worked under a code for a long time, so we automatically observe good taste in programs. We must also consider the rerun value of a film, which would be impaired if we injected controversial matter. You don't have this on live television."

Established sitcoms were also subject to the drift toward uniformity and tameness. *Burns and Allen* began as a live broadcast from New York, with one of the most idiosyncratic structures in TV history. In the first episode, in October 1950, George stood alone before a curtain at the corner of a stage. He delivered a standard Burns monologue, making fun of his lifelong role as Gracie's straight man. Then the curtain opened, revealing a set: a suburban house with a huge hole cut in one wall to expose the living room. George bid his audience adieu, stepped over the bricks bordering the hole, and entered his house, where Gracie immediately began chattering to him. He had moved from one reality to another—from the audience's to the sitcom's—and self-consciously brought his audience with him.

George began every show that way and often stepped back out of sitcom reality during the story to comment on the action. He, like the audience, existed on a separate plane from the other characters, beyond the dramatic "fourth wall." Unlike the audience, he could cross that wall. He was the viewers' metaphysical confidant. Once, just before stepping through the hole, he said, "Don't worry, I'll wave at you." And he did.

As the episodes proceeded, George's comments expanded to embrace the very mechanics of the show. One monologue was interrupted by an off-camera call of "George!" He explained, "That's my neighbor Harry Morton calling me. Excuse me. Oh, by the way, Hal March, who has always played Harry, is going off to New York to do his own show with his partner, Bob Sweeney. Gracie and I wish them the best of luck. So tonight Harry Morton is played by John Brown." George then stepped through the hole to meet with . . . whom? His old friend? An actor pretending to be his old friend? Or some unreal, benighted soul not even blessed with the knowledge of his own fictionality?

At the end of most episodes Burns scrambled the levels of reality and unreality further by leading Gracie through the broken wall for a final dialogue directed at the audience. Gracie, however, true to her character, never seemed to understand what was happening. Once, when he tried to explain that they were on television, she was skeptical: "Supposedly I've been on the radio for seventeen years, but I've never heard me." Now she wanted George to buy her a TV set so she could sit home and watch herself performing live.

When George did install a TV in the living room, it only made things stranger; he could click it on and watch his own show in progress, thereby checking on Gracie's escapades in other parts of the house. This was a cute, self-referential twist on an established gag; it was also, intentionally or not, a deft metaphor for television's ability to simulate experience while distancing and deadening it.

The domestic mix-ups upon which George commented were slight sitcom fare. "We usually had more plot than a variety show but less than a wrestling match," Burns said. "Our plots were simple. Gracie puts a dent in the car. Gracie's aunt comes to visit. . . . Gracie thinks a surprise party planned for Harry Morton is for me. Here's a good one: Gracie and I have a fight. It's amazing that we could come up with such innovative ideas with only five full-time writers." As Burns and his writers knew well, the plots were only an excuse for Gracie's lines and George's assaults upon fictional reality.

Those assaults had their roots in the cynical wisecracks of '30s radio and the self-referentiality of modern literature ("It was an original idea of mine," Burns claimed. "I know it was original because I originally stole it from *Our Town*"). Both traditions were a little too strong for '50s sitcoms, and *Burns and Allen* steadily began to emphasize domestic plot over absurdist humor. In the fall of 1952, post-*Lucy*, it moved to L.A. and onto film. Structural holdovers from radio—like musical numbers and guest stars—were abandoned. George violated the fourth wall less and less often, and the opening monologue and closing dialogue gradually evolved into discreet bookend sequences around an integral story. Burns later joked that plots became more important because "it was cheaper to have them than to hire a guest star," but a change of philosophy was clearly under way. By the mid-'50s *Burns and Allen* had become just a "dizzy wife" sitcom with vaudeville bits at beginning and end.

By that time even *I Love Lucy* seemed to have traded its heart for a flashy veneer. Its edge had been blunted slightly by the end of its third season anyway, but as the big-name guest stars and the Hollywood locales came in, it began to lose all contact with daily realities. It, like most of its sitcom contemporaries, seemed to be appealing more to Americans' love of shiny, well-crafted diversion than to their need to laugh at their anxieties.

America had now moved beyond the stresses of its postwar transition and well into the 1950s. The public was weary of the Red Scare and Korea, no longer much alarmed by inflation or recession, content that the world wasn't going to blow itself up any second. The country was wealthier than ever before, and that wealth was finding its way quickly into the hands of the great public. America was going on a spending spree, buying the sleekest, biggest, most futuristic gadgets it could lay hands on. Maybe the new glamorous, slick, and utterly empty sitcoms were just a new kind of consumer good.

The only prominent exceptions came from the studio best prepared to exploit the success of *Lucy*, Desilu itself. Almost immediately after their first series became an obvious hit, Ball and Arnaz acted to bring *Our Miss Brooks* over from radio. Eve Arden, who played spinster schoolteacher Connie Brooks, was a movie and radio veteran of approximately Lucille Ball's vintage and celebrity. But Connie was no Lucy. Arden played her with a brassy, wisecracking self-assurance that made her more than a match for her three running battles: her power struggle with her pompous principal, her endless effort to drum knowledge into the head of a dim-witted student named Walter, and her battle to snare the shy biology teacher who never seemed to pick up her amorous hints. No other TV woman was as combative. Says Walter to her; "I'd say you were in your late twenties or early thirties or—" And says she: "Quit now. Teeth become you." Connie was the only one of those dames of the depression mold to win a place in TV comedy. In keeping with the times, she worked at a nurturing, surrogate maternal job, and her prime goal was to get married and quit. Yet in her struggles the tension of changing American life was preserved.

Desilu followed with two more shows in the next two years. The first was *Make Room for Daddy*, a *Lucy*-like vehicle that developed into one of the liveliest family sitcoms of the late '50s. Next came *December Bride*, another radio transfer, about an adventurous widow and her young in-laws. The old lady's wild schemes were not unlike Lucy's, but in this context they played off generational conflicts rather than sexual ones.

December Bride was the biggest hit of the sitcom flood, placing tenth in the ratings in its first season and later rising as high as fifth. Coming at a moment when America's popular culture was swinging more and more toward youth, that was an impressive showing (although the fact that it followed *I Love Lucy* on Monday nights certainly helped its ratings). Spring Byington played her heroine with vitality and charming eccentricity. Through her little rebellions and rejections of propriety she demonstrated the older generation wasn't willing to be swept away just yet by progress or the baby boom; through the inevitable reconciliation at the end of each episode, she demonstrated that the American consensus had room for her, too. Fan mail indicated that the show had a tremendous following among older viewers, who may have seen some of their own anxieties about the new youth-oriented America played out safely within it.

All three Desilu creations were relatively fresh, lively programs and solid successes. Perhaps it's no surprise that the creators of *I Love Lucy* were the only ones insightful enough to exploit the success of that show by preserving its heart and not its outward form.

Another sitcom star-turned-producer was George Burns, who came up with *The Bob Cummings Show* (about a swinging glamour photographer), *The People's Choice* (with Jackie Cooper and a basset hound that thought out loud), and, later, *Mr. Ed* (about, of course, a talking horse). Burns's productions were far less successful than Desilu's, maybe because Burns and his people were too sharp and too cynical for their medium. As Burns said, "Television was still so new that nobody knew what kinds of shows the audience would watch, but I figured that people would like the same things . . . that they liked in vaudeville, so we did shows with pretty girls and animals." As stupid as TV can be, the sitcoms that really seize an audience are almost never condescendingly "dumbed down." The most successful ones usually display a particularly shrewd insight into the concerns of the vast American public and a special kind of integrity of their own.

The bulk of sitcoms, of course, rarely displays either, and that was never truer than in the flood of '52, '53, and '54. Still, there were a couple of shows that used the bland style of the times to touch upon the public's most cherished dreams, to open a new and complex phase in the sitcom's development. *The Adventures of Ozzie and Harriet* and *Father Knows Best* were beginning to mythologize the nuclear family in ways that still haunt us.

7

Inventing America

When the pop culture eye turns toward the mid-1950s, it almost invariably sees a time of placidity and changelessness, an eerily homogeneous landscape of spacious houses and smiling, self-satisfied WASP families. This was the image that most advertisements and entertainments of the time seemed determined to project. Yet this willfully quiet veneer was hiding—and facilitating—the biggest shift in the American way of life since the spread of industry and the great immigrations in the last century. The sitcoms of those years, which have done so much to shape our impression of the era, were conceived to explain and exploit and take some of the fear from that shift. In the process they came to crystallize some of the great American self-delusions of the 1950s.

The postwar boom had never turned to a bust. America had come out of the war as the only major industrial power not severely damaged or depopulated, by far the richest country on earth, and with rampant cold war defense spending it was able to maintain and even exceed its wartime industrial productivity. By the early 1950s the boom was being normalized and absorbed by a new middle-class suburban society.

The vets had come home, gone to college on the GI Bill, and found jobs in the rapidly expanding corporate world. In the decade after the war the national income rose at double the rate of population increase. In 1929, on the eve of the depression, five and a half million American families, about an eighth of the national total, were classified as having "middle-class" incomes; by 1953 their number had soared almost to eighteen million, over a third of the total. And where the older middle class had consisted largely of independent professionals and small-business owners, the bourgeoisie of 1953 consisted overwhelmingly of salaried corporate employees.

The vets and their new wives wanted housing. More specifically they wanted it in the suburbs. Between the depression, the decaying urban infrastructure, and rising crime rates, the city seemed to have lost its hold on the American imagination. The little house on a quiet street—Henry Aldrich's house—had become the place of dreams. The postwar abundance of automobiles and the growing network of highways now made such a house practical; the salary-man could live wherever he wanted within a reasonable commute to his downtown job.

Perhaps most important, the cheap, quickly built houses of the suburb could be owned, ending forever the economic entrapment of rent and the power of the landlord. In the late 1950s, for the first time since the early years of the Republic, the number of American homeowners surpassed the number of renters. The suburbs began to seem like a mass market Jeffersonian dream.

By 1953 one out of five Americans lived in the suburbs, and the number kept growing. The burbs were growing at fifteen times the rate of the rest of the country. *Fortune* calculated that the annual number of new arrivals exceeded the number of immigrants Ellis Island had ever seen during a single year.

Clearly the powers that were supported the exurban flight. Federal Housing Administration and Veterans Administration housing loans, the last great programs of the New Deal, accounted for nearly half of all new home mortgages during the first decade of suburban expansion. The vast majority of that federal money was concentrated on brand-new houses; government money withdrew from the cities. This policy was justified with the same magic word that explained stepped-up highway construction: defense. During the war Britain, Germany, and Japan had been virtually crippled by concentrated bombing of cities. Planners for the next war concluded that America would be far safer and better able to respond if the population were kept spread out and mobile.

There were other political supports for suburbia. Conservatives con-

sidered cities breeding grounds of discontent and trouble. Homeowner-
ship was believed to create stabler, happier citizens. William Levitt, the
master builder of the earliest mass market suburbias, put it most succinctly: "No man who owns his own house and lot can be a Communist.
He has too much to do." Not that he's too happy or has too much to
protect, just that he can't think about revolution while the backyard needs
rototilling. (Of course, Levitt's observation begs the question of what
happens to the children of the homeowners, those idle nestlings of that
quiet, unthreatening, prosperous world, those who had *nothing* to do.)

Few complained about being manipulated, however. Some sociologists assailed the sterility of the suburbs, and a flurry of sensationalistic
books warned about young suburban couples being driven to drink,
adultery, and even madness through sheer boredom. But most Americans
dismissed such attacks as just bad-tempered cant by envious city
dwellers. Or they just ignored them completely. Young America knew
what it wanted.

Corporate America knew what it wanted, too. The new suburbanites
were prime consumers, prime targets of the manufacturing and advertising worlds. By 1952 they already accounted for about a third of the
American middle class. No one, it seemed, dragged old furniture and
appliances from the city apartment to the new "ranch house." Besides,
there were so many astounding laborsaving devices rolling off the assembly lines. Everything was bought new and at remarkably low prices:
refrigerators, deep freezes, barbecues, washer-dryers, butterfly chairs,
massive cars, and, of course, televisions.

The suburbs were the cradle of a new secular religion, a faith in
Goods—colorful, modern, affordable, nearly uniform, soon-to-be-
obsolescent goods, the consumer culture that the journalist Thomas Hine
has called Populuxe. One ad exhorted consumers: "Live your dreams and
meet your budget." *House Beautiful* told its readers, "You will have a
greater chance to be yourself than any people in the history of civilization." The suburbs were freedom, wealth, happiness, personal fulfillment. Paradise had become a commodity, and an affordable one at that.

By the early 1950s producers and consumers, government and citizens, advertisers and audience had pulled together in a consensus of
unprecedented size, power, and harmony. There were, of course, people
outside the consensus. Blacks, for instance, had been virtually barred
from the suburbs. Developers wouldn't sell to them, and if they did, white
neighbors found quiet ways to keep them out. When a black family

challenged William Levitt's color line, a federal court supported the developer. Asians and Hispanics had similar experiences. At the same time nonwhites were being barred less calculatedly but just as thoroughly from mass culture. The black domestics and mammies who had appeared in so many advertisements before the war suddenly vanished, to be replaced by prim white suburban Betty Crockers. Amos and Andy were gone from the tube.

Conditions were better for ethnic whites. Jewish leaders wrote of the remarkable openness of the new suburbs to Jews, in contrast with the "exclusive" upper-middle-class suburbs of the prewar era. The key to acceptance in suburbia seemed to be appearance: If you could look like a solid all-American family and dress like a solid all-American family and act like a solid all-American family, then no one really cared about your roots. Whoever could leave his ethnicity at the gate could be admitted to the paradise of Levittown. Jake and Molly Goldberg moved to the suburbs in a last effort to save their sitcom; the ratings were cruel to them, but the neighbors were not. The suburbs were a place for fresh starts.

The prime motivation—or at least the excuse—for this headlong rush into the new life-style was "the good of the kids." The postwar baby boom that demographers had expected to spend itself quickly only seemed to pick up steam as young couples moved into their new homes. The statistically average young man of the early '50s had fathered three kids by the time he reached the age at which his father had married. Births in 1951 actually exceeded the record numbers of 1947, and the numbers kept climbing for seven straight years, reaching a terrifying height of 4.3 million in 1957. Over 80 percent of America's population growth during the 1950s was in the suburbs.

The nuclear family took on a special significance in this new context. Suburbia separated people from their neighbors, sealing them in the comfort of their dens and family rooms. It pulled people from familiar neighborhoods and ethnic conclaves. Along with fertility and prosperity, the new life brought unprecedented mobility. Corporate positions could mean frequent transfers. For those who were simply seeking a new promised land the abundance of jobs made it easy to pull up stakes. Extended families were left behind in the cities or rural areas, often a continent away. Spouse and children were often the suburbanite's only close, long-term social group. Said *The Woman's Guide to Better Living* in 1953: "Whether you are man or woman, the family is the unit to which you most genuinely belong."

Mom and Dad wanted to buy the kids a better life than they themselves had known, wanted them to grow up healthy and employable and "well adjusted." The shepherds of the consumer culture seemed to realize this even before the parents. They were ecstatic about the baby boom, seeing in it the antidote to a shrinking buyer pool brought on by the low birthrates of the '20s and '30s. Advertisers moved in quickly on new parents, then on the children themselves, largely through television.

TV had hooked the first wave of boomers in the early '50s with *Howdy Doody*; advertisers knew they had a gold mine. In 1954 the hostess of one of the most popular kid shows, Dr. Frances Horwich of *Ding Dong School*, told an ad convention: "Never underestimate the buying power of a child under seven. He has brand loyalty and the determination to see that his parents purchase the product of his choice." Thus did educators, entertainers, and advertisers work together to bring the newest generation into the corporate coalition.

For young parents, the consumer culture's attentions were often quite welcome. With Grandma and Grandpa far away—and with the "old ways" in disrepute anyway—nervous new fathers and mothers turned for examples and information to commercial products: books, magazines, TV shows. (Under the guidance of Dr. Benjamin Spock they fed their babies on demand, gave their toddlers security and freedom, and turned the doctor's *Baby and Child Care* into the second best-selling book in American history, trailing only the Bible.)

As the baby boomers grew a little older, it became clear that they would have an ever-greater impact on prime-time ratings. Researchers were finding in the early '50s that TV was, more than any medium before it, a family concern. A 1952 study by Raymond Stewart found that over half of all TV viewers preferred to watch it with someone else; 15 percent reported that they would never watch it alone. A year later Eliot Freidson conducted a survey showing that American youths treated moviegoing as a peer group activity and TV watching as a family one. Other reports found that while TV hadn't cut too severely into the time people allotted to such solitary activities as reading, it had made huge inroads into America's radio listening, mealtime, and other activities associated with the bosom of the family. By the mid-'50s the movie industry was gearing its product more and more toward specific age-groups, particularly teenagers and young adults; TV swung toward shows accessible to little kids, teenagers, and parents alike. As one industry ad put it, "Family Time is Prime Time."

The first sitcom to tap into the new mass culture was, like *I Love Lucy*, a product not of committees or TV insiders but of a determined, self-producing entertainer. Ozzie Nelson had been half of "America's Favorite Young Couple" on radio for seven years when he decided to take the leap into television. He wrote, produced, and starred in his own pilot (which he then released theatrically to recoup his investment); he reserved complete creative control of the show, wrote most of the scripts, and directed nearly every episode. He and his wife, Harriet, supervised the building of a set that duplicated their real-life home, in the interests of authenticity, and he hired his sons, David and Ricky, to play themselves, as they had on radio. Following *Lucy*'s lead, he hired a movie cinematographer, William Mellor, to give the show a polished, expensive look. *The Adventures of Ozzie and Harriet* was a classy product. It was also one of the most determinedly bland programs ever broadcast.

Ozzie made some subtle changes in moving his show from the old medium to the new. The Nelsons were no longer introduced as a young couple but as "America's Favorite Family." The celebrity guests and musical numbers were abandoned in favor of straight-ahead family stories. The locale was no longer identified as Hollywood but played as a more typical American neighborhood, full of normal, easygoing folks. One character, a sour, complaining maid named Gloria, was eliminated. With her went not only a source of discordant, burlesque comedy but any sense that the Nelsons might be of higher than dead-center middle class.

More important, Ozzie lost his job. Or, rather, his job just disappeared. No longer a swinging bandleader, he now just hung around the house, read the paper, and made folksy remarks, day after day. No mention was ever made of work or of money; the household just seemed to have all it needed, all the time. Nelson once said that "by not designating the kind of work I did, people were able to identify with me more readily." He no longer wanted any Hollywood glamour in his Everyman characterization, but "we always filmed the shows with an aim toward honesty. On our radio show I had always been shown as an actor and a bandleader. For me suddenly to become an insurance salesman or a plumber just wouldn't have sat right." (Too much honesty would have been a bigger problem; this was supposed to be Ozzie himself, after all, and showing him in the career we knew was his—directing and starring in a TV show about himself—would have created a surrealism more self-eroding than that of *Burns and Allen*.)

For viewers at the time Ozzie's constant presence in the house carried a special poignancy; one of the side effects of suburbia was absent fathers since more men commuted some distance to get to work and fewer families owned small businesses or farms that combined livelihood and residence. For many baby boomers and their parents, the eternal nearness of Ozzie was an echo of an earlier, cozier order. Thus, even as TV ventured tentatively into the new realm of suburbia, it offered a wish fulfillment fantasy that was essentially nostalgic. This was the first note of an odd tune that was to run through all the suburban sitcoms of the '50s.

The "adventures" of the Nelsons were the thinnest of comedy situations. A mix-up with a furniture store results in four unwanted chairs being delivered to the Nelson home, then in two of Ozzie's own chairs being taken away. Ozzie and Harriet suddenly develop a yen for tutti-frutti ice cream and have to drive all over town looking for it. David gets his first phone call from a girl, making Ozzie feel like he's growing old. That's about as tough as the conflicts ever got.

The only real source of emotion in these stories came from the boys, who were the most natural and authentic kid characters yet seen on a sitcom. In radio comedies, kids were generally cute caricatures of youth, cloyingly scripted and played by adult actors. Most early TV comedies shunned them altogether; only *Mama* and *The Goldbergs* used them extensively and then mainly as vehicles for lessons about life. But David and Ricky Nelson were real-life teenagers, interacting with their real-life family. They were preboomers by several years, but they were exciting role models for little kids looking forward to the day they could be as talented and funny and impudent as "the irrepressible Ricky." Ricky was cool. He sang and tap-danced and tromped around the house in an oversize lumberjack shirt and jeans with the cuffs rolled up. He insulted his brother and questioned his father and slammed the front door no matter how many times he was told not to. Parents liked him, too, because he resembled a real pubescent kid—rebellious and ill tempered and full of himself—yet he never really rocked the family boat. When push came to shove, he was a good kid. In one episode he seemed to be bratty as he insisted on having a party on the night his parents wanted to celebrate their wedding anniversary, but it turned out that his party was really a surprise celebration for *them*.

This was the formula for *Ozzie and Harriet*'s success: By ensuring that the stories never contained any real conflict, the characters were allowed to tease and provoke each other in an authentic-feeling but completely safe manner. Ozzie himself was perfect for the formula: an endearingly small and vulnerable fellow with crinkling eyes, a hesitant, embarrassed smile, and a voice that was just fine for chuckling at his own foolishness but always quavered when he tried to yell. He played at having a high opinion of himself, but he could never boast without laughing awkwardly at his own remarks.

A typical Ozzie soliloquy followed his discovery that a girl has phoned David: "Well, you know, I was just thinking, if David's going to have little girls phonin' him and chasin' after him, maybe I ought to have a little talk with him and tell him some of the little tricks his ol' Dad learned when the girls were chasin' after him . . . hah hah hah hah . . . marvelous." (Harriet, in accustomed fashion, only frowned at him in amused dismissal.)

Everything was "little" with Ozzie; everything was "maybe." As a father he was just "ol' Dad," and the smallest things were marvelous. Ozzie was a big kid who'd been forced to grow up by the depression and the war, who could now finally afford a little timidity and triviality. He was the picture of an America that didn't have to be tough and serious anymore. If other TV shows let viewers live exciting lives vicariously, then Ozzie let them slack off vicariously. He was the antithesis of Ricky Ricardo and a couple of evolutionary steps beyond him; all the conflicts of the postwar world were comfortably behind him, and now all he had to do was sit back and think about tutti-frutti ice cream.

He was a ridiculous figure, but ridiculous in a much subtler and more complex manner than the "bumbling dads" of so many short-lived sitcoms. For the thousands of men who had braved the horrors of war to save the world for democracy, only to come home to barbecue burgers in the backyards of Cape Cod tract houses, the course of history must have had a faintly ridiculous quality. No one would say out loud, of course, that the endless quiet twilights of suburbia were a bit of an anticlimax to the tumult of the '40s, but many a man must have shaken his head over the contrast between his past as War Hero and his present as Domesticated Dad.

With sly self-parody Ozzie helped American men chuckle at their retreat from heroic maleness. In the episode in which David's girlfriend calls, Ozzie and his friend Thorny begin to speculate sentimentally on what the future will bring. As they talk, they seem to age before our eyes, growing frail and melancholy, until they're shivering in tiny drafts and saying good-bye as though it's forever. At the end of the show, when David has cheered his father up and restored his lost youth, Ozzie frantically strums cornball '20s tunes on his ukulele while Harriet looks on in wifely bemusement.

Now, most adult viewers knew that Ozzie Nelson had been an Ivy League quarterback, a glamorous crooner, and the leader of a commercially successful swing band that had waxed such grooves as the sexually suggestive "The Man Who Comes Around." So what was this self-effacing jive about "the little tricks ol' Dad learned" or this Mickey Mouse ukulele shtick? Nelson seemed to be mocking his own media-engendered passage from youthful hipness to dopey blandness and inviting his viewers to participate. *Ozzie and Harriet*, like many other successful sitcoms, had it both ways: While kids were dreaming of being like Ricky, Ozzie was telling their parents that this whole business was just a game. Even in its role as a sponsor's shill, it was peculiarly transparent. When Hotpoint sponsored it in its first four seasons, a disproportionate number of scenes took place in the Nelson kitchen, the better to show off the snazzy appliances. When Kodak took over sponsorship later, the episodes tended to move outdoors for picnics and garden parties, in which every member of the family seemed to have a camera around his or her neck.

The Nelsons created the suburban Neverland of family sitcoms, in which details of locale and occupation are intentionally evaded and a homogeneous, threatless world is shown as being already in place, waiting to welcome the new exurbanite. As TV critic Rick Mitz has written, "there was something appealing about it all, because it took family life— a hotspot of American insecurity—and trivialized it to the point of innocuousness, while squeezing out all the humor like puerile pulp. *Ozzie and Harriet* was the ultimate in home movies—with an annoying laugh track." Although not an instant hit, the show gradually built a large and stable audience and went on to be the longest-lived sitcom of all.

❏

Two years after the Nelsons' debut, another cute radio family strolled to TV but transformed itself far more significantly in the process. It worked within the same milieu as the Nelsons but used it to entirely different ends, creating one of the most revealing icons of American mass culture.

The year 1954 marked a subtle turning point in the national consciousness. The last echoes of the conflicts and scandals of the early '50s were fading. The Korean War was over, Stalin was dead, and the United States declined to go to the defense of the French in Vietnam. Dwight Eisenhower was now firmly installed in the White House, and to the disappointment of doctrinaire conservatives, he had quietly institutionalized the social programs of the New Deal under the label "moderate progressivism." The Army-McCarthy hearings ended with the military cleared of suspicion, left-wingers scared into silence, and the Red-baiting senator disgraced.

It seemed that threatening voices on both the left and right had been stilled. Political philosophers were talking about "the end of ideology" and "the vital center." Spokespeople for liberal reformers and Wall Street conservatives were calling themselves "natural allies." Even the most portentous event of the year, the Supreme Court's decision that racial segregation of public schools must end, was greeted at first as the end of a conflict, the decisive victory of moderate integrationism. Blacks, it seemed, were truly being invited into the consensus. The postwar adjustment was over. The American political establishment was settling down to the great corporate adventure of managing the richest economy on earth, and soon nothing would stretch ahead but the long afternoon of middle-class satisfaction.

But were Americans ready to enter the promised land? Many thought not, and saw in the mass media a classroom for teaching them how to behave in the perfect society. Entertainment had always come under scrutiny from citizens' groups and moral leaders, of course, but never had popular culture been so explicitly linked to social education as in the early 1950s. Academics and psychotherapists expended great energy to link comic book reading to juvenile delinquency, leading to a national furor that in 1954 crippled the racier publishers and imposed a strict "prosocial" censorship code on the survivors. The movies self-importantly shouldered the burden of enlightening the public with "message pictures" and "adult dramas," which explored the pains of postwar love, sex, and work.

Even pop music, in its less coherent way, trumpeted the new American coalition. The wailers and belters like Frankie Laine and Johnnie Ray, the late swing bands, and the few widely popular modern jazzmen gave way to bland, overharmonized waves of nonconfrontational sweet sound, mishmashes of ethnic, classical, and pop motifs that asserted, in the words of 1954's biggest hit, that "Little Things Mean a Lot." Cool, soothing jazz caught on while bop and funk retreated into esoterica. Rock and roll was nascent, but the big teen hit of '54 was the Crew Cuts' "Sh-Boom (Life Could Be a Dream)."

Television, as the new engine of democracy, the centerpiece of every suburban living room, took center stage in this wave of pop culture pedagogy. Attacks on the morality of TV programming led to self-policing codes by networks, stations, and sponsors that emphasized their "social responsibility." Drama anthology programs shifted during those years to an almost complete dependence on "problem dramas," playing out the various pains of evolution from old ways to new. *Marty* led viewers from provincialism into homogeneity; *Printer's Measure*, from craftsmanship into technocracy; *Patterns*, from narrow old business ethics into modern boardroom politics. Countless dramas dissected the troubles of the modern family, with confused parents and confused youths generally saved by the school system or a therapist or some other outside agency. The big Emmy winner of 1954 was Reginald Rose's *Twelve Angry Men*, which the film critic Peter Biskind has astutely analyzed as a blueprint for the new consensus politics and the transcendence of individual beliefs.

By far the most thorough social instruction came, however, from a sitcom. Like *Lucy* and *Ozzie*, it was principally owned by its star performer, and like them, it reflected its owner's ideas of quality and the nature of television. In this case those ideas were loftier than the sitcom norm, as suggested by the production company motto displayed at the end of every episode: "Ars pro multis" (Art for the masses). This new show was unabashedly intended to uplift the broad American audience; the nature of the uplift was suggested by its title, *Father Knows Best.*

In its five years on radio *Father Knows Best* had evolved from a "bumbling dad" vehicle to a family heart-warmer, trading on star Robert Young's movie persona as a handsome but modest young chap. When Young and his producer, Eugene Rodney, brought it to TV, they dropped all supporting actors to build a new cast: Jane Wyatt as Margaret Anderson, Elinor Donahue as seventeen-year-old Betty (or "Princess"), Billy Gray as fourteen-year-old Jim, Jr. ("Bud"), and Lauren Chapin as nine-year-old Kathy ("Kitten"). Young was Jim Anderson, an agent for the General Insurance Corporation. And they all lived happily in a big two-story house in a town called Springfield, state unknown.

The Goldbergs and *Mama* had set a precedent for sitcom morality plays, but in nostalgic contexts. No sitcom had ever attempted to teach social lessons in a contemporary mass culture setting. *Father Knows Best*, however, flung itself into the task of demonstrating proper family conduct with all the ingenuous confidence of a Sunday school film.

The Anderson family was a model social unit for the new suburban society. Jim made the money, owned the house, laid down most of the family rules, refereed most disputes. Margaret, his ornament and facilitator, was pretty, witty, and socially astute. She kept things clean and tidy and supported her husband's authority when the kids strayed. Like the Virgin Mary, she was also an intercessor, interpreting the subtleties of juvenile (especially feminine) behavior for Jim and getting him to soften his stance when his power went to his head. Princess was a budding, though still insecure, replica of Margaret. Bud was basically decent but easily confused, desirous of being like his perfect father but still too wrapped up in himself. Kitten was wet clay, learning the most basic rules of socializing, still wrestling even with sex roles, given to cute remarks.

What the Andersons were not—compared with the Ricardos, the Burnses, and even the Goldbergs—was funny. Jack Benny was once asked by a midwestern matron why most comedians seemed to be Jewish or Irish. Benny responded gently, "Madame, have you ever met a funny Lutheran?" The Andersons may not have been Lutheran, but they certainly were Protestant. In one episode Jim is being honored by his townsfolk as a model father; he daydreams, and in an odd fantasy sequence— presented completely without irony—he meets a very WASPy St. Peter at the pearly gates. Peter tells him that he's just the sort of fellow they want in heaven: a good father; a constructive member of his community; an honest businessman. No, these characters could never be very funny; they were too pure to ridicule. They might be witty in a genteel way, but they were too sweet to be acerbic. Even their laugh track was restrained.

They were well-to-do. They were not new arrivals to the suburbs from cramped city apartments but habitués of wide, shady streets, members of the established professional class. Margaret could easily have been what Jane Wyatt herself was: the daughter of a banker and a drama critic, a graduate of Barnard College. Princess lived up to her name, with a high-cheeked, almond-eyed beauty that somehow suggested Audrey Hepburn while still seeming safely Middle American. They were also quite likable, with their palpable affection for one another, their willingness to take in orphans and stray dogs. Even their arguments were restrained and cour-teous. They were unfailingly democratic; for a time they hired a Latino gardener, toward whom Jim displayed an unpretentious noblesse oblige, indulging his desire to be known as "Fronk Smeeth" with a quiet smile. And why shouldn't he call himself "Fronk Smeeth"? Surely, like any sensible immigrant, he wanted to be another generic WASP, just like "Meestair Ahndairson."

Father Knows Best preached many basic lessons: Fulfill your prom-ises; respect others; don't lie to your parents; always do your best work. But if it had one driving theme, it was this: Learn to accept your role.

Bud is feeling unneeded by his family and runs away. Jim knows that he's just staying with a friend in town and talks Princess into a little deceit to make her brother feel wanted. She breaks her radio, then tracks Bud down by phone and asks if he could please drop by and fix it. Bud happily obliges, returning home never to run away again.

Princess goes through a spell of feeling ordinary. When she wins a trip to Hollywood in a movie starlet's look-alike contest, it turns her head. She goes around Tinseltown impersonating the starlet, committing the family sitcom sin of sins: pretending to be what she's not. Finally she's publicly humiliated and wants to cancel her scheduled TV talk show appearance to hurry home. But Jim calls her from Springfield, telling her, "To your friends and family, you are a celebrity." Princess goes through with her interview, directing a loving greeting to her family at the end.

Margaret feels inadequate because she's the only Anderson who's never won a trophy for some accomplishment (this is a remarkable family indeed). She enters a ladies' fishing contest, and with the help of an expert fisherman who knows Jim, she becomes a real contender. Then, fatally, she loses her humility. Rushing up a neighbor's stairs to boast of her imminent triumph, she falls and sprains her wrist. So much for Mom's trophy. Ah, but the family comes through. Each kid gives her a trophy for great domestic accomplishments, such as a frying pan labeled "Most Valuable Mother," while Jim gives her a rod and reel. She is touched and amused. It's a pointed moment. Jim acknowledges her athletic achievement while stating ironically—to the reassurance of the family and the viewer—that he knows she will never pursue this particularly crazy course again.

The message that emerges from all these little comedy-dramas is that tradition can function in modern life if incorporated in a mutually respectful discussion. Margaret, although a modern, intelligent, college-educated woman, is content with a life of washing dishes and vacuuming floors because her contrary urges are respected and she is given the opportunity to fail honorably at something else. By implication, Lucy Ricardo is unhappy in the same role only because Ricky yells at her and won't give her an honest chance to learn the truth about the female role.

The hollowness of the message is obvious, especially when one considers the contrivances needed to get it across. What if Margaret hadn't fallen and sprained her wrist? What if she had won the fly casting contest, had tasted the joy of athletic triumph, had proved herself outside the home? *Father Knows Best* had no interest in wrestling with questions like that. Nonetheless, it is revealing of the ambivalence in popular social thought at the time. Modernity was good, but so was tradition. Americans wanted hard, immediate, scientific (or monetary) proof of the value of any system yet at the same time felt a powerful yearning for earlier, less complex social orders. It was the golden age of both science fiction and the western. Tomorrowland and Frontierland were straight across from each other in that amazing new amusement park opened in 1955, Disneyland, and to get to either one, first you had to go through Main Street U.S.A.

It's no wonder that the suburb and the small town were always blurred together on television. Springfield is clearly an established small town, with its sense of belonging and deep-rooted mores, but just as clearly it is meant to stand for the uniform whiteness and social fluidity of the new suburbs. No "suburban" sitcom ever really showed the blank, barren developments, populated by recent strangers, with economies dependent on nearby cities and commerce concentrated in shopping malls. *Ozzie and Harriet* hinted at this self-deception; *Father Knows Best* made it complete.

This deception was probably not conscious, but even had it been, the Andersons might have played along. Concealment of truth was part of their family modus operandi. In one show Jim and Margaret explode into an argument when Margaret is incapable of learning to drive a car and Jim (forgetting his role) loses his patience. The kids gape at them. The perfect parents? Fighting? Jim and Margaret become self-conscious, floundering to find a way to deny what's happening, when Princess bails them out. She bursts into applause, praising them for their convincing imitation of an argument, thanking them for demonstrating what living in a less harmonious family would be like. Jim and Margaret gratefully play along. Bud and Kitten shuffle off, utterly duped. Only Princess, who presumably is old enough to handle these things, is permitted to know that anger is part of adult life.

Lying in most comedies was a character's way of getting his own at the cost of the group, and it always resulted in humiliation. It was often that, too, on *Father Knows Best*, but it was also often an effective management tool. Communication—such as the respectful discussion of conflicting desires—could help the family function smoothly, but it could also be suppressed and manipulated to the same end. This was an eerie undercurrent of a picture of family life that strove so hard to be wholesome, traditional, and Christian. It was an unintended admission that the image could not be maintained without general acceptance of a whole set of lies.

The feelings that *Father Knows Best* and its successors inspire in contemporary viewers are complex, often unsettling. Such shows haunt the reruns with a far greater frequency than any of the other shows of their time, many of which were originally more popular. *Leave It to Beaver* (the most vividly remembered of them among baby boomers because of its focus on childhood) has inspired a popular sequel series on cable TV, several published and televised parodies, even a reasonably successful book of satire. As David Marc points out, different cable networks sell the same reruns to different viewers in a variety of ways: For Christian Broadcasting they are positive instructional images; for Turner Broadcasting they're easy ways to evoke memories of cozy juvenile evenings in the living room; for Nickelodeon they are amusing trash, useful in ridiculing past generations that were supposedly simpler and dumber.

For Billy ("Bud") Gray, they are a painful embarrassment: "I wish there was some way I could tell kids not to believe it. . . . I think we were all well motivated, but what we did was run a hoax. *Father Knows Best* purported to be a reasonable facsimile of life. . . . Looked at from a certain slant, it's an incredibly destructive pattern for emulation."

For some viewers, like this writer, they are strangely seductive horrors, which deny reality as they pretend to engage it, which offer an image of secular paradise that could just as easily be viewed as hell. They are ingenious, complex, self-contradictory labyrinths with bafflingly bland, casual surfaces. They are the products of profound national confusion masquerading as confidence.

Reaction to *Father Knows Best* at the time of its debut was not nearly so complex. Critics liked it. A *New York Times* reviewer, weary of bumbling dads and scatterbrained moms, felt it had "restored parental prestige on TV." Amateur cultural watchdogs liked it even more. In 1955 the Family Service Association of America presented Robert Young with a plaque for his Constructive Portrayal of American Family Life. The government liked it very much. In 1959 the Treasury Department underwrote a special episode of the show, never aired on TV but shown to civic and church groups, to promote a bond drive. That episode, "Twenty Four Hours in Tyrant Land," showed what life in Springfield would be like under Communist rule. On the surface it was an attempt to show average Americans how the Reds might threaten their daily happiness. By implication, it was a federal endorsement of the Anderson family as the American

101

ideal, the diametrical counterpoint to Nikita Khrushchev. The fact that it was difficult to conceive any scenario in which Middle America could go Communist was ignored; that would have been as impolite to mention as Jim and Margaret's quarrel.

Many parents believed the show was as instructive as the Treasury Department did. Rick Mitz recounts the experience of one Susie Hearn, a midwestern suburban child whose weekly allowance was dependent upon her watching *Father Knows Best.* As each episode ended, Mrs. Hearn would ask her child, "Susie, why can't you help make our family be like that?" Ratings breakdowns suggested that the show was indeed reaching millions of families, families watching together, children and parents perhaps testing their own experiences against those of the Andersons.

Father Knows Best entered the ratings fray at a bad time for sitcoms: After an initial burst of success, nearly all the products of the post-*Lucy* avalanche had died. Filmed adventure shows and prime-time game shows were on the ascendant. The number of new sitcoms dropped from nineteen in 1954 to seven in 1955. The Andersons almost joined the casualty list. CBS, in one of its few programming errors of the period, plopped them into a ten o'clock Sunday night slot, evidently thinking that their intelligent domesticity would appeal mainly to parents winding down after the kids were put to bed. Ratings were poor, and CBS canceled the series.

Then came the first sign that viewers were connecting with this show as more than a half hour diversion. Thousands of letters poured in, demanding that the network keep the Andersons on the air, many asking specifically that it be shown earlier when families could watch it together.

CBS had never encountered such a thing and didn't know how to respond. NBC figured it out, picked up the show, and gave it an eight-thirty Wednesday slot. Its audience grew steadily then, until it hit sixth place in the ratings in 1959, a period in which scarcely any comedy was doing well on TV. At the end of that season, Young and Rodney abruptly pulled the plug, saying that "we'd done all we could with it." The show was still popular enough to hold its own through three years of prime-time network reruns.

As *Father Knows Best* climbed the charts, it transformed sitcoms all around it. Moral lessons became an accepted, even expected, part of the form, even when the content didn't seem to justify it. Satire and absurdity became harder to put on the air. The sitcom became mainstream America's candy-coated teacher, and the lessons were usually about the same kind of centrist, ambitionless harmony.

8

Sweet Subversion

Not everyone bought into the mid-'50s consensus. The Beat and Bop scenes, so-called "sick" comedians like Mort Sahl and Lenny Bruce, Harvey Kurtzman's *Mad* magazine, even the horny, rackety subculture of rock and roll and the smug self-indulgence of Hugh Hefner's *Playboy* advanced alternatives to family life and suburbia.

In a quieter way TV comedy produced its own alternative tradition. Even while the Andersons were bonding together to transcend their weekly difficulties, a few gutsy sitcoms celebrated discord and cynicism, greed and hypocrisy. They eschewed laugh tracks and went for the audience's jugular. They zeroed in not on what America wanted to be but on what it was: rich, swaggering, ambitious, nervous, and self-deluding.

The roots of these shows were in the noisy vaudevillian comedy hours of the Berle era. By the mid-'50s those shows were being hit hard from all sides. The democratization and ruralization of television meant that urban constituencies weren't enough to support a national program anymore. In Charlotte, North Carolina, in 1954, for example, Berle posted only a 1.9 rating, against the syndicated *Death Valley Days* with a rating of 56.3. A few years earlier that wouldn't have made much difference, but by

1954 there were a lot of Charlottes plugged into the TV networks. That was the first year Berle dropped out of the top ten in national ratings.

The networks didn't help their own cause. NBC had a solid hit in *Your Show of Shows*, a brilliant comedy showcase starring Sid Caesar and Imogene Coca, with Carl Reiner and Howard Morris supporting them and a writing staff that included Woody Allen, Mel Brooks, Neil Simon, and a couple of major sitcom writers of the future, Mel Tolkin (*All in the Family*) and Larry Gelbart (*M*A*S*H*). Then, in 1954, trying to head off the ascendant CBS, the network went for a "triple success," splitting up Caesar and Coca into their own shows and giving their producer a variety showcase of his own, *Max Liebman Presents*. The chemistry was gone, and NBC got itself a triple failure.

Network executives and producers were in part relieved by the decline of the comedy-variety shows. Their broad style of humor drew heat during the censorship debates; radio commentator Paul Harvey spoke for many critics when he complained of "bawdy New York comedians imposing their taste on the other forty-seven states." Filmed sitcoms and adventure shows were more dependable products; game shows and talk shows were far cheaper and easier to produce. The pressure to produce original skits every week also chewed up writers and burned out performers. In 1952 Milton Berle hired Goodman Ace, creator and writer of the radio sitcom *Easy Aces*, to rework his show around interrelated skits to give it a sitcomlike feel. It didn't slow his decline. Three years later Jackie Gleason tried to spin a recurrent sketch into a half hour sitcom, but that didn't save him either. Fred Allen dropped out of TV entirely in 1951. The next year the host of NBC's *All Star Revue*, a young nightclub singer and comic named Danny Thomas, did the same, with particular vehemence: "TV is for idiots! It has lowered the standards of the entertainment industry. . . . You work years building routines, do them once on TV, and they're finished. Next thing you know, you are, too. . . . When and if I ever do my own TV show, I'd like it to be a half-hour on film."

Thomas got his wish, thanks to Lucy and Desi Arnaz. They used him as the centerpiece of their follow-up to *I Love Lucy*, another sitcom about a nightclub entertainer and his family but with the comic emphasis solidly on the husband, not on the wife.

Make Room for Daddy, premiering two years after *Lucy*, displayed a decided shift toward the domestic: Danny Williams had an eleven-year-old daughter and a six-year-old son, and his wife, Margaret, was far more content with the housewife's lot than was Lucy. But the Williamses did live in a Manhattan apartment with a sassy black maid; they never made the move to the suburbs with the Ricardos, and Margaret, played by the sharp-tongued comedienne Jean Hagen, never hesitated to cut her husband down to size. The kids were no Bud and Princess, or even Ricky and David; they were cynical, manipulative, back-talking brats.

The Williams household was never presented to us as an ideal. The Treasury Department never asked Danny and his brood to show us the horrors of the Red menace; if they had, communism might still be alive today. The Williamses were a family that tried to live by the rules of the mid-'50s but simply failed to do so. The debut episode concerned Danny's neglect of his family because of his constant touring, rehearsing, and preparing. He tries to repair the rift with his wife by setting up a romantic weekend, but his daughter sniffs an opening and snags him for a school show. Danny "lays an egg" there, tries to get away with his wife again, but gets hooked by his son for another show. The episode ends on Danny's exasperated defeat. In the Williams family there was no group solution that left everyone happier than before. There was only constant competition and unsatisfying compromise.

The vanity and falsity of show biz were constant undercurrents of Williams family conflict. In one episode Margaret tries to convince Danny that her expensive hairdresser is a worthwhile expense because of all the compliments she's been getting on her hair. No sooner has Danny challenged her to name one person who's complimented her hair than the kids appear, oohing and aahing completely out of character about her coiffure. She thanks them and dismisses them, but they won't let up: "No, really, I've never seen your hair look so lovely." Finally Danny tumbles to the fact that he's being had, and Margaret grouses at the kids that they've overplayed their parts. Replies her cute little daughter: "What do you expect for fifty cents? Lunt and Fontanne?"

Danny himself was a puffed-up pretender who seemed to need his kids mainly as an audience for his paternal performance. Like Ricky Ricardo, he was a stubborn resister of compromise and consensus, with an explosive temper and a dependence on old-world (Lebanese) traditions. But whereas the universe generally conspired to support Ricky's positions, it worked to undermine Danny's. Nearly every episode involved some assault on his vanity, some exposure of his authoritarian pretense. He was an old-style man strutting for a sophisticated, cynical world that simply was not impressed.

Even the kids were self-consciously aware of themselves as kids in the filiarchic '50s. Most of their childish antics seemed calculated to upset their parents and give themselves something to smirk about in private. They even saw their lives as genre pieces; when they wanted Dad to do something and he refused, they whined back, "But fathers always do it on television!"

Daddy never grappled as frankly with domestic conflict as *Lucy* had in its first couple of seasons, but within a mid-'50s context it did pull off a remarkably saucy mockery of the American image of the family. Thomas once said that the show was "about the private life of a man who has no private life." But more than that, it was about fakery, about people playing roles and striking poses to get what they want. Even the sentimental moments of family unity that ended many of the shows were made hollow by a kid's wisecrack or by that look of Danny's that showed he was accepting defeat, not embracing a social victory. In a sense, *Make Room for Daddy* was about what happens when real people decide that it's in their interest to be like the Andersons.

It was a sharp, funny show. Its scripts were tight; its actors, real comedians. Its executive producer and principal director was Sheldon Leonard, a movie and radio comic with a sharp eye for the absurd, who became a big force in sitcoms in the next decade. Reviews were good from the beginning, but ratings were only passable. At the time Desilu developed the show, NBC and CBS were entangling themselves in an expensive race to get into color TV. ABC, having just concluded its merger with United Paramount Theaters and with big-money sponsorship from Kraft and U.S. Steel, decided to make its move, leading with slickly produced sitcoms and adventure series. It tried *Daddy* in a couple of different time slots, changed its title to *The Danny Thomas Show*, and even tried a change of format: When Jean Hagen left the show after three seasons, Margaret was declared dead, and Danny spent a year as a bachelor father, dating various women.

The show didn't really reach the vast public until the fall of 1957. Desilu had called it quits for *I Love Lucy* while it was still TV's top-rated program, and CBS needed something to fill its Monday night time slot. *The Danny Thomas Show* was the natural replacement, and Desilu negotiated the switch with the networks. Thomas said at the time that he hoped to retain half of *Lucy*'s audience. In fact, he held on to 80 percent of it and for the rest of the decade had the highest-rated sitcom on the air.

The show mellowed a bit in its new incarnation. Danny had a new wife, Kathy, a more housewifely creature than Margaret, played by a quieter actress, Marjorie Lord. With her came a new addition: Linda, her daughter by a previous marriage, played by the painfully cute Angela Cartwright (who was packaged as "America's Little Darling" and soon had more than a hundred fan clubs across the country). But even Linda had her moments, slyly turning those crinkly eyes and that pug nose into tools to manipulate her father. A little more sentiment crept into the stories, the final resolutions were made a little more convincing, but Danny's blustering and screaming went on. Still, millions of Americans tuned in every week to see a family battling and conniving and not quite making things work.

Despite *Daddy*'s success, TV resisted its example. Where one would expect a flood of sitcoms in 1958 and 1959 about brawling households with blustering fathers and scheming kids there were, in fact, none. Every family comedy stamped out during the years of Danny Thomas's reign was in either the *Father Knows Best* instructional mold or the dreary old "bumbling dad" or "scatterbrained wife" mold. Most of them failed while Thomas continued to flourish, yet the pattern continued well into the '60s. The assumption that TV always gives people what they want, that the ratings system guarantees a sort of entertainment democracy, clearly doesn't explain everything about TV programming. It seems evident, from *Lucy* and *Danny Thomas*, that the public had an appetite for rough-edged lampoons of family life, which the networks were failing to satisfy.

Sponsor worries were probably the greatest cause of the disparity between public taste and televised product. Advertisers were always concerned about the image their merchandise would develop through association with a particular show and would unhesitatingly nix or alter concepts that might run counter to their chosen personae (which were invariably conservative, dependable, wholesome, and very, very American).

Network timidity certainly played a part, too. Since ratings could never be predicted, it was always safer to go with a concept that would at least not incur any public wrath and then hope that somehow it would succeed. For both sponsors and networks, the approval of government and public do-gooders was a subtle but effective goad. Danny Williams may have been more popular than Jim Anderson, but Jim Anderson won the citizens' groups' awards. And those awards could be awfully handy in negotiating conflicts with the FCC.

So the official wardens of society systematically—though never quite consciously—kept a lid on even the mildest TV satires of American family life. Probably few people could ever have been offended by *The Danny Thomas Show*, just as hardly anyone ever seriously assailed *I Love Lucy*. Yet there were disturbing elements in such shows that prevented the controllers of TV culture from encouraging more of the same. The incredible obstacle course the Arnazes had to negotiate to get *Lucy* on the air is one indication of that; the fact that only the independence and financial clout of Desilu could subsequently bring a family like the Williamses into existence is another. American mass culture was trapped in Springfield by far more than popular taste.

Dead center in the 1950s, however, there was one jubilant, defiant explosion of noise and pain and marital rage. *The Honeymooners* was a ratings disappointment that left no immediate heirs, but the popular culture of the 1950s would look very pale without it.

It too grew from the comedy-variety tradition, but much more directly than *Make Room for Daddy*. Jackie Gleason began hosting the DuMont Network's *Cavalcade of Stars* in 1950, with Art Carney and Pert Kelton as regular performers. Like everything on DuMont, it was a low-budget show; it was sponsored by Whelan's drugstores, and an industry joke at the time held that the cast was paid in toothpaste. But Gleason's verve and mastery of comic shtick were unrivaled on television. He was a tremendously inventive creator of characters: The Loudmouth, the Bachelor, the Poor Soul, Joe the Bartender, and Reggie Van Gleason III fueled dozens of energetic skits. According to Art Carney, however, the show didn't take off until Gleason and his writers created the cantankerous bus driver Ralph Kramden and his irascible wife, Alice: "We were on against tough opposition, Friday night at ten, opposite the fights. One week we dropped in the Honeymooner sketch among all the other stuff we were doing. Whammo! We started to build an audience."

In the first five-minute skit Kramden was just a tired working stiff at the end of his day who blows his top when Alice, played by Kelton, asks him to go out and buy some bread. Their squabble escalates quickly into a pie fight that gets them in trouble with a cop. The routine's only real appeal was the energy and verbal imagination of the loving couple's combat.

Gradually, however, Ralph evolved into a classic American type, a perennial loser who persisted insanely in seeing himself as a man of the world, a master of his destiny, an opportunist eternally on the brink of making it big. Alice, meanwhile, mellowed from a shrieker to a survivor, hanging in doggedly, naggingly, as Ralph tried to dominate her with the sheer force of his voice and self-importance.

A couple of years earlier Gleason had played a similar figure on the first TV incarnation of *The Life of Riley* but was constrained by the tameness and sentimentality of sitcoms. Now, controlling his own material for his own variety show, he could rip off the gauzy veneer and let all the venom of a frustrated blue-collar Brooklyn marriage pour out. The results were hilarious, and they struck a chord. *Cavalcade*'s ratings soared, and audience surveys pinpointed "The Honeymooners" as the single biggest cause.

Art Carney played assorted supporting roles in the early skits, including the cop in the first one. But soon one regular character was developed for him: Ed Norton, the moronic but proud sewer worker, Ralph's neighbor, friend, and foil. At first his function was just to wander into the middle of the Kramdens' fights and make them worse, usually for Ralph. As the bits grew longer and more complex, he became more of a co-conspirator, joining Ralph in harebrained quick-money schemes that led to more battles with Alice. Carney played Norton as the perfect comic dupe, innocent and eager but with a weirdly obtuse perceptivity that always enabled him to slip out of a tough situation and leave Ralph holding the bag.

Near the end of that first "Honeymooner" season a fourth character was added: Trixie, Norton's wife and a former burlesque "dancer," played by Joyce Randolph. Trixie was just smart enough to be a friend to Alice and just dippy enough to tolerate Ed. Her background, with its redolence of sleaze and sweat and questionable morality, neatly completed the Kramden milieu. To Ralph and Ed, representatives of the lowest echelons of public service, was added this embodiment of phony glamour, of the dregs of show biz. Toss in Alice, the homemaker who seemed utterly helpless against the perpetual degeneration of her shabby apartment, and we may have the bleakest picture ever of working-class life in American entertainment.

"The Honeymooners" became a regular skit during the fall of 1951, at the same time that Lucy and Ricky were winning America's hearts with their loving warfare. In 1952 CBS saw a good thing in Gleason and wooed him away to star in *The Jackie Gleason Show*. It was a deadly blow to DuMont, one that may have sealed its demise only two years later.

Carney moved with Gleason to CBS, but Pert Kelton was replaced by Audrey Meadows, a strikingly pretty young actress who had the nerve and the ability to be convincingly dowdy and hangdog. As Alice Kramden she provided a pragmatic balance to Ralph's dreams of wealth and glory, a nasal voice of reason that always cut through his bombast. She stood blank and immovable in the face of Ralph's rages and his never-fulfilled threats of violence: "One of these days, Alice! One of these days . . . bang! Zoom! To the moon!"

The Honeymooners as we remember them were now complete; their skits were also the centerpieces of nearly every Gleason show and now sometimes ran to a half hour and more. The plots were simple. Ralph has a scheme: become a prizefighter; marry off Alice's meddling aunt to the local butcher; form a songwriting team with Norton; hypnotize Alice so he can go to a convention of the Raccoon Lodge. The scheme backfires horribly; Alice gives Ralph his comeuppance; he rages at her, his volume and ferocity increasing as his own idiocy becomes more painfully apparent. Finally he accepts his own humiliation and feels grateful that for some reason, Alice goes on loving him. "Baby," he says, "you're the greatest!" The honeymoon continues.

Gradually the inevitable fight with Alice became the icing on the cake rather than the cake itself. The real conflicts of the mature "Honeymooners" episodes were all within Ralph. He hated his poverty and hated himself because of it and so refused to acknowledge its permanence. He hurled himself into money-making schemes with the frenzy of a religious zealot trying to hold together his crumbling faith. Alice was his bitch goddess, judging him; all his schemes were aimed at proving his worthiness to her, and all his mad rages were fueled by the belief that she was scorning him. The contrast between her long-suffering deadpan and his mad theatrics made it clear that Ralph himself was really his only judge. Alice accepted him, as she accepted her dreary lot in life. Ralph only projected his self-loathing onto her. Her love and Norton's friendship always overcame Ralph's lunacy, for the time being. But they never brought anything resembling happiness.

Norton was a different kind of creature. He wasn't ashamed of his sewer work; he was proud of it. He once declared that his fondest dream was to visit Paris and see its famous sewers firsthand. He rarely fought with Trixie. He certainly didn't seem to worry about what she thought of him. Norton was a big kid who got involved in crackpot schemes for the fun of it, because he caught Ralph's enthusiasm. Ralph was a very poignant type, in his place and time: the low-income, no-talent schmuck in a society based on money. Ed was a lovable, transhistorical dope whose inability not to enjoy life only made Ralph's plight more painful.

The result of this combination was a portrait of life that was both comically eternal and uncomfortably relevant to life in '50s America. "The Honeymooners" fused the structure of sitcoms with the improvisational energy of live TV, the liveliness of vaudeville with the acting precision of movie comedy. Carney was a great admirer of Laurel and Hardy and compared the comic repetition of "The Honeymooners" with their great short films: "You know the plots, you sit back, and even though you know exactly what's coming, it doesn't matter. You still enjoy it. Even more so *because* you know it."

Carney called Kramden and Norton the "Brooklyn-type version" of Stan and Ollie, "the same sort of fumblers." But he and Gleason brought more than Brooklyn into the type; they brought an awareness of the pain of men who are barred from the national dream. Ralph Kramden didn't resist the new national consensus like Danny Williams: he was never even invited.

One can wonder what might have happened had Gleason and CBS decided right at the start to develop a *Honeymooners* sitcom; perhaps the tenor of the times would have helped the public accept it more than it was able to three years later. Still, no one involved in the show could have been disappointed at the way things were working out: Gleason's new program reached eighth in the ratings in its second year and in January 1955, driven mainly by the Kramden sketches, actually surged into first place, ahead of *I Love Lucy*. As if to mark his triumph, Gleason then stole Milton Berle's sponsor; Buick decided to abandon "Mr. Television" and give Gleason an astoundingly high-paying contract for exclusive sponsorship of his 1955–56 season.

Gleason was cocky—rightfully so, but also dangerously so. Feeling limited by the comedy-variety format, he decided to shake things up. He saw filmed sitcoms as a wise investment, since they could be sold and resold eternally, and so proposed converting his Kramden sketches into that form; the subsequent success of *The Honeymooners* in syndication has borne out his judgment on that subject well. But he had less sensible plans for the remaining half hour of his time slot. He'd created a pet variety program, *Stage Show*, starring Tommy and Jimmy Dorsey, as a summer replacement the year before, and though it did poorly in the ratings, he wanted to bring it back. Worse, he wanted it aired *before* the sitcom, so that viewers waiting to see *The Honeymooners* would be inclined to sit through it. CBS and Buick balked, but Gleason wouldn't listen. If they wanted him, they'd have to buy his package. They relented, of course.

The result was painful. *Stage Show* flopped, and too many viewers who drifted to competing programs didn't drift back when *The Honeymooners* began half an hour later. NBC, meanwhile, had finally found someone to counter Gleason, a frighteningly calm, quiet singer named Perry Como. If one had tried to imagine the exact opposite of Ralph Kramden, the embodiment of everything that Ralph could never be and his fans would never have wanted him to be, it would have been Como. But Como was popular, and with the aid of *Stage Show*, he became even more popular than Ralph. Como's show rated eighteenth that season. *The Honeymooners* rated nineteenth.

Had a brand-new sitcom weighed in at nineteenth it would have been counted a solid success. But as the replacement for a top-rated show it was a disaster. Gleason reversed the order of his two shows at mid-season, but it wasn't enough. With the next season he abandoned *Stage Show* and reincorporated the Kramdens and Nortons into *The Jackie Gleason Show*. He'd lost Buick, and a large chunk of his budget, but he picked up a couple of new sponsors. Unfortunately he'd lost most of his audience as well. In a turn of events that would have seemed inconceivable two years before, Perry Como eased his way into the Nielsen top ten while Jackie Gleason plummeted out of the top thirty. The next year there was no Gleason—and no Kramden—on television.

The *Stage Show* blunder was certainly a large part of this sudden change (although in its short life *Stage Show* was an odd sort of cultural watershed. It was the last mass audience forum for swing era bandleaders, the first TV show to feature Elvis Presley, and the last thing jazz pioneer Charlie Parker ever saw, since his heart failed as he was watching an episode). But the drop was so precipitous that other factors must have been involved. After all, if Americans had really wanted to see Ralph Kramden more than Perry Como, they could have switched channels at the half hour break, and they certainly could have returned to the fold the following season, when all was back to normal. Instead, they seemed content to listen to a sweatered man crooning on a stool while the Kramdens were raging unheard on another station. Nor was the quality of *The Honeymooners* the problem. By any standard nearly all of the thirty-nine filmed episodes were better than the variety show skits that have been preserved on kinescope. Something bigger was going on.

Maybe the national self-image finally caught up to old Ralph. As the Desilu gang had apparently intuited, Americans seemed to want to believe that the postwar battle of the sexes had quieted into domestic harmony. Even on the noisy *Danny Thomas Show*, open marital warfare rarely erupted. The Kramdens were a harsh reminder of a conflict being ardently denied by popular culture.

As for the get-rich-quick schemes that drove most of the plots forward, weren't those out of date now? America was on its way to becoming a land of universal prosperity after all, and soon everyone who wanted to be—or deserved to be—would be a member of the contented middle class. Audrey Meadows has reported that every season hundreds of viewers mailed her pretty aprons and hairbrushes and curtain rods so that she and her environs wouldn't have to look so damned dowdy. Maybe the viewers just finally got tired of waiting for her to move to a tract house and refurbish herself in Populuxe.

Or maybe there was a problem in the sitcom form itself. When "The Honeymooners" was a sketch within a variety show, it sat one step further from reality. Set up by Gleason's monologue as emcee, buffered by kitschy numbers with the June Taylor Dancers, the sketches had the quality of nonsense, of grotesque fantasy. TV viewers were used to broad excesses in such shows: Berle in his dresses; Sid Caesar doing goofy accents; Gleason himself playing his menagerie of weird characters. But a *sitcom*—with no reality other than the play itself, with no grinning host to gloat, "How sweet it is!" and reassure us at the end that it was all a joke— was another thing entirely. Suddenly the Kramdens existed on the same plane of reality as the Andersons, the Nelsons, and the Williamses.

As such, they were disturbing. They reminded people that even the new America had its losers, that maybe everyone was more a loser than anyone wanted to admit, that maybe the ultimate happiness of our secular, suburban paradise was just as unattainable as Ralph Kramden's dreams of wealth. *The Jackie Gleason Show* skits had played on deep anxieties, as most great humor does. But *The Honeymooners*, as a sitcom, may have brought those anxieties a little too close to consciousness. Even when the Kramdens returned to safer ground, it may have been too difficult for viewers to see them as they had before. The Kramdens, and Gleason, would have to lie low for a few years, while Americans watched new families like the Cleavers and the McCoys go through their far more comforting paces.

The Honeymooners has been a big influence on sitcoms, from *The Flintstones* to *All in the Family* to *Married . . . with Children*. It returned fairly successfully to the variety show venue in the 1960s. It's been a continual favorite in rerun and on videotape, particularly among hip baby boomers not inclined to be nostalgic for the "happy days" of the '50s. But its own times proved not to be right for it. Americans watched it by the millions for a few years, then suddenly shut their eyes.

❑

An oddly similar fate was suffered by another sitcom premiering in 1955, *You'll Never Get Rich*. Of the comedies positing antitheses to the dominant TV worldview, it was by far the wickedest. As bleak as *The Honeymooners* could be, it never challenged conventional American values and social systems. For the most part it reinforced them; Ralph's painful lessons usually taught that he should just stick to his steady job and predictable marriage. *You'll Never Get Rich*, on the other hand, gleefully and unabashedly made a hero of a con man, a con man flourishing, no less, in the very military that was defending our liberty.

Phil Silvers was a wide-mouthed, expressive veteran of Broadway, movie comedy, and TV variety shows who had perfected an unctuous, charmingly obnoxious wise guy character. In 1954 he emceed a Washington Press Club dinner for President Eisenhower at which, in addition to much of the top echelon of the U.S. government, was a CBS vice-president named Hubbell Robinson. Robinson was so taken with Silvers that he signed him to create and star in his own sitcom. The producer, director, head writer, and owner of the series was to be Nat Hiken, a New York comedy writer with whom Silvers had worked successfully in the past.

Hiken and Silvers ground out countless premises for sitcoms, trying to find one that would use Silvers's smart-ass con man persona to good effect. Some were trite: Silvers as the obnoxious brother-in-law of a regular American husband. Some were bizarre: Silvers as a Turkish bath attendant. Finally they found one that would be perfect: He would be U.S. Army Master Sergeant Ernest T. Bilko, a gambling, scheming, parasitic exploiter of the system at a dreary base in Kansas.

The concept was guaranteed to strike a chord with GIs and ex-GIs, who at that time would have included nearly every American male between the ages of eighteen and fifty. Anyone who had served time in the military—especially the bloated, unused peacetime military—knew how hypocritical the whole system was, knew how little liberty defending or character building really went on. The infantry inductee spends his two or four years desperately seeking ways to kill time, augment his measly income, and dodge mind-numbing duties. Every soldier would have loved to have had a Bilko in his barracks, an enemy of officers, a friend of any enlisted men who'd play his game, the one unbeatable power at Fort Baxter. An authority-fearing private said in one episode, "Bilko'll get his." Another soldier, who knew the master sergeant, replied, "Oh, he's already got his. And he's got yours, too."

It was guaranteed to strike a chord with kids, too. Like any kid, Bilko is officially powerless, subject to the arbitrary edicts of his moronic superiors. But like a superkid, like every kid's dream self, he was a master at getting his own way, at lying and subverting authority, at throwing the system into chaos and then slipping to safety with a huge grin on his face. He was Bugs Bunny in a uniform.

Bilko's perpetual victim was the stuffy, hapless Colonel Hall, played with an absentminded stiffness by Paul Ford. Ford's hesitant delivery, balding pate, and homely heartland looks inevitably brought to mind Dwight Eisenhower. Appropriately Hall ran his base the way Ike seemed to be running America: smiling genially, desperately maintaining an appearance of respectability, while letting the profiteers and the silver-tongued salesmen run the system for whatever they could get out of it.

Of course, Bilko wasn't entirely selfish. He never fleeced the really likable characters, and he often defended the defenseless. He saved the fat, ugly Private Doberman's pride when a boneheaded army error got him picked as the All-American GI. He outfoxed a military court to save a chimpanzee that, through another boneheaded army error, was inducted as a private. Bilko's targets were all those who were too officious or too respectable or too authoritarian for their own good. His enemies, in short, were the wardens of American society.

Like *The Honeymooners, You'll Never Get Rich* was a New York product. It was, in fact, the last major network sitcom to be produced outside Southern California and the influence of the Hollywood entertainment machine. It was shot in a small studio on East Sixty-seventh Street, right on top of a show biz delicatessen. It was written by a brilliant bunch of veterans of live TV and radio and the nightclub circuit: Leonard Stern, Arnold Auerbach, Arnold Rosen, Coleman Jacoby, and many others (including, briefly, Neil Simon, fresh from Sid Caesar's show). The supporting cast—Herbie Faye, Harvey Lembeck, Elizabeth Fraser, Maurice Gosfield—was theatrically based and developed a sizzling chemistry. *You'll Never Get Rich* was the smartest and funniest comedy of its time.

It was also the boldest and most honest. Its themes were simple and need no clever critical analysis to be discovered: The army is pointless; bureaucracy is inept; authority is hypocritical; superiors are there to be outfoxed; the cold war is a joke; it's fun to be a crook. Bilko didn't live the American ideal of Jim Anderson, nor did he struggle with it like Danny Williams or snatch at it uncomprehendingly like Ralph Kramden. He just saw right through it. Ernie Bilko's America ran on self-interest, money, and deceit, and Bilko knew how to take advantage of it. His popular success would prove that millions of Americans sympathized with his viewpoint. As Silvers himself once said, "Inside everyone is a con man wiggling to sneak out."

The pilot episode impressed everyone at CBS with its verve and nonstop humor. Network head William Paley called it "money in the bank" and gave it the green light to find a sponsor. With typical insouciance, Silvers wanted Jackie Gleason to sponsor it with some of the money from his multimillion-dollar Buick deal, telling Gleason he'd run "Jackie Gleason is good for you" commercials. The makers of Camel cigarettes actually picked up the tab, figuring that a wisecracking GI show would fit their manly image well. Hiken and Silvers, with a cynicism that would have made Bilko proud, obligingly inserted a number of comedy bits involving packs of Camels into the show.

CBS programmers decided that Bilko was just the weapon they needed for a battle that had seemed hopeless a few years before. They scheduled his adventures for Tuesday night, directly across from Milton Berle. Berle had finished a solid eleventh in the ratings for the previous season, but he was clearly a wounded beast. He'd just lost his sponsor to Jackie Gleason, and now here was another old vaudevillian—and a personal friend—going after him with a sitcom. Silvers won the time slot; Berle's ratings crumbled. In 1956, only six years after he had seemingly owned the airwaves, Berle was canceled. His time slot was given to an unsuccessful game show, and *The Phil Silvers Show* (as it was soon renamed) rose in the ratings, ranking third among sitcoms. Ernie Bilko became a national figure, imitated at parties, used as a reference point by pop journalists. Silvers, Hiken, and their crew won nine Emmys in three years for acting, writing, directing, and best series. CBS, it appeared, had found another rich sitcom resource.

Then, in his third year, Silvers met his Perry Como. Or, rather, a foursome of Comos. NBC weighed in against him with a variety show cofeaturing Eddie Fisher, the bland singer who had risen to stardom with a bit of quasi-ethnic treacle called "Oh My Papa," and the mildest of mild '50s comedians, George Gobel. Bilko might have held his own against them had he been able to keep his numerous younger viewers, but ABC devastated him there. For this was 1957, ABC's "Year of the Adult Western," and an alternating pair of Warner Brothers productions, *Cheyenne* and *Sugarfoot*, played on Tuesday night, beginning a half hour before Silvers. *Cheyenne* became ABC's second-highest-rated show, twelfth overall, a key part of the western and adventure strategy that finally made ABC a contender among networks.

Although the network liked to call them "adult westerns," using the label film critics had hung on the cycle of John Ford-Howard Hawks-Anthony Mann movies that dominated the big screen in the early '50s, it was no secret that most of the audience for the shows was comprised of children and their captive parents. ABC's corporate chief, Leonard Goldenson, and his new dynamo of a president, Ollie Treyz, understood demographics. They packed their seven-thirty and eight o'clock slots with what advertising insiders were calling "kid vid": *Disneyland, Maverick, American Bandstand, Circus Boy, Rin Tin Tin, Zorro, Cheyenne.* When *Rin Tin Tin* clobbered *Leave It to Beaver* and CBS dropped the Cleaver boys, ABC quickly picked them up and pitted them against CBS's prime-time reruns of *I Love Lucy*, as a lead-in to *Zorro*. Beav won the time slot.

CBS and NBC, of course, wasted no time in leaping onto the western chuck wagon, with *Gunsmoke* and *Wells Fargo* and countless others. The four biggest veteran comedians still on the air—Red Skelton, George Burns, Jack Benny, and Bob Hope—astutely saw the westward migration as a major threat and vowed to "laugh the westerns off the air." From the very beginning of the 1957 season they mocked and lampooned and spoofed the new wave of horse operas mercilessly. By season's end the westerns had corralled three of the top four ratings spots, seven of the top ten. Jack Benny, up against *Maverick*, plummeted from the top ten to the outskirts of Palookaville. CBS eventually had to move him to a ten o'clock time slot to save him. Only Skelton held his ground: He was already on late, up against Bob Cummings and a drama anthology. It was a sobering lesson for satirists.

So the baby boomers had finally taken over the airwaves, at least in the prebedtime hours. And they wanted to see snorting horses and twirling guns even more than conniving army men. CBS moved *The Phil Silvers Show* to a more grown-up, nine o'clock Friday slot, where he fared well against *M Squad* and *Man with a Camera*. His ratings were not what they had been, but they were solid.

Then, in 1959, the network dropped its bombshell. Bilko, the programmers decided, was still hot but was fading. Nat Hiken had sold ownership of the show to the network a couple of years before, and CBS foresaw potentially huge syndication income if it moved quickly to package the reruns. The problem, it claimed, was that no stations would buy the reruns as long as new episodes were being produced. The show would have to be canceled before it got "cold."

Silvers was devastated. He'd delivered big ratings, rave reviews, and several Emmys to his network, and now it was jerking the rug out from under him for some quick cash. He admitted later that his enthusiasm for television was destroyed by the cancellation. Subsequently he made only occasional specials and guest appearances and then vanished from the tube entirely.

CBS's decision was, most likely, purely a business one, but the assumptions guiding it are difficult to comprehend. Would the continuing production of new shows really have hurt the reruns? It certainly didn't one year later, when CBS began rerunning *The Danny Thomas Show* five days a week. For five years the Williamses' new and old episodes coexisted profitably.

Why syndicate the reruns in any case? CBS filled its own daytime schedule with sitcom reruns for years, yet it chose to sell the Bilko shows to independent stations, as if hoping to end their association with the network.

As for the show's losing its heat, a CBS vice-president once explained that the network tried to guard against "the fatigue factor." "If a show begins to wear thin on the ear and eye," he said, "you don't just say, 'Well, the tread is thin, but I'll wait till next year to buy new tires.' You change now and avoid a blowout." Silvers's ratings were down from a couple of years before, but so were Jack Benny's, so were Danny Thomas's in 1960. The network never pulled the plug on them to go into rerun.

It may be that the programmers' perception of *The Phil Silvers Show*'s marketability was shaped by its content. With prime-time TV utterly dominated by citation-winning families like the Andersons, by courageous cops, and by brave American cowboys taming the wilderness, with the raucous old comedy-variety giants wilting before the soporific onslaughts of the Perry Comos and George Gobels, maybe the cynical anti-authoritarianism of Ernie Bilko just *had* to be out of step with its times. It just *had* to be on the verge of bombing.

At a deeper level, the Silvers show must have been vaguely unnerving to the powers at CBS. Here was an unblushing satire of the U.S. military establishment, a satiric rejection of all the ideals of the cold war, airing weekly in the backyard of Bill Paley—Bill Paley, the friend of presidents, the former head of U.S. Psychological Warfare, a nobleman in New York society. CBS was viewed as the "liberal" network, but liberal only within the great government-corporate coalition—liberal mainly in that it worked with the government rather than chafed against it. Paley laid down dress and decor codes for his employees, requiring a look that he called "modern but conservative." That same phrase might have described CBS programming policies or the American political center as of 1959.

Only a year and a half after Bilko's demise the great Colonel Hall in the White House, in his farewell address, warned America of the growing power of the "military-industrial complex." But by then the country had already elected the perfect "modern but conservative" president, a snappy, forward-looking young man who embraced the military-industrial complex wholeheartedly. And half a year after that CBS premiered its sitcom version of the Kennedys, the very modern but inherently conservative Rob and Laura Petrie. Theirs would be a sassy, hip series that CBS could embrace comfortably. The satire of *The Phil Silvers Show* may have cut a little too close to the heart of that complex of which CBS was a part.

There was surely no conscious conspiracy to suppress Ernie Bilko as a threat to the cold war establishment—not even network programmers have ever taken sitcoms that seriously—but if the subtext of a show causes discomfort for people in decision-making positions, they may unconsciously devise reasons to turn against it. They may even convince themselves, conveniently, that the public is about to repudiate it.

The programmers were wrong, of course. The rerun package, under the title *Sgt. Bilko*, remained hugely popular for years and retains a loyal audience to the present. Just three years after the show's cancellation ABC struck gold with a half-assed imitation, *McHale's Navy*, kicking off an explosion of cynical military sitcoms during the Vietnam years. CBS joined the trend with *Gomer Pyle* and *Hogan's Heroes*, but none of those series dared to be as real or contemporary or biting as the Silvers show.

By the end of the 1950s the television comedy scene was bleak. TV had been an established mass medium for several years and was settling into comfy respectability. CBS was no longer the hungry underdog but the lordly overdog, confident enough even to toss away a hit like Silvers. ABC, the new up-and-comer, was basing its attack on wholesome kid stuff. NBC, falling into second and then third place, chose caution over daring.

In 1956 Pat Weaver, the visionary of cosmic communications, relin-
quished his post as president. Control of the network passed to Robert
Sarnoff, the son of one of the founders of RCA and NBC, and to Robert
Kintner, the former head of ABC. TV writer Max Wilk called Weaver's
departure "the end of an exciting, venturesome era."

The old comedy giants were gone or in retreat. Few new ones were
coming up, largely because live American comedy (perhaps partly in
reaction to the nature of TV comedy) was taking a sharp turn toward the
combative, political, and obscene. Steve Allen put Lenny Bruce on the air
in 1959, but Bruce was too hamstrung by the medium to be any good.

A series of music payola and game show–fixing scandals had humiliated the industry in 1958, and now the networks believed they had to earn
the public's good will all over again. Anything daring or caustic was
considered dangerous. Of course, that had been a growing tendency in
network decision making even before the scandals. Maybe the show trials
of Dick Clark, payola suspect, and Charles Van Doren, game show fraud,
had simply facilitated what needed to be done.

Bilko, the Kramdens, the Ricardos, and the Burnses were gone. The
Nelsons and Andersons were going strong, and new families were following their example. The Williamses were getting softer: The 1959–60 season of the Thomas show was dominated by daughter Terry's engagement
to a mild young singer (shades of Como and Fisher). Several episodes
also swirled around the visit of an Italian exchange student, played ever
so sweetly by Annette Funicello. Both sequences were heavy in sentiment, as Danny learned to surrender his old-fashioned ways and accept
these new elements into his family.

One new sitcom character, Dobie Gillis, promised something different, but as yet one couldn't quite be sure. His was a sly and quiet show
that wouldn't fully reveal what it was about until the 1960s had begun.

Maybe the clearest statement of the condition of the sitcom at decade's end was the most popular new show of the 1959 season, an instant
top twenty member, *Dennis the Menace*. Hank Ketcham's six-year-old
troublemaker had been one of the most refreshing creations of '50s pop
culture. He was an explosion of chaos, an unconscious anarchist, a pint-
size id running rampant through suburbia. Then TV got ahold of him.

The Dennis who appeared on CBS Sunday nights was a whining,
epicene little creature driven by an impossible naiveté and a cloying
desire always to do the right thing. His antics would have made Beaver
Cleaver puke. In a typical episode Dennis's father is throwing a party for

his boss, and Dennis becomes inexplicably worried that the guests won't find the house. Having seen an "Open House" sign on someone else's lawn earlier, he decides to move it to his own front yard. As a consequence, dozens of strangers tromp through the party, checking the house out for possible purchase. Various bits of confusion lead to a fight between the boss and Dennis's irascible neighbor, Mr. Wilson. Only Dennis's gleeful explanation of his helpful deed averts a social and financial disaster.

TV had broken the beast, tamed the child. It had turned him into a confused but harmless denizen of conflict-free suburbia. Yet viewers liked him, at least for a couple of years.

The vision of the nuclear family sitting contentedly in its tract home, of an America that had solved all its problems through prosperity and consensus, was defeating its mockers and detractors. The sponsor-pleasing concept that TV comedy should present ideal situations that make us feel good about the world had squeezed out the philosophy of comedy that comedians and satirists preferred: that humor should dredge up our ugly aspects and allow us to laugh at them. The sitcom, apparently, could no longer be a fun house mirror, but only a candy-coated lesson.

Television knew best.

9

Meeting in the Middle

During 1955 and 1956, while the Kramdens fell and Bilko soared, a wave of familial suburbanity washed over the rest of sitcomland. Inspired by the Nelson kids, George Burns and Gracie added their teenage son, Ronnie, to their show, completing their steady drift to domesticity. Gertrude Berg brought the Goldbergs from the Bronx to the suburbs, although it didn't save the show from cancellation. Then even the Ricardos and Mertzes made the move. Lucy summed up two dominant strains of current thought when she said she wanted to move to Connecticut so that "little Ricky can grow up in the country." Doing it for the kids and identifying the suburbs with a small town or the countryside: the Andersons would have been quietly pleased to hear her.

At the same time the family sitcoms flowed out to absorb parts of the world beyond the tube. In 1956 Elvis Presley had turned rock and roll into a youth craze. Citizens' groups, religious leaders, and psychologists flew into paroxysms of revulsion and terror, convinced that the new music would inspire juvenile delinquency and undermine the morals of decent white youngsters. Plenty of respectable kids liked the new sounds, though, and many grown-ups saw no danger in it; in fact, many grown-ups in the entertainment industry saw great profit in it.

In early 1957 sixteen-year-old Ricky Nelson decided he'd like to cut a rock and roll record. His dad, the old bandleader, set him up with a friend at Verve Records to do a white version of Fats Domino's "I'm Walkin'." Never one to miss a trick, Ozzie then had Ricky sing the song on the family TV show. The disc hit the top of the charts, and the irrepressible Ricky, with his sexless version of the Presley sneer, was on his way to being one of the most popular young performers of the late '50s. Along with Pat Boone and other "good kids," he helped tame rock music, turning it from a biracial moan of passion into a safe white pop phenomenon. *The Adventures of Ozzie and Harriet* had played a big role in the process.

By 1957 new shows were appearing in clear emulation of *Father Knows Best*. Of eight sitcoms premiering that fall, three offered instructive families. Only those three survived the season, and each was a solid success, going on to last five or six years. Each also went a step beyond *Father Knows Best* in social education. Where *Father* offered a nearly impossible ideal of the family, its followers showed Americans who were not so wealthy or so settled just how they could remake themselves in the Anderson image.

The best of them was also the one that hewed closest to the Anderson model—*Leave It to Beaver*. Its derivation is transparent: Springfield became Mayfield, Jim and Margaret became Ward and June Cleaver, Bud became Wally, Princess was eliminated, and the girl called Kitten became a boy called Beaver. *Beaver* was always funnier and less contrived than *Father*, but its tone and intent were about the same. It was, nonetheless, quite an original series, and it made some key contributions to '50s mythography, thanks to the backgrounds of its creators.

Bob Mosher and Joe Connelly were only about halfway through their transformation of Amos and Andy from dumb darkies to mainstream middle-classmen when that show was canceled. They tackled various writing projects over the next four years; the most successful was a screenplay called *The Private War of Major Benson*—about a cute little boy who melts a military school commander's hard heart—ostensibly inspired by the experiences of one of Connelly's seven kids. It netted them an Oscar nomination and made them a hot commodity in Hollywood. It also inspired them to create their own sitcom, taking a kid's-eye view of growing up.

Connelly explained *Beaver*'s approach: "We weren't doing a situation comedy in the sense of situations created for some certain effect. We

123

wanted a natural storyline growing out of events that might really happen. . . . When we hired a writer, I told him to look for situations from his own background." Both writers drew story ideas from their childhoods and from their own kids' escapades. (One anecdote, perhaps too perfect to be true, has it that one of Mosher's kids, upon being punished, yelled at him, "I'm never going to give you another idea for your show, ever!")

The great charm of the show was its attention to the details of kid stuff: the daily small terrors of school; the aimless amusement of catching frogs and spitting off bridges; the disgustingly ambivalent emotions evoked by "icky girls"; the wicked fun of sending away for a baby alligator and trying to raise it in the toilet tank without Mom and Dad knowing. The kids were convincing; Jerry Mathers and Tony Dow played Beaver and Wally with an engaging lack of self-consciousness and precocity. Their friends, whose main function was to lead them into innocent trouble, were a weirder—and yet more believable—menagerie than any sitcom had attempted: oily wise guy Eddie Haskell; thickheaded, thin-skinned Lumpy Rutherford; fat, selfish Larry Mondello; belligerent, jealous, rat-finking Judy Hensler.

Beaver created a much clearer picture of time and place than *Father Knows Best*. Mosher once said that the show was intended to "celebrate everything that's good about small town life," but more specifically it celebrated what *could* be good about the *new* "small town" if we managed it correctly. The Cleavers weren't confidently established as the Andersons were; they lived not in the reality of middle-class dreams but in a world still in economic flux.

Ward was pure *nouveau bourgeois*. He lost his temper when Beaver failed to understand "the value of a dollar." At times he'd moan about the lost past, grouse about how soft kids were today, resort to a bit of archaic patriarchalism (though he always recanted). He had a clearly defined background, unusual for a sitcom man: He'd grown up on a farm in Shaker Heights, Ohio, where his old-fashioned father laid down the law and whipped him for breaking it; he'd been a surveyor with the Naval Construction Battalion during World War II, gone to college with June, then joined the corporate world and raised his two fine boys. He reminisced frequently about skating on frozen ponds, making his own kites, and walking twenty miles to school. He expressed fond memories of *Weird Tales* magazine and the *Our Gang* comedies, a couple of marginally subversive bits of depression era kid lore.

For Beav and Wally he was "the neatest dad in the whole world" because he remembered what it was like to be a kid and sympathized with their fallibility. In a broader framework he was a carefully constructed link from the prewar world to the present: farm to office; authoritarianism to consensus; real small town to generic one. (Mosher and Connelly were especially well suited to capture the sense of family solidity being forged in the midst of change; both were products of broken homes who worked hard at being good family men in their own lives. Perhaps that explains the special poignancy their best scripts bring to the ideal of family togetherness. Hugh Beaumont was also especially well suited to play Ward; he was a progressive Methodist minister from the Midwest who'd taken up acting largely to fund church projects. Ward's gentle but firm, traditional but empathetic manner came naturally to him.)

Prominently set in the middle of Ward's transformation was the war. For millions of real-life men it was a similar watershed. For millions of kids it was the myth of their ancestors, the great John Wayne adventure in which their very own fathers had participated. In one especially revealing episode the kids in Beaver's class are boasting about their fathers' military exploits. Beaver makes Ward out to be a regular Audie Murphy, capturing sixty-five enemy soldiers by himself, dragging home tons of guns and grenades. Challenged to back the story up, Beav breaks into Ward's old footlocker but finds only surveying scopes and T squares. Beaver is crushed, but with patience Ward finally convinces him that the engineer's role in the war was a valid one: "There were thousands of us in the service who weren't heroes. They put a man where they thought he could do the best job." Thus the violent past was symbolically put away; the day of the manly hero had yielded to the day of the builder, the planner, the quiet team player.

The most striking difference between Springfield and Mayfield, however, was that Springfield didn't have an Eddie Haskell. Bud had a couple of rambunctious pals, but they were basically good kids. Any other troublemakers appeared only once, just long enough to cause a family complication; none of them was a long-term friend of the Anderson kids, who picked their companions as carefully as Margaret picked her china. But Eddie, the creep who schmoozes with parents, torments little brothers, and tricks his pals into mischief, was Wally's best friend. He was a regular supporting character who frequently got more screen time than June. Played with engaging, grinning obnoxiousness by Ken Osmond, he became many young viewers' favorite character. And although his influence over Wally and the Beav was always broken by episode's end, he himself was rarely fazed.

Eddie knew the angles, or claimed to: "This is vacation! Your parents aren't allowed to make you work all the time. It's a state law!" He was a hipster, greeting his buddies with "Hiya, Gertrude, what's cookin'?" He was remorseless in his pursuit of pleasure: "Nothing's a dirty trick if it's funny enough." He posed as a sexual demon. When Beaver admitted, "I'm not allowed out on school nights," Eddie answered, "Hey, that's rough. If that ever happened to me, eight or nine girls would kill themselves." He knew how vicious the world was. When Wally asked, "How come you're always giving Beaver the business?" Eddie explained, "I'm just trying to wise him up. I don't want him going out in the world and getting slaughtered."

Most of all, Eddie was an enemy of authority, who referred to Wally's father as "the warden" and to moving out of the house as "going over the wall." He would play the grown-up game ("Mrs. Cleaver, you've done something new to your hair!"), but family guidelines were meant to be subverted. He knew a kid couldn't win through confrontation, but there were ways: "My pop made me stay around the house one Saturday. You know what I did? I went out in the yard and started bouncing a ball off the roof. Pretty soon my old man came out and told me to get lost." Whenever Beav and Wally felt frustrated by parental dicta, Eddie offered them the forbidden fruit of in-group solidarity: "If we don't stick together, we're gonna lose the cold war with the adults."

Eddie wasn't just a "bad kid," a symbol of self-indulgence or of the big world waiting to seduce the innocent (although he was often both). He was trying to prove a point about natural conflicts, irreconcilable differences, clashing ideologies. Like the Kingfish, he was a retrograde figure, resisting the forward movement of the group and pursuing happiness in willfully contrary directions.

Eddie's way is shown to be tempting; he is easily able to talk Wally into adopting a "hip" hairstyle and dismissing Ward's objections as "square." But it is also shown to be a dead end, because, say Mosher and Connelly, the world simply isn't as hostile as he thinks, at least not anymore, not in the new America. It's individualism that is hostile now. In order to protect his rebellious haircut, Wally has to skip trying out for the swim team. When Lumpy copies Wally's hairstyle, his manhood is impugned by his father. The final straw is when little Beaver emulates Wally's 'do. Poor June is mortified; the generations are in danger of division.

Even then June doesn't fall back on arbitrary authority. She counsels Wally to think beyond his own agenda; she reminds him of how embarrassed he felt when Beaver used to insist upon wearing stupid hats to Sunday school. Wally now understands the wisdom of the group, the utility of tradition, the importance of maintaining the delicate equilibrium of social comfort. He returns to the "nice" haircut of which his parents approve and remarks cutely that Eddie should be so lucky as to have parents who "yell at him." (Being "yelled at," in the sweet irony of the Cleaver house, meant being enlightened through a lecture.)

Just as the Kingfish was Mosher and Connelly's strongest comic figure on *Amos 'n' Andy*, Eddie was their funniest and sharpest creation for *Beaver*. Obviously they felt a kinship with both characters, enjoyed getting in their heads and seeing how they'd act and talk. Yet ultimately, perhaps sadly, they saw such characters as losers.

Both the Kingfish and Eddie were occasionally presented as objects of pity. The Kingfish's problem was that he had never transcended his background, never let go of his ex-slave conniving and laziness and resistance to the work ethic. Eddie's problem was that he was unable to transcend the archaic dynamic of his family. Eddie's homelife was rarely seen, but there were many hints that it was marked by poor communication, arbitrary parental authority, and needless conflict. Like the unreconstructed old radical who won't sit down with the lords of Wall Street or the stubborn old rustic who won't cooperate with the government, Eddie was appealing and almost admirable, but in the end pathetically ridiculous.

A subtle but constant theme of the show was that the Cleavers were the only functional family around. Larry Mondello's father was always away on business, his mother was an ineffectual nut, and his sister was an undisciplined adolescent; the implication was clear that these were the causes of Larry's compulsive eating and disobedience. Fred Rutherford smothered his son Lumpy with preposterous expectations and a projected self-image; Lumpy was therefore a simpering mess who we knew would be destroyed by the real world. Whitey Whitney, a high-strung kid prone to psychosomatic ailments, once phoned the Cleaver house and asked June, "If you're not yelling at Beaver, can I please talk to him?" June asks, "Why would we be yelling at him?" Whitey responds, "I don't know. They're always yelling at me around here." June smiles bemusedly, with a flicker of pity in her eyes. She—and we—now know all that needs to be known about nervous little Whitey.

Ward and June appeared to be the only parents in Mayfield who used the "lecture" technique of guiding a kid to the proper conclusion while making sure he internalized the lesson. Wally and Beaver, in turn, seemed to be the only kids who weren't crybabies, bullies, or liars. Ward was the perfect father, as Wally and the Beav told each other more than once. But it wasn't because of his moral superiority; he just knew the techniques. In moments of anger he'd declare that a "trip to the toolshed" could be good for a kid. "It didn't do me any harm!" Then his modern understanding would return (often with the aid of a nudge from the gentle, well-bred June), and his disciplinary actions would be tempered by respect for his son's agendas. As a consequence, his boys would be successful, cooperative members of modern society.

Where *Father Knows Best* demonstrated ethical and systemic problems, *Beaver* brought the same lessons to the psychological sphere. In both cases the conservative American tradition was brought for discussion and possible modification into the household boardroom, the father's den.

❏

A different twist on this family formula came with another 1957 show, *Bachelor Father*. This John Forsythe vehicle, about an amorous Hollywood lawyer who inherits his thirteen-year-old niece after her parents are killed, featured a father who didn't know best—often knew less than the kid, in fact—but was learning as fast as he could. Its purpose seemed to be to show not how kids should be raised but how adults should be prepared for the role of parenthood. It seemed calculated specifically, in fact, to tame the *"Playboy* Man."

The *Playboy* Man was a peculiar product of overwhetted '50s appetites, a fantasy figure who embraced the prosperity, social mobility, and penile pride of postwar America while rejecting the compensatory push toward family life. He was sold as an ideal to the regular guy frustrated by the constraints of domesticity and to the sexually itchy adolescent yearning for the power and freedom of manhood. He was presented as a hipster and a rebel against the mainstream, but in fact, he was just a consumer with a slightly different shopping list. An advertisement in one of the first issues of *Playboy* tried to plug readers into Allen Ginsberg and Jack Kerouac for a small fee: "Join the beat generation! Buy a beat generation tieclasp! A beat generation sweatshirt! A beat generation ring!" The fantasy enabled men to feel they were rejecting the smug hypocrisy of the bourgeoisie while never actually leaving the American feast.

The '50s playboy was Hugh Hefner's gold mine, but not his creation. George Burns's sitcom factory had even put a comic example of the type on the small screen in January 1955, a few months before Hefner's magazine hit the stands, with *The Bob Cummings Show*.

Cummings was an affable but smug-seeming movie actor whose best performances emerged when he was cast as a grinning, oily womanizer. That's precisely how his sitcom cast him. Bob Collins is a fashion photographer and a bachelor, through whose life sashays an endless parade of busty, beautiful, vapid models. Bob is constantly sexually inflamed and goes after every dame who crosses his path with comically obnoxious charm. And most of the time—to judge by the models' reactions—he scores. He even has one regular model, played by former cover girl Joi Lansing, incurably desperate for him.

The masturbatory fantasy of Bob's life is complicated by two women who don't fit the curvaceous mold: his plain, scrawny secretary Schultzy, who is as hungry for him as his models are but who doesn't suit his appetites, and his widowed sister, Margaret, a respectable sitcom matron who disapproves of his life-style. Complicating it further is Margaret's teenage son, Chuck, who, despite his mother's lectures, admires his uncle's sybaritic adventures. He declares, in fact, that he wants to grow up to be just like him, and none of the formulaic comeuppances that Bob suffers at the ends of most episodes will dissuade him.

The Bob Cummings Show deftly compromised its own fantasy, enabling itself, like so many successful sitcoms, to have it both ways. Those of a "swinging" mind could enjoy Bob's adventures and join him in mentally undressing the dishes who were regularly trotted before the camera. Viewers of more "respectable" attitudes could chuckle at Margaret's dry jabs and take satisfaction in Bob's frequent humiliations, content that justice had been served. Both could enjoy Schultzy's misery: Was the universe punishing her for desiring an unworthy man or just for being an ugly broad? The show never made it clear. Both types of viewers could root for Chuck to make the "right" choice: to overcome his gonads and join the ranks of female-dominated civilization or to rebel against the hypocritical prudes and go for the gusto. In four years of episodes, of course, Chuck never made an irrevocable decision.

This ability to play on both teams at once was the peculiar genius of the series' developer, head writer, and co-owner, Paul Henning. He'd been writing for *Burns and Allen* since the early '40s, first on radio and then on TV, and had mastered their strange blend of absurdity and domesticity, self-parody and lovability. He displayed a remarkable acumen for pressing wild extravagances into accessible formats and for enabling a wide variety of viewers to feel he was winking especially at them while bamboozling the others. He was bound for huge success in network comedy, not so much with his various '50s products but certainly with his '60s creations, *The Beverly Hillbillies* and its spin-offs.

Bachelor Father was a response to *Cummings*, one that did take a side: Margaret's. Its two principal plot elements were the struggle of playboy Bentley Gregg to learn to settle down into fatherhood and niece Kelly's efforts to pick an appropriate wife for him from the mob of women who made themselves available to him. Kelly's friend and helper was Ginger, a typical suburban girl whose parents were solidly married. Bentley's advisers were his sassy secretary, representing a prodomestic female viewpoint, and his cute Chinese houseboy, a eunuchoid fount of vague ancient wisdom. Everything conspired to draw Bentley away from the temptations of the flesh and into the family fold.

Bachelor Father's ratings weren't much better than *Cummings*'s, and it didn't last much longer, but it made a far greater impact on sitcoms to come. TV in the '60s abounded in shows about single parents and odd couples learning how to make a family work. Bentley Gregg marked the desexualization of the single man in sitcomland. Through him, Bob Collins was turned into Steve Douglas of *My Three Sons*.

The third successful sitcom of 1957 looked like the one most likely to flop. It had been a hard sell. A couple of New York comedy writers named Irving and Norman Pincus saw a market on TV for character actor Walter Brennan and conceived a vehicle about a cantankerous old hillbilly who moves to Southern California and has to adjust to modern life. Brennan thought it was a loser. NBC was momentarily intrigued, then decided that only rural viewers would watch it. The Pincuses hammered away. They secured financial backing from Danny Thomas Productions, overcame Brennan's doubts, and finally got the desperate ABC to put *The Real McCoys* on the air.

The few critics who bothered to comment at all on the new show blasted it. "Cornball, hillbilly comedy," said *Variety*, lumping it in with the hick-mocking *Ma and Pa Kettle* movies. Ratings were low at first, but word of mouth must have been good. The Nielsens were rising by December. By its second year it had reached eighth place, becoming ABC's first top ten sitcom and helping the network slip ahead of NBC for second place in the 1958–59 season.

It's difficult to reconstruct what that word of mouth might have conveyed, but most likely it was the fact that the new show put a lot more emphasis on family sentiment and quiet domestic conflict than on dumb hick shenanigans. Despite its rural surface, its roots were in New York television writing. Along with the Pincus brothers its principal writers were Jim Fritzell and Everett Greenbaum, who had scripted nearly every episode of *Mr. Peepers* up until two years before. More than any other show *The Real McCoys* made a conscious effort to articulate the changes America was going through at mid-century.

While the national imagination was taken with the image of city dwellers abandoning their cramped apartments in favor of suburban homes, a similar trek was being taken by country folk. Since before the war automated farming and big agribusiness had been undermining the small farmer and sending rural youngsters to seek new life in the towns. Postwar prosperity accelerated the trend. Booming coastal economies sucked millions of people out of the continental interior, particularly to California.

The journey of the McCoy family was a sweetened version of that of the Joads. American popular culture was no longer willing to confront the realities of economic failure, such as the fact that the depression had never ended for much of rural America. The sitcom never quite said why the McCoys were pulling up stakes and making a long, hard trip from the Alleghenies to California. The first episode just shows them arriving, tired but hopeful, at their cute little San Fernando Valley ranch, right at the border of suburbia. But the background, as all adult Americans knew, was that while the corporate middle class was prospering, other classes were being broken. The nation's rapid confluence into a homogeneous suburban pool was not being accomplished without loss and pain.

Grandpappy Amos, the Brennan character, was the series' comic nexus for that pain. He was incorrigibly wedded to his old ways, constantly yearning for his backwoods past and running down everything new and strange. At the opposite extreme were his cutesy-poo great-grandchildren, who wanted desperately to fit in with the kids and their new school and recklessly shed all their hillbilly accoutrements.

The middle generation, Luke McCoy and his wife, Kate, were the transitional figures, optimistic young parents creating a new society. Solid but flexible, they always managed to preserve traditional American values while embracing modern systems. They were in the process of inventing the world Jim Anderson already lived in: a rich, sophisticated, uniform human community, solidly grounded in Christian, conservative ways.

They suffered their stresses, too, of course. In one early show Luke refuses to learn how to read, considering that a skill suited only to "sissies." To shatter this resistance to civilization, Kate locks him out of the bedroom. Amos encourages his grandson's primitivity, of course, telling him that he can do without his wife's attentions with the aid of a little "willpower and cold water." But the down-home Lysistrata wins her war, of course, although Luke's surrender seems motivated more by a desire to restore sweet domestic harmony than by any baser urges. He admits that his resistance to reading was based on his own insecurity and enters the new world of literacy (which he masters quite easily). Amos can only limp and mutter his way into the past.

Kate, like Ma Joad, was the organizing and civilizing force in her family. She was the one who reminded Amos of biblical morality ("The Lord is warning you what's gonna happen if'n you go through with that deal") and the one who brought the spirit of modern compromise into the family dynamic ("But, Grandpa, there's two sides to everything." "Yeah. And I'm on the right side!").

That in itself was a reflection of an earlier, rustic view of sex roles, in which men were believed to tend naturally toward the harsh and violent, while peace and culture were the responsibilities of women. But in the boardroom of the modern family the civilizing function had been given to Dad, while women were relegated to powerless domestic management functions. Interestingly, in its sixth season, when ratings had begun to slip, Kate was written out of the show, and Luke (following the lead of the popular new *My Three Sons*) was made a widower. The result, however, was just another hollow formula piece. Ratings dropped further, and the show was canceled.

An intriguing sidelight to the McCoy family dynamic was their jolly Mexican farm hand, Pepino Garcia. The younger McCoys treated him with the same kindness that the Andersons showed to "Fronk Smeeth," but Amos was constantly impatient and overly judgmental with him. Implicit in their conflict was Amos's provincial ethnocentricity. He came from an exclusively white Protestant world, in which everyone lived and spoke about the same. Pepino was a representative of the new America, the great melting pot that TV had been so loath to acknowledge since 1953. Amos simply couldn't accept him, but Pepino didn't mind. He treated Amos with the same patronizing mixture of exasperation and affection as

Luke and Kate did. Amos was harmless and not long for this world. The proper course was to be charitable with him and wait him out.

This was the ultimate message of these sitcoms of 1957: As we move into our new society, we will still be haunted by ancient prejudices, dead ideologies, infantile selfishness. But we need not be threatened by them. We can distill the most positive, most universal values from the past and wait for those stubborn negatives—Amos McCoy and Eddie Haskell—to die a natural death, while we head toward the American center. It doesn't matter where we come from: West Virginia, Mayfield, or swinging Beverly Hills. If we remain responsive to the needs of the group, hold fast to family harmony, and stay open to compromise, then we are all going to make it.

10

Homesteaders of the New Frontier

By the opening of the fall 1960 season the rambunctious, inventive days of the sitcom were over. The form had been locked into patterns that persisted for a decade with only slight variations. All through the 1960s TV's prime-time families reflected American social turbulence only in cautious and oblique ways.

TV ownership was now a nearly universal American condition. Control of prime time rested comfortably in the hands of the three networks, in a sort of tripartite monopoly, with CBS entrenched at the top of the ratings heap and ABC and NBC not far below, trading off the number two spot. With the medium as profitable as it was, and programs as expensive as they were, the spot advertising system was now standard; the networks, not sponsors, made nearly all programming decisions. Entertainment production was centered in L.A. and happily wedded to the movie community.

In the time-honored manner of big business, such prosperous stability meant a shift away from scattershot innovation and toward the calculated refinement of proven products. The networks seemed to have found the answers to the challenges posed by their medium, and all three networks had found pretty much the same answers. Now they could get down to fine-tuning.

The sitcom, now as safe and dependable as any TV product could be, enjoyed a resurgence from its mid-'50s doldrums, with thirteen new ones launched in 1960 and seventeen the next year. Most of them folded, but for every one that fell there seemed to be two more just like it to take its place. Ten new sitcoms in 1962, twelve in 1963, nineteen in 1964, seventeen in 1965, sixteen in 1966: They never stopped flowing.

There were bachelor-father and bachelorette-mother shows, families-enlarged-by-adoption shows, families-with-wacky-maids shows, single-guys-with-goofy-occupations shows, adaptations of popular movies, spin-offs of *Danny Thomas* and *December Bride*, and retreads for Lucille Ball, Bob Cummings, Robert Young, Gertrude Berg, George Burns, and Phil Silvers. As the '60s progressed, there were goofy military shows and screwy hick shows and silly magic shows, nearly all well produced, expertly filmed, with expensive stars, factory-tooled scripts, and no guts at all.

Each network had its special emphases, but it took a subtle eye to distinguish them. This was network TV's Golden Age. Even the movie business in the big-studio era had never enjoyed such snugness, accord, and optimism.

At first glance the mood of the nation at large would seem to have been quite different, but there were corollaries. The postwar challenges of creating a vast suburban middle class, transcending economic and political ideology, and turning the nation into a global power had been largely accomplished. The economy was dipping and wavering at the end of the '50s, but a new boom time loomed ahead. Although political debate was growing louder, most of the issues being debated were growing smaller and more specific.

In 1960 America's two political parties pitted a pair of remarkably young candidates for president against each other, each a representative of the new generation, the war vets, the founders of suburbia, the fathers of the baby boom. They were not much different in platform or viewpoint. Both fit comfortably within the new centrist coalition, accepting as givens the notions that we must contain communism across the globe, aid our impoverished allies, build up the defense business, use some of our affluence to uplift our own poor, bring the private and public sectors together, continue the centralization of power in Washington, and gradually end racial segregation. They differed mainly in style and in the speed with which they thought government should move. Nixon wanted to maintain Eisenhower's "moderately progressive" pace. Kennedy said:

"America is moving in the right direction. We're just not moving fast enough." That, and his modern-but-conservative bearing, struck a chord with voters.

Kennedy was the voice of a cocky country that believed it had found the answers and wanted to apply them energetically to those problems still facing us. Like the networks, government and society seemed to have settled the big issues and could now get to fine-tuning.

It's appropriate, then, that the two most intelligent and spirited sitcoms of those years would attempt to apply the "suburban solution" to two groups seemingly well outside the middle-class mainstream: small-town southerners and New York entertainers. Both were products of the Danny Thomas-Sheldon Leonard combine, both were created by clever veterans of the New York comedy tradition as vehicles for talented young comics, and both were considerable critical and popular hits for CBS. *The Andy Griffith Show* and *The Dick Van Dyke Show* are like bookends, cut from the same stone yet supporting different ends of the centrist American worldview.

Andy Griffith was a singer and musician from North Carolina who made his name as a folksy stand-up comic in the early '50s, creating the character of a pleasant but ignorant hick who attempts to describe the bizarre world of mainstream America in his words, with the manner of a tall-tale spinner (his best-known routine was "What It Was, Was Football"). He portrayed the ultimate angelic bumpkin Will Stockdale in the Broadway, TV, and movie versions of *No Time for Sergeants*, which made him a national symbol of rural innocence. In *A Face in the Crowd* he darkened and expanded the character, playing an angelic-seeming con artist who becomes a TV star.

When Danny Thomas hired him for a one-episode appearance on his sitcom in early 1960, Griffith played a country sheriff—an apparent rube—who nails Danny Williams for speeding through his town. But as Danny grows more and more arrogant, contemptuous, and abusive, Griffith grows more and more sly. Danny rants his way from a five-dollar ticket to a day in jail and finally to a self-humiliating outburst on television. It turns out that Griffith (who is also the mayor, justice of the peace, and jailer) has sagely staged it all to teach this cocky New Yorker a lesson.

This was a role well suited to Griffith because just above that sloppy Dixie grin were a pair of sharp and calculating eyes and a beetling brow that could suggest sternness, hostility, even villainy. Griffith was, in fact, an astute businessman and a sharp comic. He was something of a modern southern type himself, the master manipulator who can drop a mask of bucolic buffoonery over his face whenever it suits him. As he told one interviewer, in an overplayed drawl, "If I was to lose my accent, I'd have to compete with *actors*. And I wouldn't do that for a hundred-dollar bill." But of course, he was an actor, a competitive one, and a hundred-dollar bill wouldn't mean much to a man who would soon make himself a millionaire several times over.

The episode was a huge hit. Viewers wrote and called in, demanding to see the sheriff of Mayberry again. Thomas obliged them by arranging for Sheldon Leonard and Aaron Ruben to work with Griffith on developing a series. Ruben was a veteran of radio comedy—*Burns and Allen, Fred Allen*, and others—who had written for Berle and Sid Caesar on television and then become a director of *You'll Never Get Rich*. He was scarcely a southern boy, but he was from good comedy lineage. Griffith himself owned 50 percent of the show and involved himself heavily in production and story conferences.

The Mayberry, North Carolina, they created for the series was no suburban community. It was a classic fictional small town, complete with old families, gossipy widows, a town drunk, eccentric bachelors, obnoxious rustics, and a backlog of ancient loyalties and hostilities. Griffith's character was the widowed father of a cute little boy, but he was no Jim Anderson or Bachelor Father. As sheriff he was responsible for running his little microcosm, not just participating in it as a team player. And as the fussed-over ward of his spinster Aunt Bee he was himself something of a son, undergoing socialization by an embodiment of the old feminine South. He and Mayberry represented not the blank slate of the new communities but the continuities of the old.

Mayberry lacked one thing that real southern towns tend to have: black people. A southern show produced seven or eight years before would no doubt have featured black comedians playing domestics and dumb field-workers. But by 1960, when most Americans thought of race conflict first when they thought of the South, even those figures would have been too explosive. On February 1, 1960, precisely two weeks before Griffith's episode of *Danny Thomas* hit the air, students in Greensboro, North Carolina, started a sit-in to integrate a Walgreen's lunch counter. By the time the show aired, sit-ins had spread to most of the big towns in the state. Barely over a month before Griffith's own show premiered, the sit-ins were still going on. Yet the good folks in Mayberry never heard of any such thing. The only way prime-time entertainment had of dealing with an issue that divisive in the new America was ignoring it.

Even so, in oblique and abstract ways the world of Mayberry did comment on such issues. The Griffith character took a step beyond the schemer-rube to become a nonauthoritarian father figure for the town. He used all his guileful folksiness to forge social compromises, to open lines of communication between feuding parties, and to trick clot-headed citizens into doing whatever was for their own good. He applied the same techniques to raising his son, Opie, mixed with a fair amount of reasoning and gentle lecturing in the most progressive sitcom manner.

Constantly snagging Andy's efforts to work out smooth, modern solutions was Mayberry's population of idiots and provincials: Aunt Bee, good-hearted but overly concerned with appearances; Gomer Pyle, the cretinous but affectionate gas station operator, incapable of believing or comprehending anything he couldn't see and feel for himself; Floyd, the barber, an old gossip, quick to think evil of others; Emma, an aging hypochondriac with a paranoid streak. These characters might have represented the traps and limitations of old southern ways, but the biggest single thorn in Andy's side represented something far different. This was his deputy, a wired-up pop-eyed lunatic named Barney Fife (played with quivering intensity by Don Knotts).

Determined to play the role of the modern lawman as he saw it, Barney insisted on wearing a gun; Andy permitted it, as long as Barney packed only one bullet and carried it in his shirt pocket. Barney was obsessed with filing reports and interrogating suspects whereas Andy did everything by memory and intuition. Barney sought trouble where there wasn't any, to boost his sense of self-importance. Once he threw the town in an uproar by fanning the flames of a long-forgotten feud because he insisted upon clearing an unclosed police report out of an ancient file. Barney was, in short, a mockery of modern bureaucracy.

Barney was supposedly Andy's cousin, which explained why Andy felt obligated to give him the job. But where Andy was clearly southern—like nearly all the others on the show—Barney was pure North. Knotts delivered his lines at twice the rate of the other actors, moved frantically and jerkily through their slow and genteel ranks, used clumsy hard-boiled slang, and always wore his full uniform and hat. In some episodes he had a girlfriend, but otherwise he never meshed with the town at a social or familial level. He didn't even seem to share a past with the other townsfolk; where Andy related to everyone as lifelong neighbor, Barney could relate only as a lawman.

Barney was an outside intrusion into Mayberry. For southern audiences, faced with federal involvement in their own backyards over the integration issue, he inevitably touched upon fears of dangerous external, modern forces disrupting their world. No one, of course, would have compared the pathetic but likable Barney with Freedom Riders, "outside agitators," national guardsmen, and Bobby Kennedy. But a common note struck by conservatives during those years was that Washington doesn't understand the southern community, that it understands only its abstract principles and bureaucratic programs, and that imposing those programs by force would destroy the South. That was precisely what Barney would probably do to Mayberry if the wise Andy weren't there to defuse him.

In order to find sane middle solutions to Mayberry's troubles, Andy had to negotiate this minefield of Dixie detritus and Yankee lunacy. He was a modern man, with modern sitcom answers, but his modernity was homegrown from the neighborliness and wisdom of small-town America, not brought in with exurban flight. Considering the way sitcoms had ignored the old towns in favor of the new suburbs, it's no surprise that *Griffith* was an immediate hit, particularly in the South and the rural West and Midwest.

Andy Taylor didn't emerge full-blown from the first episode, however. Even he had some lessons to learn first from mainstream America. During his first season he was often a less wise and effective figure than his girlfriend, Ellie, the local drugstore manager. Ellie was played by Elinor Donahue, coming straight from her role as Betty on *Father Knows Best*; in switching from upper-middle-class midwestern college student to southern businesswoman, she changed her persona not a bit. She was a bright, independent, forward-thinking gal without a trace of a Carolina accent— even her connection with pharmaceuticals underlined her modernity— and she gave Andy his comeuppance more than once.

In one episode a New England collector of folk music comes to town to compile a record of local string bands, including a group of which Andy is a part. The local yokels are pleased but also suspicious. Thinking that the collector is going to profit off their music, they talk him into letting them buy into his project in return for a cut of the gross. When Andy hears about this, he concludes that this northern slicker has conned them and that they'll never see him or their money again. He turns the town against the man and sets a trap to catch him. Only Ellie, with her more cosmopolitan outlook, has faith. And sure enough, she's right. He is an honest and serious connoisseur of folk culture, but the folk themselves—including Andy, their finest representative—nearly alienated him with their parochial paranoia. Andy is humbled and learns his lesson. It's taken an unaccented gal from the suburban sitcom mainstream to help him realize how benevolent the modern world really is.

Andy continued to grow, and after the first season Ellie was gone. Andy eventually found another girlfriend, Helen, who wasn't very southern either but was considerably mousier. Andy would still be wrong sometimes, but never quite so meaningfully.

The Andy Griffith Show mellowed considerably as the seasons dragged on. In the beginning it maintained a tense energy between New York sassiness and country wholesomeness; one could never be quite sure whether the townsfolk were being mocked or sympathized with. With each season, though, it played more obviously to a low-key, rural, generally elderly audience. After its fifth season, when Helen joined and Barney left, it rambled along with treacly demonstrations of Andy's ability to help bring together his ever less extravagant friends. It rambled along to enormous popularity, however. In 1967–68 it was the top-rated series on TV, mainly because it towered in southern and heartland markets; it failed even to make the top ten in northeastern areas, where Jackie Gleason and the Smothers Brothers sat on top, but more people watched TV for more hours in Griffith country than anywhere else.

Griffith decided to leave the show and try his hand at the movies after that season, handing the lead over to the blandly wholesome Ken Berry. Berry played a newcomer to town, an émigré from somewhere beyond the realm of southern accents, who quickly became a peacemaker for the locals. Even this new version of the show—called *Mayberry R.F.D.*—was hugely popular for a time. The sitcom mainstream had finally conquered the South and the small towns, not by bringing in the suburbs but by teaching the yokels to behave like the denizens of sitcomland.

❑

The Dick Van Dyke Show was to New York what *Griffith* was to North Carolina. It split its time between the entertainment industry of Manhattan and the quiet streets of New Rochelle, showing how a family from the heartland could create the perfect suburban life in the shadow of the giant city. It argued that the new America offered solutions not just to the drones of the middle class and the rural poor but to urban sophisticates as well. Ultimately it modernized the image of the sitcom family and gave it an explicitly Kennedyesque glamour.

Its origins lay in the Jewish ghettos of the Bronx, in the stages of Manhattan, in the studios of early New York TV, and in the bridges and tunnels that reached out from the island to the burgeoning towns of New Jersey and Connecticut. Carl Reiner had come south from the Bronx in 1938 to work in Manhattan's WPA Drama Workshop, then performed overseas during the war and came back for both Broadway and television comedy, writing and performing for Sid Caesar's *Your Show of Shows*. The son of immigrants, he was assimilating and moving upward in American society. Unlike some of his peers, however, he virtually never did Jewish shtick; he was frequently the "normal American" straight man for Caesar's dialect routines. He was also moving to the suburbs, to New Rochelle, with his ex-painter wife and his son, Rob.

Reiner was a suburbanite, commuting from tract home to steady job and back again daily, except that his job was in a business still very urban, very sophisticated, very Jewish. He had made a long social journey from depression to the late Ike Age, longer even than most Americans had, and his working world kept him acutely conscious—*self*-conscious—of where he had come from and where he was going. On the Caesar show he worked on comedy sketches dealing with that journey, about couples called the Commuters and the Hickenloopers, which David Marc has called "minidomesticoms" that "exploited the self-amused peccadillos of emerging alrightnik culture in post-World War II America: dented fenders, forgotten anniversaries, wives with charge accounts, impossible in-laws, that darned plumbing, and so on. If there could be no poetry after Auschwitz, there could at least be New Rochelle."

So the domestic sitcom was a natural direction for Reiner to explore when the comedy-variety shows died. He decided immediately not to crank out just another bachelor-adopts-orphan or French-girl-works-for-senator riff. Appropriately the idea for his sitcom came to him during a commute: "I was driving my car downtown from New Rochelle, wondering, what grounds do I stand on that no one else stands on? I thought, I am an actor and writer who worked on the Sid Caesar shows." So came to be Rob Petrie, husband of Laura and father of Ritchie, resident of New Rochelle, head writer for the Alan Brady show.

Reiner wrote a pilot for a sitcom to be called *Head of the Family*. Then, pumping with enthusiasm, he went on to write thirteen more episodes.

He wanted to "guard against supposition." He wanted it clearly known what he intended. What he intended was "the first situation comedy where you saw where the man worked before he walked in and said, 'Hi, honey, I'm home!'" More than that, he intended "examining my life and putting it down on paper." This was the first sitcom conceived from the start with autobiographical intent.

Considering the New Frontier image that the show eventually projected, it's fitting that Reiner was initially funded by the Kennedy clan. Peter Lawford, Senator Kennedy's brother-in-law, was trying to set himself up as a TV producer in 1960. With the senator running for president, the patriarch, Joseph Kennedy, insisted upon looking over all of Lawford's prospective projects to be sure they suited the family image. One of those was *Head of the Family*, and the old man loved it. Maybe he saw his own family history reflected in its subtext: Second-generation punk makes his fortune in a vaguely disreputable field (TV comedy for Petrie; rum-running, politicking, and theater ownership for Kennedy) and then slips into the American mainstream. In any case, he loved it enough to bankroll the pilot himself.

The pilot ran in the summer of 1960 on a CBS comedy anthology. Reiner played Petrie himself. None of the supporting actors who were later on the *Van Dyke Show* was involved. Critical reaction was moderately good; viewer reaction was minimal; sponsor interest was tentative. CBS passed on the series.

But Sheldon Leonard was looking for new sitcom properties for Danny Thomas's company. The prognosis on *Griffith* was good, and a *Make Room for Daddy* spin-off, *The Joey Bishop Show*, was in the works. Leonard took Reiner under his wing and offered to help him turn it into a salable show. He quotes himself saying, "Carl, you're not right for what you wrote yourself. I believe that if recast, the show would have every chance of making it. Do you mind if I try to rewrap the package?"

"Rewrapping the package" was a small matter with huge implications. In recasting the role of Rob Petrie, Leonard did far more than plug in just a different actor. He didn't turn to Sid Caesar or Howard Morris or anyone else who might have shared Reiner's ethnic and social background. Instead, he turned to two homespun Protestant boys from Nebraska and Missouri, Johnny Carson and Dick Van Dyke. The latter got the nod, largely because his broader musical and physical comedy skills would allow for more variety numbers within the show.

Reiner's role had never been explicitly Jewish. Petrie, after all, was one of those names one could never quite pin down. But any astute reader would have understood: Reiner's name, his looks, his character's New York show biz background . . . *Head of the Family* was clearly a story of Jewish assimilation and exurban flight.

As David Marc points out, however, Van Dyke's Rob Petrie was completely reconstructed. Flashbacks and family gatherings during the five seasons of the show filled in a remarkably thorough biography: Rob was a small-town Illinois boy with a gosh-golly enthusiasm for musical comedy and slapstick, who did a little entertaining in the army and married a wholesome seventeen-year-old dancer named Laura when she visited his base with the USO. Both their parents were solid midwestern couples, backslapping Babbitts and snooty matrons. Rob's ancestors had fought with the Union in the Civil War. He stumbled into New York show biz almost by accident, plucked from an Illinois station to give *The Alan Brady Show* some "fresh blood." Initially rejected by his hard-boiled co-writers, Buddy and Sally (he explicitly Jewish, she ethnically vague but clearly working-class urban), Rob won them over with his heartland humility and honesty. He apparently never lived in New York; there were no "cramped apartment" flashbacks in the series. Presumably he and Laura rushed directly to New Rochelle after he landed his job, thus maintaining an approximation of the small-town environment in which they'd both grown up.

Sheldon Leonard was no less Jewish than Carl Reiner, but he had less personal investment in the show and, perhaps, a better feel for what the broad American public wanted. The results, in any case, upheld his decision. CBS put *The Dick Van Dyke Show* on the air in 1961. After a shaky start it climbed into the Nielsen top ten and went on to be a perennial rerun favorite.

The transformation of Rob Petrie did more than just alter the show's flavor from matzoh to mayonnaise. It reversed the entire dynamic of the character's development. *Head of the Family* was, in effect, about *de-*sophistication; *that* Petrie left behind the bustling, competitive, cosmopolitan world of Manhattan and learned how to relax, to simplify, into the genial American mainstream. Van Dyke's Petrie was leaving behind the white bread Midwest and learning to speed up into the multiethnic, smart-ass, conniving urban world. For Reiner's Petrie, New Rochelle was itself a brave new world. For Van Dyke's, it was a familiar retreat from the new world he was exploring.

Many *Van Dyke* episodes centered on Rob's innocence in a

sophisticated world. He and Laura take art classes, improving themselves in the manner of modern, prosperous, college-educated Americans; the dangerously bohemian art teacher sets her sights on Rob, but Rob can't see it. Laura tries to tell Rob but refuses to be so gauche as to make a big scene about it. Finally Rob catches on, and although he's modern enough not to be outraged, his basic small-town goodness keeps him faithful.

Earlier sitcom couples could never have reacted like this. Lucy would have gone insane at the slightest hint that another woman was after Ricky. No woman would ever have been after Jim Anderson, because his world didn't permit such wrongness. Confronted with a bohemian seductress, Andy Taylor would never have let his fear of seeming unsophisticated get in the way of rejecting her. And none of them would have been taking painting lessons anyway.

Rob had to learn other lessons the hard way. When he loses a script for the Brady show and it's found by a bum whom Rob assumes to be an altruist, Rob blurts, "Thank you! That script is worth a fortune to us!" The bum promptly tries to hold it for ransom. When Buddy suspects his wife, Pickles, of adultery, Rob immediately takes Buddy's perceptions at face value and condemns Pickles. He has to learn a great deal about the ethically complex nature of the world—Pickles's past as a chorus girl, Buddy's mother's hostility to her, her early marriage to a forger, and his subsequent blackmail scheme—before he can bring Buddy and Pickles back together.

Alone among all sitcom characters of the time, Rob learned some things about race relations, too. Progressive in their politics, Rob and Laura attend a fund-raiser for a group based on the NAACP. Because of a mix-up with their son's costume for a school pageant, however, they end up dying their hands black. Terrified that their black friends will take this as an affront, they try to bluff their way through the event with white gloves. Rob finally realizes that this is a microcosm of America's racial misunderstandings and that only honest communication will solve our problems. He displays his black hands and explains the problem, and of course, blacks and whites join together in laughter at the embarrassing quirks of fate.

The Petries were always deeply concerned with appearances. Embarrassment was Rob's most painful and most frequent emotion. Their story was the story of innocent youth struggling to become sophisticated. They were provincial but open-minded Americans, striving to settle into this New Frontier of affluence, mobility, ethnic integration, instant communication, and *Playboy*-style sexual freedom. *Van Dyke* broke from the previous cycle of family sitcoms by denying that Americans were moving into a homogeneous small-town dream. It asserted that they were moving into a complex and frightening world—even in the suburbs—but that they could handle it if they reached out and made friends and laughed at themselves. That assertion struck a chord among millions of Americans, Americans all over the country, according to surveys, but generally a younger group of adults than were attracted to most sitcoms of the time.

Reiner had flip-flopped his own social journey in reconstructing Rob Petrie but in so doing might have captured the mass American journey more astutely than he would have his own. The great care and originality with which he built up Rob's back story showed a desire to define a real-life experience, based on American social realities (much of the material was taken from Van Dyke's real life). The flashback had been virtually unknown in sitcoms, but Reiner used it extensively, and ingeniously, to make Rob Petrie the best-developed character in the genre. In subsuming his own biography into Van Dyke's, he created a very timely comic statement.

Much has been made of Rob and Laura's supposed resemblance to John and Jacqueline Kennedy. In fact, the resemblance is restricted to a few physical details, but in their differences the Petries and Kennedys say a great deal about each other. Where the Kennedys set styles, the Petries nervously tried to adopt them. Rob filled his house with *bourgeois moderne* decor and then promptly tripped over the ottoman. Kennedy was groomed to play the role of an American aristocrat; Rob was self-created—through imitation—and never quite seemed to know what he should do. Jackie was socially infallible; Laura did her hair like Jackie's and dressed like Jackie and tried her best to play the sophisticated hostess, but she was a quaver-voiced nerve case who constantly battled her own insecurities and jealousies.

The Petries were not sitcom versions of the Kennedys but small-time folks *trying* to be like the Kennedys, and endearingly failing. This was made explicit in a two-episode story in which the charming but politically ignorant Rob runs for city council against the diminutive but vastly knowledgeable Lincoln Goodheart (played by Wally Cox); their debate before a ladies' club, in which Lincoln wins all the points and Rob wins all the hearts, was an obvious burlesque of the Kennedy-Nixon debates. Rob, ashamed that his charm makes him more popular than a candidate he sees as better qualified, quits the race, but his campaign manager tells him, "A leader can't just know what's right. He has to know how to do the job right. Goodheart knows the facts, Rob, but you know *people*." Rob throws his hat back into the ring and wins, like Kennedy, in a nerve-rackingly close vote. Rob was a suburban JFK, indeed, but still needed the experts to teach him what that meant. *The Dick Van Dyke Show* strongly implied that viewers should strive as Rob and Laura did but reassured them that it was okay if they had a little trouble outgrowing the America of Andy Hardy and Jim Anderson.

The Petries were held up as ideals over their co-workers. Sally, an aging single gal, was openly miserable, choosing the company of a dweebish mama's boy over having no boyfriend at all. Buddy and Pickles, living in a small urban apartment, endured a hostile and mutually disrespectful marriage. But Rob and Laura were the lovebirds that they all envied and adored.

Despite the glamour of Rob's work world, he found true peace only in New Rochelle and the bosom of his nuclear family. Reiner went out of his way to ridicule bohemians and pretentious literati, to establish Rob as a regular guy, despite his uncommon profession. Laura had given up dancing to be a housewife and mother and go shopping with the dentist's wife next door, and although the show biz "bug" bit her occasionally, she always reaffirmed her decision. Mary Tyler Moore played her with a febrile energy that suggested unacknowledged frustration but at the same time with a trivializing cuteness that made her dancing just a fun little thing, never a means of expression. The plots always put her back in her husband's arms, gazing up at him lovingly with her little-girl eyes.

Unlike other family comedies, this one did very little with the business of child rearing. Ritchie Petrie was a background figure that was used most effectively to help Rob learn some lessons: Rob rejects Laura's claim that he's trying to buy his friends' acceptance by grabbing the check in a restaurant, but when he sees Ritchie engaged in parallel behavior, he realizes that she's right and allows simple honesty and fairness to carry him through. Rob, in effect, was a child himself. The sitcom socialized him just as it did Wally Cleaver, teaching him "modern but conservative" systems for fitting into the new American mainstream.

Van Dyke was the most ambitious sitcom yet attempted and an impressive piece of work. It was energetic and funny and willing to take chances, alone among the sitcoms of its time in using a live audience instead of a laugh track. Yet within its sophisticated and progressive framework, it remained a very middle-of-the-road show, ideologically at peace with *Father Knows Best* and its imitators.

Van Dyke's oblique New Frontier endorsements underscored the manner in which government and broadcasting drew closer and closer together during those years. Kennedy's FCC head, a former law partner of Adlai Stevenson's named Newton Minow, immediately rejected the laissez-faire attitude of the Eisenhower administration; scarcely two months into his tenure he blasted the National Association of Broadcasters with his now-famous "vast wasteland" speech, describing a typical broadcast day as "a procession of game shows, violence, audience participation shows, formula comedies about totally unbelievable families, blood and thunder, mayhem, violence, sadism, murder, Western badmen, Western goodmen, private eyes, gangsters, more violence and cartoons."

Minow's speech didn't do much about those "totally unbelievable families" (almost exactly a year after the speech CBS put *The Beverly Hillbillies* on its schedule), but it startled the networks into adding hours of news and public affairs programs and to a degree into adding more social instruction to their entertainment programming. *Van Dyke*'s integration shows and *The Patty Duke Show*'s Peace Corps episode may owe their existence to Minow.

Late that same year ABC got called on the carpet by a Senate committee on juvenile delinquency for a violent episode of *Bus Stop*, a drama series, that starred teen idol Fabian as a small-town ax murderer. Ollie Treyz was promptly dismissed as network president, replaced by Thomas Moore, who sanitized the ABC line and went on to become an adviser to Spiro Agnew and Richard Nixon. Shortly before that ABC had hired Eisenhower's former press secretary, James Hagerty, as head of its news division.

ABC's lineup took a decided twist toward the governmental, playing into the new glamour that Kennedy brought to politicians and—through projects like the Green Berets—to the military. Among sitcoms alone there were *Mr. Smith Goes to Washington*, *No Time for Sergeants*, *McHale's Navy*, *Broadside* (about WAVEs), *The Farmer's Daughter* (about a governess to a widowed congressman's kids), and *The Double Life of Henry Phyfe* (about a genial intelligence agent). Its biggest sitcom hit, *My Three Sons*, centered on an aeronautical engineer, a respected figure in the defense industry. NBC, following suit, soon carried its share of affectionate comedies about military academies, army veterinarians, naval officers, astronauts, and air force wives, while CBS had a very popular spin-off with *Gomer Pyle, U.S.M.C.*

Meanwhile, the rest of the Mayberry gang was demonstrating that even the South was redeemable, and the Petries continued their quest for Kennedyhood until nearly three years after the president's murder. The sitcoms carried the Kennedy-Johnson, liberal-center, military-progressive coalition on through the decade, straight on into the years when that coalition was being challenged by forces that the established entertainment machine was incapable of absorbing.

From Burlesque to Bourgeois: Radio's Amos and Andy were white actors in broad "black-voice" . . . (Freeman Gosden and Charles Correll; *Amos 'n' Andy.*)

. . . but television, and the 1950s, turned them into models of middle-class propriety. Here Amos and Ruby admire Andy's gift to Arabella in the oft-repeated Christmas episode. (Alvin Childress, Patty Marie Ellis, Jane Adams; *Amos 'n' Andy.*)

The Changing View: Molly Goldberg, relic of radio and prewar urban culture, looks across a short gap to her neighbors . . . (Gertrude Berg and supporting players; *The Goldbergs*.)

. . . while the new television family turns to the corner to attend the words of Hal ("Great Gildersleeve") Peary.

The Costs of Rebellion: One of Lucy's upstart schemes finds her bound and gagged, "to teach her a lesson." She gets no sympathy from her long-suffering fellow wife Ethel. (Desi Arnaz, Lucille Ball, Vivian Vance; *I Love Lucy.*)

And the Rewards of Cooperation: The Anderson children see to the perfect appearance of their mentor, protector, breadwinner . . . although Mother suspects some ulterior motives. (Billy Gray, Robert Young, Elinor Donahue, Lauren Chapin, Jane Wyatt; *Father Knows Best.*)

ABOVE: *Strategies of Self-Interest: Manipulation . . .* :
In a moment of sentimentality that may or may not
be sincere, cute little Linda dotes on her show biz
daddy. (Angela Cartwright, Danny Thomas; *The Danny
Thomas Show.*)

RIGHT: *. . . Military Maneuvers . . .* : Bilko uses his
wiles and his uniform to compromise middle-class
womanhood. (Hildy Parks, Phil Silvers; *The Phil
Silvers Show.*)

BELOW: *. . . . and Entrepreneurship*: Ralph, sure of
imminent economic triumph, gloats to the sadder,
wiser Alice. (Jackie Gleason, Art Carney, Audrey
Meadows, Joyce Randolph; *The Honeymooners.*)

Taming the Child: Ward, June, and the Beav are *very* disappointed in Wally. He takes their glares seriously and no doubt will never transgress in quite that way again. (Jerry Mathers, Tony Dow, Hugh Beaumont, Barbara Billingsley; *Leave It to Beaver*.)

Dennis the Menace's mom and dad, on the other hand, comfort their son when it becomes clear that he's been causing trouble only out of well-intentioned innocence . . . as usual. (Gloria Henry, Jay North, Herbert Anderson; *Dennis the Menace*.)

ABOVE: *The Early '60s: Mainstreaming the Eccentrics*: American Colonel Hogan makes harmless stooges of Nazi officers . . . and corporate entertainment embraces military horror. (John Banner, Bob Crane, Werner Klemperer; *Hogan's Heroes*.)

RIGHT: Sheriff Andy uses gentle persuasion to wring social cooperation from small-town crackpots. (Andy Griffith, Howard Morris; *The Andy Griffith Show*.)

BELOW: The Petries of New Rochelle bring urban creativity to the suburban living room. (Dick Van Dyke, Mary Tyler Moore, Rose Marie, Morey Amsterdam; *The Dick Van Dyke Show*.)

ABOVE: *Young Love*: A question of dangerous sexual attraction . . . (Dwayne Hickman, Tuesday Weld; *The Many Loves of Dobie Gillis*.)

BELOW: . . . or simple chemistry? A very postromantic view from Dobie Gillis and his questionable friends. (Bob Denver, Hickman, Sheila James.)

Approved by the AMA: Professionalism, prosperity, and piety unite in a sitcom image of familial perfection. (Paul Petersen, Donna Reed, Carl Betz, Shelley Fabares; *The Donna Reed Show.*)

"Not Approved by Nobody": In the most critically reviled sitcom ever, these hillbillies cast doubt on whether the corporate coalition can ever really work. (Donna Douglas, Buddy Ebsen, Max Baer, Jr., Irene Ryan; *The Beverly Hillbillies.*)

ABOVE: *Monsters In . . .* : Wipe away the cobwebs and the makeup, and Herman and Lily Munster are Ward and June Cleaver. (Fred Gwynne, Yvonne DeCarlo; *The Munsters.*)

ABOVE RIGHT: *. . . Monsters Out . . .* : Gomez and Morticia Addams may play at bourgeois propriety, but their hearts remain dangerously wild. (Carolyn Jones, John Astin; *The Addams Family.*)

RIGHT: *. . . and Monsters in Between*: Samantha, Queen of the Witches, is inconsolable when her supernatural duties interfere with her duties as a Connecticut housewife. Mother simply doesn't understand . . . and neither do we. (Agnes Moorehead, Elizabeth Montgomery; *Bewitched.*)

Oh, Boy! More Stuff!: The family in a self-indulgent stage, united in consumption . . . (Eve Plumb, Maureen McCormick, Robert Reed, Susan Olsen, Christopher Knight, Michael Lookinlad, Florence Henderson, Barry Williams, Ann B. Davis; *The Brady Bunch*.)

. . . and in hipness. (David Cassidy, Shirley Jones; *The Partridge Family*.)

The Two Families of the Single Woman: Sisterhood, blissful but soon to be destroyed by personal agendas, marriages, and spin-offs . . . (Cloris Leachman, Mary Tyler Moore, Valerie Harper; *The Mary Tyler Moore Show*.)

. . . and the job: stressful and unequal, but enduring. At least until the company is bought out. (Gavin McLeod, Ed Asner, Moore.)

ABOVE: *Conflicts of Change*: Archie Bunker tries to dismiss George Jefferson, a more successful American than he is . . . (Carroll O'Connor, Sherman Hemsley; *All in the Family*.)

RIGHT: . . . Fred Sanford holds his would-be bourgeois son hostage with age and guilt and the support of his good-for-nothing cronies . . . (Don Bexley, Redd Foxx, Demond Wilson; *Sanford and Son*.)

BELOW: . . . while the would-be bourgeois James and Florida find themselves with an archaic racial stereotype for a son. Social "dyn-o-mite!" (John Amos, Jimmie Walker, Esther Rolle; *Good Times*.)

ABOVE: *Late '70s Solutions to Cultural Division*: Caring teachers, ethnic shtick, sentimentality, good-natured insults . . . (John Travolta, Marcia Strassman, Debralee Scott, Gabriel Kaplan, Robert Hegyes, Lawrence-Hilton Jacobs, Ron Palillo; *Welcome Back, Kotter.*)

BELOW: . . . and white paternalism. (Conrad Bain, Gary Coleman, Todd Bridges; *Diff'rent Strokes.*)

What Do Women Want?: Maude doesn't know. Told by a famed psychic that her current wedding (a remarriage to her already-fourth husband) won't be her last, Maude finds herself torn between dismay and anticipation. (Paul Benedict, Bill Macy, Beatrice Arthur, Hermione Baddeley; *Maude*.)

Mary Hartman thinks she just wants to scrape the waxy yellow buildup from her floors. But her smile can't hide the growing hysteria of a television housewife. (Louise Lasser; *Mary Hartman, Mary Hartman*.)

What Do Men Want?: Comradeship? Smart-ass sensitivity? The simplicity of '50s life with the haircuts of the '70s? (McLean Stevenson, Gary Burghoff, Alan Alda, Wayne Rogers; *M*A*S*H*.)

Or is it comradeship, smart-ass *in*sensitivity, and the sexual discussion of the '70s with the haircuts of the '50s? (Don Most, Ron Howard, Henry Winkler; *Happy Days*.)

TOP: *Recombinant Families,
Recombinant Comedy*: Sitcoms of
the '80s and early '90s tell us that we
can all be happy if we just like each
other. Ethnic employee and WASP
boss . . . (Tony Danza, Judith Light;
Who's the Boss?)

ABOVE: . . . mothers and sisters
without husbands . . . (Doris Belack,
Estelle Getty, Bea Arthur; *The Golden
Girls.*)

LEFT: . . . and the nuclear family, of
whatever race. It's all the same
family, all the same plot. (Bill Cosby,
Tempestt Bledsoe, Keshia Knight-
Pulliam; *The Cosby Show.*)

11

The Kids Are All Right, Basically

It's often overlooked that for most Americans, in the most fundamental ways, the 1960s were a less eventful decade than the one before. The '60s abounded with national and world events of the type that pop historians and news producers love: theatrical diplomatic crises, assassinations, combat, riots, extravagant life-styles. But for the average American, those were rather abstract concerns, challenging ideologies maybe, but not like changing one's place of residence, type of work, income level, or family structure.

To risk a sweeping generalization, one might say that in the '50s Americans were going through such big and genuine changes that they desperately wanted to pretend all was calm and ideal; in the '60s most felt stable enough to flirt with the thrilling idea of being on the brink of disaster.

One major new problem did force itself into the homes of millions of Americans in those years: teenagers. The front edge of the baby boom was turning fourteen as the decade began. An estimated four million kids were exploding into puberty every year. By 1965 a horrifying twenty-six million teenagers were overloading the nation's high schools, gobbling up low-paying jobs, and supporting massive entertainment, clothing, and refreshment industries.

TV programmers found a juicy market spawned by the teen boom— but not among the teens themselves. Demographic surveys showed that very few teenagers watched television; they had more exciting things to do. The viewers of prime-time entertainment, it turned out, were mainly younger children, the captive parents of those children, and the elderly. The first two groups had a strong interest in contemporary teenage behavior. The kids were curious: What does my big sister *do* on those dates? What do I have to dread or look forward to? The parents were worried. The relatively few depression and war babies had already created an assertive teen subculture in the 1950s, which had been scary enough. The possibilities for mayhem and self-destruction by this new oversize peer group seemed exponentially increased.

Several sitcoms attempted to play off the concerns of both groups. All of them, given the reassuring nature of the form, ultimately delivered the message that the kids would turn out fine, but they arrived at that message along two very different routes. Some were pro-kid, suggesting that parents were essentially incapable of managing the lives of modern youth and that kids would have to learn their own life lessons; others were pro-father, suggesting that kids could turn out well only by hewing to conventional wisdom and not experimenting with life. Neither one, as it turned out, could stand up to the stresses of the years to come, and the result was some of the most bizarre and dishonest of all TV's creations.

The most aggressively pro-kid show of all was also a delightful gem of willful peculiarity in the dreary TV schedule of 1959–60, one of the most idiosyncratic shows ever to sneak through the network factory: *The Many Loves of Dobie Gillis.* In a sense it was a follow-up to *The Bob Cummings Show,* starring Dwayne Hickman (who had played Bob's wide-eyed and horny nephew) as a sex-obsessed teenager. It could also be pegged as the last of the "subversive" sitcoms.

Dobie Gillis began in the early 1950s as a novel by a young satirist named Max Shulman. The title character was an indefatigably damestruck college boy who reflected sadly on his troubles with girls and authority figures. Through him, Shulman deftly expressed the confusion of the times, the contradictions of a hyped-up postwar America desperately trying to cover itself with a veneer of conservative decency. The book became a movie in 1953, and in 1956 Shulman turned it into a sitcom pilot. For two years sponsors and network execs passed on it, generally asserting that not enough people cared about college kids. Finally someone at 20th Century-Fox thought of taking a few years off Dobie's age, making him a peer of Ricky Nelson and Wally Cleaver. Shulman acquiesced when Fox agreed to retain him as story editor and sometime scripter, and Dobie's televised amours finally hit CBS air in 1959.

In the first moment of the first episode Dobie announces that he is no conventional TV teenager. The camera finds him sitting in profile against a blank background, fist curled under his chin in a spoof of Rodin's *Thinker.* He raises his head, looks at the camera with an ancient weariness, and says, "My name is Dobie Gillis, and I love girls. I'm not a wolf, mind you. A wolf wants lots of girls. I just want one. One beautiful, gorgeous, soft, round, creamy girl for my own. One lousy girl. But to get a girl, you need money, and standing between me and money is a powerful obstacle." The camera swings, finding a sour-faced middle-aged man in an apron, standing at the butcher counter of his tiny grocery store. This, says Dobie, is his one great obstacle to sexual bliss: his father.

Herbert T. Gillis is an astoundingly small-spirited man for a sitcom dad. Vain, stupid, and petulant, he denounces his much smarter son as a "bum" because he won't stock the shelves in his store. Dobie wants nothing from him but cash, so he can woo the money-hungry object of his desire, Thalia Menninger. But Herbert won't give him money any more than he'd give him love or respect.

In one episode Herbert goes to night school for the high school diploma he never got; learning that his instructor is one of Dobie's high school teachers, he adopts the pseudonym Fred C. Dobbs (a screwball reference to *The Treasure of the Sierra Madre*) because he's convinced that being associated with Dobie would disgrace him. As it turns out, however, Dobie knows the material far better than he, and Herbert ends up plagiarizing Dobie's homework under the guise of helping him study. All the while he keeps putting Dobie down, while his ineffectual dope of a wife can only twitter about Dobie's "potential." Ultimately Herbert is found out, humiliated, and has to eat crow for son and teacher before he can get his diploma. This is no exemplary sitcom family.

If the Gillis home is a hostile environment, then Central High School is a shark pool. Dobie's teachers are sarcastic and untouchable. Even when his female math teacher tries to take him under her wing, she ends up being sabotaged by her demanding husband, and Dobie is seduced into cheating by the scheming Thalia. The episode teases at a sappy sitcom solution when Dobie confesses his crime to the teacher, and she grins sweetly and says, "You've made me very happy. You've restored my faith." Then, with the same sweet smile, she adds, "But I'll have to flunk you, of course." She tells Thalia, "You should be proud of him, too. You have a fine, sweet, wonderful, sensitive boy." "Yes." Thalia beams. "I have a fine, sweet, wonderful, sensitive boy"—suddenly tearful, she finishes—"who's never gonna make a dime!"

Thalia is a dazzling creation, a microcosm of Dobie's world. Hypocritical, vain, greedy, and manipulative, played with dangerous sexual potency by Tuesday Weld, she is wholly unadmirable, and she is the only thing Dobie wants. She shivers orgasmically while contemplating a husband with "oodles and oodles of money," but she insists that "I do not happen to be interested in money—not for *myself*." She needs it, she claims with quavering voice, for her father with a kidney condition, and her failing mother, and her sister married to a loafer, and her brother who "is on his way to being a public charge." Dobie soon comes to memorize the Thalian litany: "If my father hadn't put braces on my teeth and sent me to dancing school so I could be beautiful and graceful and charming—the way I *am*—then he might not have a kidney condition. And you aren't making things any easier, Dobie!" At which point she comes up with a new scheme to force Dobie to better himself . . . or corrupt himself. Invariably Dobie is outraged and then instantly capitulates. In the end, like Ralph Kramden, he always loses.

And these are not the only hostile forces in Dobie's world. Milton Armitage is a high school *Übermensch*—rich, tall, handsome, athletic, arrogant (played by Warren Beatty)—against whom Dobie has no chance in competition for girls. Once Thalia manipulates them into one-upping each other with a procession of increasingly fancy suits. Armitage pulls the suits from his own wardrobe, but Dobie has to connive a deal with a local tailor, claiming that he'll use the suits to advertise the man's store. Armitage discovers Dobie's scheme and humiliates him. Money always wins in the Gillis universe (although in this case Dobie scores a small moral victory: Thalia concedes that any boy with enough savvy to cook up a scam like that must have some potential).

As the series proceeded, Thalia and Milton faded away (Beatty hated the show and quit; Weld, reportedly, was often drunk and disruptive and didn't get along with the crew). Dobie was left to chase after a procession of other bizarre (and bizarrely named) beauties and contend with the likes of Chatsworth Osborne, Jr., a grotesque caricature of the idle rich (the motto on the Osborne family arms read, "Never Touch the Capital"). Nearly every plot turned on a self-destructive obsession . . . and money.

Dobie did have two allies in this loveless world, although they were essentially useless. One was his "beatnik" friend Maynard G. Krebs, the only person who seemed to accept him unconditionally. The other was the plain, brainy girl who wanted to marry him, Zelda Gilroy. To call her the girl who loved him wouldn't be quite accurate; Zelda simply decided, at first glance, that she and Dobie were meant to be together, by accident, by "biology," and by sad social necessity. It didn't matter if they didn't like each other a bit. Eventually they'd learn to love each other. They'd have to. "Halt!" she declaimed, in weird Shulmanese. "Dobie, we are a fact, a verity. Dobie, you and I are simply a thing that exists."

Although friendship and the devotion of an honest woman were always held out to Dobie as compensation for the disappointments he suffered at the hands of his father and beautiful girls, Dobie was always spared a happy ending by the fact that he really had no use for friendship and the devotion of an honest woman. Maynard was often a millstone around his neck. Zelda was the nightmare of adult reality, the girl he didn't want but whom he—and the audience—always knew he would end up stuck with. In the meantime, he'd use her to help him with his studies while she laid the groundwork for the marriage.

Dobie Gillis can be viewed as a ferocious satiric analysis of the dehumanizing effects of modern capitalist society. There is no love between father and son; there is only mutual parasitism, only the store and the allowance. There is love between mother and son, but it is useless and unrealistic. Between men and women there is only exploitation; between men, only competition. The only man capable of love is Maynard, the childlike, idiotic nature boy, who is incapable of dealing with the real world.

Perhaps to avoid looking too closely into the maw of such satire, Shulman and his collaborators erected a wall of unreality between the viewer and the characters. The dialogue was purposely artificial, often baroque. This is Dobie hitting on a new girl in town, before he's even said hello: "Could you love a poor man?" Girl: "Are you ill?" "Please let me be your slave. I'm Dobie Gillis." "Arrivederci, sick one." "Oh, Swedish, huh?" "No, that was good-bye in Italian." "Oh. My strong suit is hygiene. Can't we go steady?"

Choppy, quick-panning camera work, phony-looking sets, and the device of having Dobie address the audience in every episode added to the quality of unreality. Characters reacted to stimuli with the comical precision of windup toys. Hickman himself played his teenager like a defeatist adult, self-consciously calm and cynical in the wake of the most disillusioning blows. He was well into his twenties when he made the show and never really tried to disguise the fact. His Dobie was like a soul in a strange purgatory, a thirty-year-old failure forced to go through the motions of adolescent striving for the second time; you knew that he knew there was no hope for anything. Everything about the show, right down to the too-hip, too-cool jazz sound track, seemed to be reassuring us that this wasn't really a teenager, these weren't really people. Maybe that was the only way to get a cute TV comedy out of the realities of modern adolescence.

As if to distance itself further from any real critique of modern life, the show introduced a genuine cultural rebel, then did nothing but ridicule him. Maynard was a cute character and a dependable source of gags, but he was a ridiculous substitute for a beatnik. The beats were notoriously sexual; that was one of the most threatening things about them. Maynard was completely presexual, alternately scared of and indifferent to girls. The beats were quite hip to the cynical ways of the world, perhaps even a bit hypersensitive to the role of money in American life. Maynard was an innocent, rarely having a clue to the conflicts played out around him. The beats, most of all, were dropouts, angry and judgmental toward the mainstream. Maynard accepted everything with total, bland equanimity (except the word *work,* which made him scream and run). Eddie Haskell was a much better beatnik than Maynard G. Krebs.

Maynard made America's most visible counterculture of the period seem safe and unthreatening. It was as if, in exchange for showing Dobie screwed over by modern life, Shulman felt he had to show the alternatives as being completely ineffectual. The result was one of the most cynical creations ever funded by American advertisers and disseminated by commercial American broadcasters. It was a funny show, sometimes brilliant. But it was ultimately safe. It didn't tell kids that the system was good, as did most sitcoms. It acknowledged their darkest suspicions about it. But it did tell them that there was no point in bucking it. Dobie Gillis was the Job of sitcomland.

A more conventional position on adolescence was held by family coms like *The Donna Reed Show,* a plastic reworking of the Anderson family elements that premiered in 1958. (And where *Dobie* lost its direction, stumbled, and disappeared after four seasons, *Donna* coasted along unchangeably for eight.) The kids in this case were prissy Mary (Shelley Fabares) and rambunctious Jeff (Paul Petersen). They were modern youths (even recording pop songs, in a commercial hook borrowed from *Ozzie and Harriet*); Mom and Dad find repeatedly that they can advise and comfort them, but strictness and discipline won't do any good. The kids have to work things out themselves. Being good kids, they do indeed work them out just as Mom and Dad would like.

For instance, teenage daughter Mary is invited to a dance at an out-of-town college. Donna fears that the college boys will induce her to do something she shouldn't, something that is never specified but that any mother or daughter in the audience could readily imagine. Donna at first denies Mary permission, but this makes Mary so depressed that she relents. Unknown to Mary, however, Mom and Dad will be lurking around, spying on her. Sure enough, a college boy puts the moves on little Mary, and Donna is about to burst from the bushes to save the day . . . when Mary tells the boy that she likes him, but she doesn't feel this is right. Mary is poised; the randy lad is humbled; Donna is abashed. Then Mary discovers Mom spying and lets her know pointedly that she need never have worried.

Thalia Menninger she ain't. But then, what can one expect from a sitcom about a pediatrician's wife that gave script approval to members of the medical establishment and actually featured the head of the American Medical Association in one episode? Modern child rearing, almost an adjunct of modern medicine, was being sold as a system that could painlessly cure all our ills.

Lucille Ball, who had always been more effective as a troublemaker than a homemaker, came down on the side of the kids in a different way. In her new *Lucy Show* she played a working widow with a couple of kids (in 1968, when that show was replaced with *Here's Lucy*, she used her real-life kids, Lucie and Desi, Jr.). All the adults on the show were ridiculous: Lucy the scheming scatterbrain; her dubious but always suckered best friend; her idiotic blowhard of a boss. The wise ones were the kids, warning her against her schemes, getting her out of trouble, making comments like a cutesy Greek chorus.

The show was never half as good as *I Love Lucy* had once been, but it brought in big ratings for a decade, with particular strength among old folks and heartlandites (it played right before *Andy Griffith* on Monday nights and shared its demographic constituency). The kid angle never seemed calculated to interest young viewers, but rather to comfort older ones with a lightweight message: These kids today understand this crazy world better than we do, and even when they get uppity, they really do mean well.

A much more self-consciously pro-youth slant was crafted by Sidney Sheldon, a screenwriter with a track record in fluffy comedy: Jerry Lewis vehicles, Jane Powell vehicles, Mitzi Gaynor vehicles. Now he was creating a sitcom vehicle for Patty Duke, the teen prodigy who'd starred on Broadway and won an Oscar before she was sixteen. *The Patty Duke Show*, airing on ABC in 1963, started out looking like a gimmick show, with Duke playing "identical cousins," the goofy Yankee girl Patty Lane and the polished, foreign-educated Cathy. But after the first few episodes Sheldon seemed to lose interest in mistaken-identity plots and focused almost entirely on Patty's familial and romantic tribulations. Cathy hung around primarily as a sympathetic but cautious counterpoint to Patty's bubbling American impulsiveness.

This was the only show that made a point of examining the mechanics of a teenager's learning to make sensible life decisions. In one episode Patty and her boyfriend, Richard, are inspired by another couple, marrying young, to make premature wedding plans of their own. There's no opportunity for Patty's parents to bring their wisdom to bear in persuading her to wait because she conceals the whole matter from them until the final scene.

In a fantasy sequence Patty sees herself as a joyful homemaker, with a perfect house and a perfect little girl (also played by Duke herself, of course) and a husband who lavishes her with presents and bad romantic dialogue. But after seeing how things are going with the other couple and realizing how much is sacrificed with an early marriage, she has a second, parallel fantasy sequence: The house is now a hovel, the daughter is a monster, and although Richard delivers exactly the same lines, he delivers them now with bitter sarcasm. Patty sensitively broaches her doubts to Richard, and they wisely decide just to continue going steady. In the last scene Mom and Dad have finally figured out why Patty's been acting strangely all episode and confront her: "You and Richard are planning to get married!" "*Married!*" says Patty. "Where'd you ever get that idea?" Mom and Dad never know what a volcanic personal development their daughter has just undergone.

They do know what's going on in the episode in which Patty decides to join the Peace Corps and go to Africa. Filling her room with African art, playing African music on her record player, and studying Swahili words, she allows her idealistic fantasy to engage every fiber of her being. Her parents are paralyzed by indecision, admiring her ideals but fearing she's too young to make such a drastic decision. Cathy saves the day by trotting a bunch of orphans into the house to tell Patty how much they need her; it turns out Patty's been volunteering at local hospitals and orphanages all along, quite unbeknownst to her parents (and the viewers). Patty realizes that there's so much to be done right near home, she doesn't need to rush off to Africa.

Patty's secret life was a frequent theme of the show. Unlike Ward Cleaver, whose omniscience often caused his sons to marvel, Martin Lane missed an awful lot going on in his own living room. He wasn't stupid or bumbling; he was, in fact, a big-time New York newspaper editor, and his wife was as sharp as a TV housewife was allowed to be. But he was a bit aloof, removed, and Patty existed in a largely separate world. This was the "generation gap" in genial sitcom terms: the old order and the baby boom loving each other and respecting each other but ultimately not connecting.

In Patty, Sheldon created an optimistic vision of American youth: flushed with energy and middle-class idealism, wiggly with wholesome sexuality, leaping from passion to passion but never fixating too long on anything. *Patty Duke* did for teenagers what *Dick Van Dyke* did for young marrieds: It attempted to seize its moment and bring the forward-rushing energies of young Americans into line with mainstream systems. With the Peace Corps episode Sheldon showed how even Kennedy's call for global activism could be adjusted to sitcom priorities—the lowering of sights, the choosing of home and hearth over the exotic—without essential compromise.

There's a certain poignancy in watching those *Patty Duke* episodes today, envisioning the collegiate world into which Patty would have graduated in 1966. In 1965 it was still possible for Patty to become infatuated with a handsome military cadet without branding herself as a hawk or evoking the escalating war in Vietnam. It was the last moment in which a sitcom about teenagers could still pretend to be hip while endorsing the status quo. It was probably for the show's own good that it got knocked out in the ratings when it did, allowing Sheldon to move on to the juvenile fantasy of *I Dream of Jeannie*.

At the opposite end of the spectrum sat that most thorough of tele-vised treatises in progressive child rearing, *Leave It to Beaver*. Mixed in with Mosher and Connelly's lessons in humane socializing had always been a strong conservative streak. By the final season, 1962–63, with Wally about to graduate from high school and a new mood of rebellion spreading among young Americans, that conservatism flared.

Eddie Haskell, always the mischief-maker, now became a central cautionary figure. Eddie, it seemed, was growing restless, in much the same way Patty Lane would be restless. He toyed with wild, youthful dreams, with dangerous dreams if we accept the show's viewpoint. He wanted to quit school and get a job, to move out of his house (which had been shown to be a bad environment) and into his own apartment, to spend a summer working on a fishing boat.

In every case Ward and June, concerned that Wally might be inspired to do something equally reckless, heard about Eddie's schemes and denounced them. Ward, by this point, had lost much of his warm, casual manner. He often wore a suit and tie while lecturing the boys in his den, as if resisting the movement toward casual attire that was afflicting the world beyond Mayfield. He became omniscient. When he forbade Wally and his pals to drive over treacherous Camelback Cut-off and they did so anyway, one of his co-workers inevitably spotted them and told him about it, enabling him to give another lecture and leaving Wally with the humbling theological conviction that nothing could be done without Dad's knowledge.

Fortunately Ward had raised Wally well; fundamentally Wally wanted only to go to his father's old college, enter his father's old fraternity, and get a good job, probably much like his father's. But even good boys could be impressionable, and Eddie's wild dreams of taking risks and charting his own course through life threatened to lead Wally off the course so subtly laid before him by Ward. Eddie was a rebel like Maynard G. Krebs, but in the context of Mayfield Eddie was a far more serious threat. Where Shulman could make Maynard cuddly, Mosher and Connelly had to make Eddie pathetic and contemptible.

The pleasant folks of Mayfield would, of course, never do anything cruel to make an example of Eddie; which was fine, because the cosmic logic of Mosher and Connelly's world made sure they didn't have to. When Eddie moves out of the house, for example, he brags about the wild parties he has and the chicks who visit him. But Wally and Beaver discover that he's really all alone, crying in his room at night, blocked from seeking companionship by his own defensive boasts. Beaver says, "You know, Wally, I feel kinda sorry for Eddie. Even if he is a creep."

Mosher and Connelly made sure Wally and the Beav got the message: The creep of Mayfield had been revealed as neither satanic tempter nor scary rebel but just a sick little boy who hadn't been raised right. If life planted a boot in his face every time he raised his head too high, it was for his own good.

A figure like Eddie was needed because *Beaver*, like other "perfect family" shows, ultimately rendered its own principals worthless. If the Cleaver method of child rearing was, in fact, perfect, then Wally had to be a near-perfect person by the end of high school. In one late episode he takes an interest in a girl he meets outside of school and brings her home to meet his parents. She plays at being a very nice young lady, but as soon as she's alone with Wally, she crushes his lips with a steamy kiss. He's shocked. Later she takes him to a "beer joint" and offers him cigarettes and booze. Not for a moment is Wally tempted. The girl sees what a square he is and suggests they go their separate ways. The story has the form of a sitcom lesson, but what does anyone learn in it? Only to screen companions more carefully before getting involved. By making Wally a sexless, viceless, untemptable model of a teen, Mosher and Connelly had made it impossible for him to demonstrate anything to real kids or their parents. The didactic cycle of '50s sitcoms died on this note of desperate wishful thinking when *Beaver* finally ended in 1963.

Another, more adaptable sitcom found a way to maintain a conservative '50s stance all through the '60s and into the '70s. *My Three Sons* premiered on ABC in 1960, showing the leisurely struggles of widowed aeronautical engineer Steve Douglas to raise three boys, with no help but that of his cantankerous, widowed father-in-law, Bub. The casting of the show was calculated to give it a wholesome, familiar, conservative air. Steve was played by Fred MacMurray, by then typecast as a mellow, genial old sort, thanks to his recent work for Disney in *The Shaggy Dog* and *The Absent-Minded Professor*. MacMurray even added to the mellowness of the character with his bored underacting; he admitted to having no interest but a financial one in the show and minimized his work by having all his scenes for each entire season shot in two months, leaving the rest of the cast to film the other scenes for later assembly. "Working on that show," he said, "was like working long weekends, that's all."

His oldest boy, Mike, the square one who emulated Dad, was played by another Disney veteran, Tim Considine. The younger boys—awkward, insecure Rob and boisterous little Chip—were played by equally mild young men, Don Grady and Stanley Livingston, less forceful even than

Ricky Nelson or *Donna Reed*'s Paul Petersen. Bub was William Frawley, familiar from years as lovable crank Fred Mertz on *Lucy*.

It was a relaxed, pleasant show, but it was also the most paternal of all sitcoms. Most episodes taught moral lessons supporting the value of traditional wisdom, like *Father Knows Best* (the principal director and some of the writers moved straight over from *Father*, in fact), but they lacked the bantering and feminizing touch of the Anderson gals. The Douglas boys were saddled with more rules and chores than Wally, Beav, and other denizens of the sitcoms. Steve was a rather aloof figure, often working alone in his upstairs office, but he was firmly in command and unfailingly wise when his direction was needed. Bub functioned like a bellowing sergeant, running day-to-day operations but deferring to Steve. At times the household had the quality of a military academy—a very loose academy, to be sure, since the boys had time to watch TV, see girlfriends, and cause minor trouble. But they rarely had to teach themselves important lessons. Steve was always there to point the way, and Steve, ultimately, was infallible.

In one episode Rob plagiarizes one of Steve's old history papers for a school assignment and gets an A. Steve is shocked, icily disappointed, severe in his punishment. Then the teacher reveals that Steve apparently plagiarized the paper himself from an old history book. Steve is humbled, eats crow, tells Rob that he understands how a human can fail his moral code sometimes. Rob thanks him for that but insists that his punishment remain intact. Then Steve remembers: He copied the history book not for a history class but for a *typing* class, where copying was perfectly legal. Bub expects him to go tell Robbie that, but Steve resists the temptation; he doesn't want to ruin the moment of humble father-son contact they enjoyed. So Steve remains an untarnished knight, in adolescence and adulthood, in morality and compassion.

The Douglas family was explicitly a part of America's booming industrial society. Steve was often seen at work, going over plans, talking to officious clients. The family traveled as no other sitcom family ever did, to Japan and Ireland and other nations in the American orbit, broadening the kids' horizons and expanding Steve's business (in Japan Mike fell for a prim Japanese girl, who helped him put his infatuation with the girl back home into proper perspective, learning old-fashioned lessons in a jet age context). Because the show was sponsored by General Motors, during one season the closing credits featured stock shots of fleets of roaring cars and trucks, which left an odd subliminal connection between the family morality play and American technology lingering in the viewer's mind.

My Three Sons was never a top-rated hit, but its large, loyal following kept it on the air until 1972, partly because it was able to change with the times. It moved from black and white to color, and from ABC to CBS, in 1965. Mike married and moved out, and a new third son, the dorky Ernie, was adopted. When William Frawley died, William Demarest—as old bachelor sailor Uncle Charley—took his place. Then, in 1967, the Douglases moved from the Midwest to California, breaking with the heartland settings of '50s sitcoms and moving into the glowing Sunbelt that attracted the genre in the '60s. There Steve met a woman, a widow with a daughter, and eventually married her; that, combined with Robbie's marriage, feminized the household.

The rebellious currents that Eddie Haskell had hinted at were becoming full blown by then: Students for a Democratic Society, the free speech movement, the Summer of Love, political folk music, weird new rock. Young women, in particular, seemed determined to shock their elders, with miniskirts, "unfeminine" Twiggy bodies, topless bathing suits, the pill, and a nascent women's liberation movement. *My Three Sons* responded strangely to the currents. On the one hand, it tried to be hip: Ernie donned preposterous fringed leather jackets; Rob's wife, Katie, had a fling as a folk singer; Steve's obnoxiously precocious stepdaughter talked back at adults cutely. But the heart of a young Steve Douglas beat beneath that fringed jacket, Katie immediately gave up her singing when her family disapproved, and all the females deferred to the wisdom of Steve. Steve himself went from being merely infallible to humorlessly omniscient; by the end he was referring to men like himself as "us Solomons," with only a trace of irony.

Like all the family sitcoms, *My Three Sons* promoted a variation of progressive, nonviolent child rearing, but on broader social issues it dug in its heels against the liberalization of America. By implication it blamed that liberalization on feminization. In the early years Steve avoided entanglements with scheming females who wanted to take over his household and work their influence over his impressionable boys. He remarried only after his sons were safely grown and he could bring his firmer fatherly wisdom to bear on his precocious but mixed-up stepdaughter.

It had the same viewpoint as *Father Knows Best*: Protestant; ethically absolutist; pretherapeutic in its view of individual responsibilities and capabilities. But in the challenging intellectual environment of the late

'60s, when family structure, sexual ethics, and male-female roles were being hotly debated, that viewpoint would have been tough to convey through a conventional nuclear family without running head-on into the thorniest questions. Indeed, those families were vanishing from TV: 1966 saw the simultaneous end of *Donna Reed*, *Ozzie and Harriet*, *Dick Van Dyke*, and *Patty Duke*, which left scarcely anything but widows, widowers, weirdos, and singles. The unreal, overlapping households of *My Three Sons* created a safe environment for a comforting conservative fantasy. The only safer way to deal with the times, the sitcom soon discovered, was to create households still more unreal than the Douglases'.

12

Fantasyland

Even in this book, which argues that situation comedies inevitably contain comments on their times, seeking any sort of social meaning in *The Beverly Hillbillies* seems like something of a conceit. Yet it was the highest-rated TV show of the 1960s, and it kicked off a whole cycle of other popular shows that dominated America's most popular medium during some of the country's most interesting years. It had to be saying something to somebody.

Demographics reveal something about that somebody. Although TV ownership and per capita viewing time had reached unprecedented heights by the early 1960s, proliferating stations and more varied programming meant that fewer people watched any one program—or even network TV in general—at any one time. The novelty of the medium had also worn off; there would be no more crazes such as Berle and Lucy had inspired. Where *Lucy* had pulled in more than two-thirds of the TV audience over the entire 1952–53 season, *Wagon Train* led the 1961–62 ratings pack with less than one-third; no show would ever top 40 percent again. A program no longer had to cut across all social strata to be a ratings leader.

Programmers began to zero in on what became known as the heavy-viewing center or, more bitterly, Bill and Mary Six-Pack. These were the watchers of several hours of TV entertainment a day: more likely to be working class than professionals; more likely to be rural than urban; more likely not to be college-educated. By inference, Bill and Mary were socially conservative and not especially political. Rick Mitz quotes one NBC executive as saying, anonymously, that they're "like a kid with candy who eats and eats. They're nice people, they have good jobs, but they don't want to think. 'Dummies,' I call them."

Specifically important to early-evening ratings was that odd coalition of little kids and old people, the former with their broad sense of humor and curiosity about adult life, the latter with their fears about the changing, threatening world. American popular culture had already become deft at pleasing oppositional audiences with the same product (as in getting both poor blacks and white bigots to like radio's *Amos 'n' Andy*), but it reached new heights of oddity in playing for old and young in the 1960s, whipping dopiness and sentiment into one frothy punch.

Neither kids, nor oldsters, nor Bill and Mary Six-Pack were viscerally connected to the youth movement, civil rights movement, Vietnam, feminism, or the other political forces beginning to shape the decade. Yet they watched the TV news; they saw the signs of trouble and heard the voices of dissent. They may have favored escapist comedy, but they liked escapism best when it acknowledged or soothed their deep anxieties.

No TV boss understood the ratings game better than CBS president James T. Aubrey. After years in middle management with CBS, he had jumped as a programmer in the mid-'50s to ABC, where his emphasis on rural- and kid-oriented filmed programs (*The Real McCoys*, *The Rifleman*) helped push that perennial loser ahead of NBC. CBS hired him back, to run the whole show, before the 1960 season. He immediately laid out a sitcom-based strategy to snag Bill, Mary, their parents, and their kids.

He picked up *The Andy Griffith Show* instantly; he passed on Rob Petrie until Sheldon Leonard and Dick Van Dyke mainstreamed him. For his six-thirty Sunday evening kid slot he picked up a syndicated show about a talking horse called *Mr. Ed*. With an appealing animal lead, goofy adults, obvious humor, and a parade of guest stars (including the L.A. Dodgers) it held a solid kid audience for six years and opened the doors to a whole cycle of fantastical gimmick sitcoms.

Aubrey really found his gold mine, though, in producer-writer Paul Henning. A Missourian who had moved into the smart-ass circles of

Hollywood radio comedy writing, Henning loved to play with the conflict of provincial Middle-Americans and crass California sophisticates. He'd done it with *The Bob Cummings Show* and again as one of the writers for *The Real McCoys*. Now he did it with a show about a family of loony hillbillies who strike oil on their Ozark farm, become instant millionaires, and are talked into moving to Beverly Hills—not because they want to but because their media-influenced kinfolk think that's what millionaires are supposed to do.

Dennis the Menace and NBC's briefly popular *Hazel* were demonstrating that comic strip sitcoms could pull in large audiences, and Henning cannily took Al Capp's *Li'l Abner* as his model for *The Beverly Hillbillies*. Pansy, Lucifer, Abner, and Daisy Mae Yokum became Granny Clampett, her son-in-law, Jed, his nephew, Jethro, and daughter, Elly May, with only slight variations. Granny was a cultural reactionary, changing her habits, her palate, and her superstitions not a bit in the move west. Jethro made lunkheaded attempts to fit into the L.A. scene and find himself a beautiful sweetheart. Elly filled the estate with homeless "critters" and scared off prospective beaus with her superstrong tomboy antics. Jed drifted along in eternal mild surprise, good-heartedly trying to understand the modern world while still yearning for the simplicity of home.

Arrayed against the Clampetts and their innocence were some harmless, comical embodiments of sterile modern values: Mr. Drysdale, the scheming banker who would use any means to keep the Clampett fortune in his bank and see that it was aggressively invested; Mrs. Drysdale, dreary snob of the California nouveau riche, who had to be nice to the Clampetts for her husband's sake but was appalled by their primitivity; Miss Hathaway, Drysdale's sexless secretary, genuinely fond of the Clampetts but ultimately loyal to her boss. There was also the inevitable procession of slickers, snobs, swingers, and potential boyfriends and girlfriends for the Clampetts to confound.

Most of the gags were old "country cousin" riffs of the sort that filled *Grand Ole Opry* performances: Jed sees his vast new lawn and wants to plow it for crops; Granny tries to find possum innards in L.A. stores for her down-home "vittles"; Jed thinks "golf" is some sort of game animal and mistakes the balls for eggs; Elly dates a navy frogman, and Granny works up a potion to turn the poor fella back into a full human.

There were also lots of sight gags for the kids, including many involving Elly's "critters": Granny boxes a trained kangaroo; guests run screaming at the sight of a lion, to Jed's quiet mystification. The critters even helped make simple social statements: The family's lazy hound, Duke, knocks up Mrs. Drysdale's pedigree poodle, sending her into a rage that the Clampetts never understand. And there were elements to titillate pubescents: Elly's swelling breasts, skintight jeans, and utter naiveté made her a luscious but nonthreatening sexual object. Jethro's moronic pursuit of the playboy life would have reassured even the most awkward junior Romeo that he wasn't so bad. This was the complete synthetic sitcom.

Even more than *Cummings*, this Henning creation deftly juggled— and refused to resolve—contradictory messages. Were viewers asked to laugh at the dumb hicks or at the phony slickers? Were the Clampetts demonstrating that we can preserve simple values in the modern world or that there's just no place for provincials in mainstream culture? Was their sudden wealth a wish fulfillment or a cautionary lesson? Conflicts erupted arbitrarily and were settled by slapstick conveniences. Viewers were left to believe what they wanted.

Yet *The Beverly Hillbillies* did work one constant theme: The consensus doesn't really work. No one learns anything. Both parties in a conflict are just as uncomprehending when it stops as when it began, and they'll start up the same mutual stupidity next week. It was a refreshing message, after years of sitcoms leading people firmly into prosocial agreements. It was also relevant: The postwar economic boom was leveling off, and millions of Americans found themselves still poor, still locked out of the middle-class dream; the civil rights movement, meanwhile, was growing bigger and more confrontational, driving an ideological wedge between poor black and poor white, between white North and white South. Moderate-progressive social forces seemed to be polarizing people, not homogenizing them. Americans were intuiting that the social promises of the '50s were not being fulfilled. *The Beverly Hillbillies* resisted bringing any social issues consciously to mind, but when it premiered in the fall of 1962, it may have made more political sense than any other show.

In any case, it drew more viewers than any other show. It stormed to the top of the ratings in its first season with 36 percent of the audience, five percentage points over its nearest rival. It clobbered Perry Como on NBC. In its second year it hit 39 percent, the last show ever to rise that high. On some nights its estimated audience hit sixty million people.

Critics assailed it. Gleaning the shrill and repetitive reviewer reactions of the time, certain words come up again and again: idiotic, inane, stereotyped, insulting, juvenile, crude. It was all that, of course. But in the beginning it was also energetic and pretty funny. And considering the cautious state of TV at the time, its rejection of the pat messages and surface refinement that always make TV critics glow is almost admirable.

Henning immediately concocted a follow-up, *Petticoat Junction*, about a widowed hotelier and her three pretty daughters—Billie Jo, Bobbie Jo, and Betty Jo—in the jerkwater town of Hooterville. James Aubrey, always adept at schedule placement, dropped it in after *The Red Skelton Show*, with its big rural audience, and it placed fourth in the ratings its first season out. Its following steadily eroded from there, however. Its characters weren't half as kooky as the Clampetts, and there was little room for conflict between yokels and slickers. Viewers wanted worlds in collision, not just amusing hicks.

Henning devised a more durable premise when he flip-flopped the concept of *Beverly Hillbillies*. In *Green Acres*, a romantic Manhattan attorney, Oliver Wendell Douglas, moved to the aforementioned Hooterville, convincing himself that "farm living is the life for me." Dragged along unwillingly was his spaced-out European socialite wife, Lisa. What he found was not the wholesome rusticity of Mayberry or even the Hooterville of *Petticoat*. It was a madhouse, a city boy's nightmare of rural perversity.

A solid cast of character actors brought the bizarre locals to life: the slow-working but indefatigable con man Mr. Haney (Pat Buttram); the idiot handyman Eb (Tom Lester), passionately seized by every notion that crossed his dim brain; pig farmer Fred Ziffel and his wife (Hank Patterson and Fran Ryan), who believed that their pig Arnold was really their son; Arnold himself, a trained pig of many tricks, who fell passionately in love with a dog and communicated his fervor through subtitled grunts. Then there was the gang at the general store, whose endless circular arguments always made fine syntactical sense, but never connected to the real world (at least as Oliver understood it).

Even more than *Hillbillies*, *Green Acres* presented a world in which nothing made sense and nothing could ever be completely resolved. Each character filled his or her own self-contained world, and none could ever communicate with any others, even when they tried. Oliver stood for the whole realm of modern systems, of precise verbal communication, yet he was at sea in the irrational American heartland. It was not the townsfolk who seemed stupid, however. In their unshakable, unselfconscious security, they made Oliver (played with constant baffled exaggeration by Eddie

Albert) appear the fool: a fool for trying to make sense out of them; a fool for thinking he could fit in among them; a fool for presuming to leave his own kind. (That is often how TV executives, comedy writers, and advertisers see themselves when they try to play to that "heavy-viewing center.")

Pointedly it was Lisa who found the greatest contentment in Hooterville. Played with trancelike dopiness by Eva Gabor, she floated incongruously through the farmhouse in extravagant evening gowns. Like the locals, she found her own reality and stayed within it. She was too dizzy to do otherwise. She believed whatever she was told (that stray dog is Eb, reincarnated? Fine, then; she'll take the dog in and treat it no differently from Eb), and she created no conflict. She was as content in the madness of Hooterville as she must have been in the madness of jet set society.

The critics blasted *Green Acres*, too, dismissing it as another bunch of dumb hick jokes, completely missing its clever lunacy. It was, in fact, the most ingenious creation of Henning's company. Had most of the plots not been so easy and boneheaded, it might have been brilliant. Certainly the characters were well realized, the acting was oddly convincing, and in an indirect way, it was very timely for America in 1965.

Since its cancellation in 1971 the show has developed a loyal following among young adults with a bent for the peculiar. Jack Mingo, founder of the Couch Potatoes, called it "the most misunderstood TV show of the past thirty years," adding, "There is a surreal sensibility hidden in the show that's absolutely hilarious." Critic Steve Sonsky went as far as to call it "a Kafkaesque nightmare . . . almost like *Alice in Wonderland* . . . like an acid trip." The cable channel Nickelodeon coyly promoted its reruns with the line "Remember: it's not dopey. It's surreal." Its viewers at the time, numerous enough to place it as high as sixth in the ratings, wouldn't have used such analogies, but at some level they must have responded to its worldview.

Aubrey's country hits appalled the relatively intellectual faction of the TV community. Jack Paar, who quit network TV in disgust in 1962, described television as "a medium today that's operated strictly by survey and committee. . . . Eventually, when those network guys got their heads beaten a bit, can you blame them for losing their enthusiasm? Then Jim Aubrey came along at CBS with his theory: give them the lowest common denominator, the worst stuff. And his theory worked. . . . And that was the end of it as far as I'm concerned. . . . I don't see any renaissance possible."

Aubrey's theory had indeed worked, according to the only standard by which TV shows were then judged. In 1961–62 CBS had held eight of the top fifteen ratings positions, with third place its best showing. Two seasons later it held *fourteen* of fifteen, including the top spot. Most literate commentators saw in this a victory of reactionary idiocy over the efforts of the cultural establishment to uplift the masses. One of the ideological fissures of the late '60s was opening.

❑

The growing importance of children to ratings enabled some of the more dangerous spirits of '50s TV to return to prime time, but only in compromised and juvenilized forms.

ABC, with its kid-vid strategy, commissioned four prime-time cartoon sitcoms from the Hanna-Barbera animation studio: *The Flintstones*, a Stone Age reworking of *The Honeymooners* but with a reasonably contented, suburban caveman version of Ralph Kramden; *The Jetsons*, a space age spin on the same concept; *Calvin and the Colonel*, about a southern-accented fox and bear, played by Freeman Gosden and Charles Correll, who were essentially Amos and Andy without race; and *Top Cat*, a *Bilko* adaptation about a conniving alley cat, with comedian Arnold Stang contributing a Phil Silvers imitation as T.C.'s voice. These were all socially defused versions of touchy '50s properties; all but *The Flintstones* soon retreated to Saturday morning.

Nat Hiken, the man behind *Bilko*, tried to repeat his success with a comedy about New York cops, *Car 54, Where Are You?* Hiken said he got the idea when he visited a police station and noticed that the cops "sounded and acted just like any group of men at work." He created a station house full of nutty but believable characters, blue-collar guys more concerned with keeping their lockers neat than with battling deadly criminals. They were an ethnic grab bag: Schnauser, Antonnucci, Rodrequez, O'Hara, Abrams, and Anderson (the last being black). They played cards and dodged tough duty and struggled with harping, frustrated wives.

The trouble was, Hiken didn't give them a Bilko. The principals were a garrulous, lovable dope (Officer Toody) and his stoic, silently vulnerable partner (Officer Muldoon). There was no con man, no self-created leader to make sense out of the nonsense, to expose the shams of urban bureaucracy. The nation's police executives objected to the show, but only because, as a deputy police commissioner of New York noted, they were "saddened to see a couple of buffoons masquerading as police-men." Hiken had created an appealing show, with none of *Bilko*'s bite. Kids liked it, but few others. It died after two years, and that was it for Hiken and the sitcom.

Yet *Bilko* reruns—usually played in afternoon kid hours—were grow-ing increasingly popular. The networks couldn't ignore them. Beginning in 1962, through various strategies of trivialization and depoliticization, producers and networks created a popular sitcom cycle out of the Ameri-can military.

During the Truman and Eisenhower years the entertainment business had been rather ambivalent about World War II and war in general. There were some flat-out war hero movies, but they were outnumbered and overshadowed by the likes of *From Here to Eternity* and *Attack!* When they drifted at all toward humor, it was a dark humor (*Mr. Roberts, Stalag 17*). Television, uncomfortable with ambivalence, tended to avoid the topic entirely.

But by the time *The Wackiest Ship in the Army* was released in 1960, a new mood was being signaled: The war was well past; the nation could laugh it off and move on to future challenges. That year, after all, America's most prominent living reminder of the reality of the war was about to step down as president. His successor was a handsome young war hero, an obscure figure onto whom the public could project what-ever romantic image of the war it chose. In 1962 *The Longest Day*, emotionally cool and technically spectacular, reinterpreted the Euro-pean theater as a historical epic. In 1964 the sequel to *Mr. Roberts*, *Ensign Pulver*, took all the complexity out of the original and left the war manageable and cute.

During this transition TV programmers finally felt comfortable grap-pling with the military through entertainment. The public responded. Kids were curious about their dads' roles in the war; dads were ready to look back without flinching. More important, there were signs of new war on the horizon: Kennedy had talked about the "missile gap" during his campaign, and now he was closing it rapidly. He and Khrushchev were butting heads, and we were scraping up against Castro all over the Caribbean. The Green Berets and the all-military astronauts were being held up as ideals to kids. Advisers were shipping out for Vietnam in greater numbers every year.

The shows poured from the networks from 1962 to 1965, and many met with solid ratings. There were gritty dramas (*Combat*), romantic dramas (*Twelve O'Clock High*), and heroic dramas (*The Gallant Men*, *The Rat Patrol*). And there were sitcoms, three from NBC alone in 1962: *Ensign O'Toole*, about sailors in World War II, an obvious watered-down version of *Mr. Roberts*; *Don't Call Me Charlie*, a cutesy piece about a veterinarian who got drafted and assigned to a stuffy superior in Paris; and *McKeever & the Colonel*, with a precocious military school cadet whose mischief confounded the stuffy but likable headmaster.

Far more successful, however, was ABC's entry, *McHale's Navy*. Like *Top Cat*, it went directly to *Bilko* for inspiration, and though this series was live action, its characters might as well have been cartoons. Lieutenant Commander McHale, played broadly by Ernest Borgnine, was a paternal, antiauthoritarian con artist, but his schemes were childlike and harmless compared with Bilko's. The loafers and screw-ups serving under him were two-dimensional versions of Fort Baxter's grunts. His superior, Captain Binghamton (Joe Flynn), was a screaming nut, a kids' version of James Cagney's obsessive martinet in *Mr. Roberts*. Ensign Parker (Tim Conway) was a reduction of the "green recruit" archetype to the figure of a slapstick idiot.

McHale's Navy does deserve some credit for iconoclasm: It got up in front of the kids of America every week and showed GIs in World War II as far less than gallantly self-sacrificing. But it wasn't well enough connected to reality ever to be more than an innocuous pastiche. McHale's gang were not in Bilko's present-day military but in a PT boat on a tiny Pacific island during World War II; at the same time the sense of tragedy and difficulty that *Mr. Roberts* had used to balance its humor was excised. *McHale* was mainly popular for the cute slapstick bits between Borgnine and Conway, which had a Laurel and Hardy flavor. It found a formula to take viewers' growing interest in the military and plow it into harmless nuttiness.

More military sitcoms followed: set in World War II (TV versions of *The Wackiest Ship in the Army* and *Mr. Roberts*); in peacetime (*No Time for Sergeants*); in long-ago wars (the cavalry spoof *F Troop*). Most were short-lived, but CBS, in 1965, found a solid hit in the most extreme comedic trivialization of all. *Hogan's Heroes* was a reworking of *Stalag 17*, but with all of Billy Wilder's bitter irony surgically removed. The heroes in question were a cute international group of POWs in Germany, secretly working for Allied intelligence. The camp commandant was a vain, impotent bureaucrat who became dependent on the resourceful Colonel Hogan and so let himself be easily fooled. The barracks sergeant was a big, lovable dope. Thanks to them, Hogan and his boys were able to broadcast secrets and leave and reenter the stalag at will.

In contrast with the cheap sets and juvenile screwiness of *McHale's Navy*, *Hogan's Heroes* created a weird veneer of realism: Lighting was moody; music and editing worked at creating suspense; the good-guy characters were relatively restrained; Bob Crane played Hogan like a hard-boiled straight man. Rather than announce, as did *McHale*, "Let's forget reality and amuse the kids," *Hogan* suggested that war really could be this easy, this harmless, for the tough, intelligent American.

Critics and citizens' groups attacked *Hogan's Heroes* loudly for its tastelessness, but viewers latched on to it (the critics' noise, of course, no doubt fueling curiosity). The government didn't say a word against it or against any of the military comedies. Congress had helped shove Ollie Treyz from the presidency of ABC when *Bus Stop* toyed with youthful violence in the American heartland, but no one grumbled at the trivialization of war. After all, the current war effort didn't need the same kind of propaganda as the one in 1941. America wasn't hurling itself into Vietnam as a national effort but rather being eased in by escalation and executive deceit, and it would all go more smoothly if the populace were sitting at home, chuckling at the harmless vicissitudes of combat.

Most of the war-coms lost their audiences as the real war got realer. *Hogan's Heroes* hung on until 1971 but not as a top-rated show. The others disappeared. Only one military sitcom sustained its popularity, even increased it, during the heat of Vietnam and the antiwar movement.

Gomer Pyle, U.S.M.C. premiered a month after the trumped-up Tonkin Gulf incident, which guaranteed a full-scale war in Vietnam and the election of Lyndon Johnson. It was a James Aubrey masterstroke, taking the moronic but loving naïf of *The Andy Griffith Show* and making him a marine. Hick show, military show, gimmick show, and spin-off of a dependable hit, all in one. It was a guaranteed hit with kids, old-timers and country folk. Sure enough, it enjoyed five years of huge success before its star, Jim Nabors, quit to try a comedy-variety hour.

Gomer, played by Nabors with retarded cuteness, arrives among the cynical, self-interested troops of Camp Henderson, California, as the ultimate goof-up. Gradually, though, his unquestioning love and trust of the world begin to warm up the platoon. The other privates rediscover their own loving natures and take Gomer under their wings. Sergeant Carter, the hard-boiled platoon commander, at first thinks Pyle is a wise guy, trying to make a laughingstock of him. But finally even Carter is revealed to have a heart of gold. He becomes Gomer's shepherd and benefactor. He screams at Pyle every time his good-natured impulsiveness leads to another embarrassing complication, but Gomer's dumb, loving grin always melts his wrath.

This was Bilko in reverse. What if the boys at Fort Baxter had been given a Christ-like simpleton instead of a conniving city slicker? Might not those same scraggly, flawed average Americans have become much better people? *Gomer Pyle*'s message was far simpler than that of any corporate-suburban sitcoms with their lessons in compromise and role-following, far simpler even than *Andy Griffith*, with its systemic complications. It said merely that the oldest, most basic, least sophisticated sort of sweetness could redeem even the toughest modern types.

Sheldon Leonard and his cocreators astutely chose a Southern California marine base for their hero. In various episodes Gomer connected with the movie and TV industries, the music business, the surf scene, the Beverly Hills rich—all the easy symbols of modernity. Everywhere he went he left a trail of fond smiles and innocence—at least temporarily—restored.

One thing Gomer never, ever connected with was the Vietnam War. He somehow existed in the peacetime military when there was no peace. He lived in a timeless, slow-paced idyll: five years as a private on the same base, answering to the same sergeant who got him in boot camp.

The same TV that brought this idyll into living rooms was pouring out far stronger images at the same time: combat, body bags, protesters in the streets, police clubbing students in Chicago. The more *Gomer Pyle* resisted those images, the stronger its following grew. After outrating all other sitcoms in its second year, it stumbled a bit; then, in its final season, 1968–69, it was back on top of the sitcoms, second among all shows. This after Tet, after Johnson threw in the towel, after Chicago, as Nixon took over.

Gomer Pyle can't strictly be called a pro-military show; Gomer was making the military better, not the other way around. Nor was it exactly trivializing the military, for it acknowledged the military as an important social force that can work for good or ill. In its simpleminded way it offered hope that in this hostile, divisive world, simple goodness might yet save the day. With all the corporate and progressive systems of the postwar world seemingly breaking down, it was a message that attracted millions of uncritical viewers. Most of its audience—older, rural, conservative—no doubt supported the Vietnam War. But even those with doubts about the war found a reassurance in *Gomer*. It helped them pretend that Vietnam really didn't matter. And that, from the viewpoint of the political and economic establishment, was the next best thing.

❏

James Aubrey, meanwhile, was merrily following up on the success of *Mr. Ed* with more fantastical kid shows. Two of the great fascinations of preteen subculture had become science fiction and monsters. *The Twilight Zone*, *The Outer Limits*, and the cycle of '50s SF movies—now finding their way onto weekend TV—fanned the flames of the former, abetted by Kennedy's space program and the new stress on science in schools. Monsters were more an underground fascination, inspired by the bloody Dracula movies coming from England's Hammer Films, by sleazy gore flicks running in cheap matinees, by fan magazines like *Famous Monsters of Filmland*, and by Universal's recent release of its moody '30s horror movies (*Frankenstein*, *Dracula*, et al.) to television. Both provided ways for kids to grapple with the stresses of rapidly changing times. Science fiction was a quasi-respectable means for them to entertain fantasies and fears about the future; monsters were a way to mock standards of taste and decorum, to affirm themselves as dangerous little misfits.

CBS took on both trends in Milquetoast sitcom form, with *My Favorite Martian* in 1963 and *The Munsters* in 1964. Neither one quite got the idea. *Martian* was about a bachelor reporter in L.A. who befriends a stranded alien and passes him off as his uncle. The plots revolved around little mix-ups, which "Uncle Martin" dispensed with his Martian magic: moving things telepathically, talking to animals, disappearing. The special effects were good, the chemistry between the leads (Ray Walston and Bill Bixby) was appealing, but the fantasy was too sanitized, too safe, to give kids any thrills or chills.

The Munsters was similar. It was, in fact, a sitcomized undermining of the whole spirit of the monster fad, selling itself to kids with visually effective facsimiles of Frankenstein, Dracula, Vampira, and the Wolfman. Its creators were Bob Mosher and Joe Connelly, jumping from the uncomfortable quasi reality of *Leave It to Beaver* into this safer realm. Their characters were a good-natured monster family that was desirous of living normal lives in normal surroundings but that never understood why they made people nervous. The teenage daughter was a typical white bread American who feared she was ugly because she looked so unlike her folks. Most episodes helped the Munsters win normal friends or fit into society. (No mobs of frightened suburbanites ever came after them with torches.)

Mosher and Connelly had gone head to head with the monster fad a couple of years earlier, in a *Beaver* episode entitled "Sweatshirt Monsters." In it Beav insisted on wearing a shirt emblazoned with a hideous monster face to school, in defiance of an astounding array of authority figures: father, mother, friends' fathers and mothers, teacher, and principal. For this offense he was sent home and confined to his room. The show never mustered any dramatic evidence to support the wrongness of such a shirt, but Beav folded before the force of Ward's lecture: "Wrong is wrong even if everyone else says it's right, and right is right even if everyone else says it's wrong." With the naive, assimilation-minded Munster family, Mosher and Connelly no longer had to ban the monsters. They had made the monsters safe. As lead actor Fred Gwynne described it, the series was *"The Donna Reed Show* with monsters." Looking back on his role, Gwynne said, "It was fun to be as much of a household product as Rinso."

The Munsters produced an interesting by-product, however. When ABC execs heard that CBS had the show in the works, they smelled a potential juvenile hit. They cast about for a competing item and found that producer David Levy was working with Charles Addams on a TV version of the latter's perverse cartoons for *The New Yorker*. They snapped it up and got it onto the air a week before *The Munsters*.

Addams did not have a TV sensibility. He had avoided entanglements with the medium before and agreed to work with Levy only because they had a mutual acquaintance in novelist John O'Hara. Levy had him develop his nameless cartoon characters and their world for TV needs, which gave the show a cockeyed twist from the beginning (compare the names Gomez and Morticia, Uncle Fester, Pugsley, and Wednesday to Herman and Lily Munster, Grandpa, Marilyn, and Eddie). He drew a different type of talent, too. Movie actress Carolyn Jones had avoided TV series work but auditioned for the role of Morticia because Addams "appealed to my snob instincts." She turned in a wonderfully campy performance as the morbid sexpot mother of the family.

The Addamses lampooned genteel middle-class society. They had a butler: a seven-foot, cadaverous, ominously laconic brute named Lurch. They had a maid, sort of: a disembodied hand in a box, called Thing. They kindly supported older relatives: Grandmama, a wild-haired old loon;

Cousin Itt, a hairy monster; Fester, a hairless, jittering, high-voiced madman who illuminated light bulbs by popping them into his mouth. They had all the accoutrements of the elegant home: a bearskin rug (that growled), a garden (full of deadly nightshade and roses with the blooms chopped off); houseplants (an "African Strangler" that nearly killed a few guests); a stuffed fish on the wall (with a human leg hanging from its mouth); and even decorative swords (which Gomez swallowed when Morticia wasn't in the mood for sword fighting).

They also had a couple of cute kids: Pugsley, who followed in his proud daddy's footsteps by playing with dynamite, and Wednesday, the darling preschooler who played "Marie Antoinette" by guillotining a doll and then burying it—along with "Bluebeard's Wives" and "Mary Queen of Scots"—in her doll cemetery in the backyard. They were the envy of every kid feeling stifled by the parental world.

All this would have amounted to no more than gimmickry, however, had they not had one other thing: life. Gomez and Morticia were the only set of parents in the sitcom world who ever expressed lust for each other—frenzied lust at that. Let any French word pass his wife's seductive lips (even "pie a la mode"), and Gomez would throw himself at her, kissing her hand and arm all the way to the neck. Much of the time she would stall him with a cool "Don't, Gomez. It wouldn't be right." In that one stroke they presented their young viewers with a blunt affirmation of sexuality and a sly mockery of middle-class propriety.

Gomez, played with grinning glee and manic élan by John Astin, was a man of passion such as the sitcoms have never seen, before or since. Whether blowing up his model trains, engaging in rapier-clashing foreplay with his wife, or gobbling up eye of newt, he lived every moment. He wanted nothing from the world that he didn't have, least of all the acceptance of the mainstream. He never quite understood normal perspectives, never knew quite why people were afraid of him, but he had an inkling. More than once, when a visitor ran shrieking from the house, Gomez would say sympathetically, "Poor man. He must be working too hard."

The Addams household, creepy and kooky and ooky as it was, was a self-contained counterculture. It's no surprise that the punk singer Siouxsie Sioux later said, "My role model, inspiration, and heroine is Morticia Addams." It's revealing that such a family could only be presented in such a gimmicky, safely unreal context. Perhaps it's just as revealing that its ratings were no better than those of *The Munsters* or *My Favorite Martian*. All three shows were canceled in 1966.

ABC scored the one huge hit of the fantasy sitcom cycle in the same season that the Addamses premiered, but with a diametrically opposite point of view. *Bewitched* was as antifeminist, antisexual, and procentrist as a sitcom could be. It was also, however, peculiarly ineffective in selling its own point of view. It was a visibly uneasy and phony show. Yet it struck an immediate chord; in its first season it was the highest-rated sitcom of the year.

Female discontent was becoming an issue by then. The Pill had gone to market in 1960 and was in common use by 1962, diminishing the one great fear that had prevented so many women from testing the new sexual mores. Books like Gael Greene's *Sex and the College Girl*, from 1964, were revealing a leap in premarital female sexual activity; medical statistics showed a frightening increase in venereal disease among young women. Beyond the bedroom, women were beginning to test the boundaries of their roles. The year 1963 saw the publication of Betty Friedan's *The Feminine Mystique* and the first vocational workshops in Seven Sisters colleges. Late that same year a *Time* article stated, "Nobody is more noisily dissatisfied these days than that symbol of stability—the fortyish housewife with teen-age children and a reasonably successful husband." For those women the suburban revolution had been accomplished, and now they found that—in an age of laborsaving devices, affluence, and social fluidity—mere homemaking was not enough.

Bewitched's premise was a riff on a couple of movies—*I Married a Witch* and *Bell, Book and Candle*—worked up by some executives at Columbia/Screen Gems. Originally intended as a vehicle for perky musical comedy star Tammy Grimes, it was adapted to the demure All-American appeal of Elizabeth Montgomery when Grimes passed on it. Montgomery was much of the reason for its success. Wholesomely pretty with a faint touch of sexuality, able to play an absurd scene with a self-conscious irony that made it believable, bright but not aggressive, she made herself appealing to boys and girls, men and women. She personified mass culture's ideal wife, in that last moment before mass culture tried to encompass the women's movement.

Montgomery played Samantha, a witch who falls in love with a New York advertising man named Darrin Stevens. She doesn't tell him until their wedding night that she can do virtually anything just by twitching her nose. When she does tell him, he's aghast. He forbids her from ever using her powers. She agrees. It isn't power she wants; it's domesticity, with Darrin as her breadwinner and boss.

She also fails to tell him that because marrying a "mortal" is frowned on among witches, they will be constantly harassed by Sam's relatives, particularly her mother, Endora, a sophisticated free spirit who uses her powers to taste all the sensual and cultural delights of the universe. Endora never understands how Samantha can prefer doing housework in the suburbs and hiding her powers from repressed old neighbor women and enduring her husband's tedious outbursts to such a glorious life. Frankly neither can any reasonable viewer.

The show's creators seemed to go out of their way to make Samantha's magical relatives far more interesting and sympathetic than her husband and his fellow mortals. Endora was played by Agnes Moorehead, with charismatic self-certainty. She got all the good wisecracks, leaving Darrin fuming impotently and demanding his wife's help in throwing the old witch out. Sam's cousin Serena, played by Montgomery herself, was full of bubbling sexuality and love of life. Her father, Maurice (Maurice Evans), was elegance personified. Her Uncle Arthur (Paul Lynde) was a likable image of, implicitly, a liberated gay man.

Darrin, played by Dick York, was a pop-eyed, nervous, intolerant goon. When another actor, Dick Sargent, took over the role, Darrin became a stiff-backed, crabby jerk. In both incarnations he ranted about "my home" and "my wife." He was owned by his job, dominated by his shallow, oily boss. In episode after episode he humbled himself to please stuffy, arrogant advertising clients. Darrin seemed to have no friends, and the neighbors were detestable. As TV historian Harry Castleman noted, "You inevitably come to the conclusion that [Samantha's] family was right—she shouldn't have married a human at all."

Samantha's domestic life was like a satire of the sterility of mainstream sitcom values. Her daughter was cute but drained of personality and initiative. Her house was militantly devoid of personality. Darrin's job—advertising—had already been an icon of parasitic, soul-deadening modern careers in pop culture for years (*The Man in the Gray Flannel Suit*, *Will Success Spoil Rock Hunter?*, Stan Freberg's *Green Christmas*). Her community (ostensibly Westport, Connecticut) gave her nothing but conformist assaults.

On the other hand, Sam's family represented all the rich diversity of sophisticated society. Endora was a self-sufficient divorcée who never regretted the dissolution of her marriage; it was strongly implied, in fact, that her life reached its fullest when she dumped her husband, a pointed message to Samantha. In one late-'60s episode she popped into the living room wearing a psychedelic muumuu and holding an enormous hookah, declaring that "the Sultan of Xanadu was getting too enthusiastic" but that she was "hooked on his hookah." The references to Coleridge's opium-inspired pleasure dome and the pipe of choice of Carroll's caterpillar made for quite an explicit reference, by sitcom standards: Endora was bold enough not only to travel the world and dally with exotic men but to explore the drug culture as well. And no negative denouement ever turned her into a cautionary figure. She, like most of the witches and warlocks, was freer and happier than Darrin could ever be.

One could not have laid a more thorough groundwork for a satire lambasting Middle America and demonstrating how a poor confused woman allowed her spirit to be suffocated by the patriarchal dictates of traditional domesticity. Indeed, Sam opted for that domesticity again and again and again, no matter what tempted her. Yet as Montgomery played her, she was so content, so hip to herself, so much smarter than everyone else on the show that every episode asked viewers to believe that she was doing the right thing. What was going on here?

There was an odd clue to the underlying dynamic of *Bewitched* in the credits of the first episode featuring Sam's identical cousin, Serena. The role is attributed to "Pandora Spocks." The Pandora's box of the American mainstream was female power. Serena was the Sam-that-might-have-been, the sexy sprite who loved every moment of her own life but brought terror and trouble to poor schmucks like Darrin. (And was Pandora Spocks a cousin to Benjamin Spock? Would her box be opened by the coming generation, the adolescents raised on the psychology of personal fulfillment?)

Sam struggled in every episode to keep that box slammed shut. She was tempted to use her powers often, usually allowed herself a little magical cheat. She wasn't resisting magic for her own happiness but for Darrin's. She helped him so often with his work and personal life that we knew he'd never be able to survive without her. She didn't need him; we knew she'd be happier in that life of power and glamour. She kept the lid on that box so that he and his boss and the neighbors could go on living their sad but safe little lives. *Bewitched* was a concession and a plea from American men to American women—or girls. "We know you'd be happier if you broke from domesticity and led the lives you secretly desire," said the men, "but we'd be lost without you. Stay in this life and take care of us poor inferior fellows . . . not for your sake but for ours." It flattered women and played on maternal guilt as effectively as any male boor trying to talk his wife out of leaving him. Sam was a sitcom savior, smiling as she bore her vacuum cleaner cross.

Bewitched was a savvy show when it started, simply by virtue of its acknowledgment of growing female power. Just a few years later shifting trends had rendered it merely quaint. As if in a trade-off, it flirted with liberal politics in the late '60s, turning out a few bland sermons about race prejudice. The changing scene was too much for it, however; its ratings plummeted in 1969.

The amazing ratings of the gimmick shows didn't hold very long in any case. From second season to third *The Beverly Hillbillies* dropped from nearly 40 percent of the audience to 25, where it held steady for a few years. The networks kept grinding them out: CBS's *Gilligan's Island*, an extremely stupid show aimed at kids, hung in for three years. Sidney Sheldon's *I Dream of Jeannie*, on NBC, got five seasons out of a kiddified male sex fantasy with a dose of *Bewitched*. *The Flying Nun* hovered for three years with the help of sappy, quasi-religious messages. Others—*My Mother the Car*, *The Second Hundred Years*, *It's About Time*—withered quickly in the late-'60s heat.

The fantasy sitcom cycle was largely a demographic product, which was hurt by the aging of the baby boomers and the shrinking of the kid audience. It was a novelty, too, that lost its appeal when new fads came along. Yet it was also an expression of a particular moment of nervousness in the national consciousness, when the American imagination was plagued by fears that popular culture didn't yet have the nerve to confront openly, when the social agreements of the late Eisenhower days were being called into question but the demons of Pandora's box had not yet hit the air.

13

Cracks in the Pot

James Aubrey fell in 1965. He had not made himself a popular man with his co-workers; his arrogant, unsentimental management style had earned him nicknames like the Smiling Cobra. Rumors flew about a perverse personal life and mob connections. Then he entered into a business deal with an actor-producer of tainted reputation named Keefe Brasselle, which put three bad and unsuccessful shows— *The Baileys of Balboa*, *The Cara Williams Show*, *The Reporter*—on the 1964 schedule. ABC, led by *Bewitched*, briefly overtook CBS's ratings lead. And then the FCC started investigating the Brasselle connection. In February 1965 CBS eased Aubrey out the door.

Aubrey's fall was a major crack in the TV coalition. The medium had lost its most forceful programmer, right when pop culture trends were shifting more drastically than ever before, when even the rules of sponsorship were changing. No one seemed able to get a handle on it all. CBS-TV had four presidents in the next four years; most new-program decisions fell to the less imaginative programming head, Mike Dann, and the network coasted for the rest of the decade. NBC and ABC, meanwhile, stumbled confusedly—and usually too cautiously—to keep up with the times.

Even Aubrey, though, might have been overwhelmed by the challenge of keeping a thumb on the American pulse in the mid-1960s; any executive dedicated to dead centerism might have been, for the mass culture that had been forged by radio and movies and consumer goods between the wars was rapidly splintering along lines of race, age, class, and politics. Lester Maddox was elected governor of Georgia with no other qualifications than his willingness to swing a pick handle at blacks who wanted to eat in his restaurant. Lyndon Johnson tried to spend the country's way back to harmony, but too many had been barred from the postwar coalition for too long. Riots burned the cities—including Watts, in the heart of the postwar promised land of suburban California—letting whites know forcibly that while the courts had been debating educational rights and pop culture had been ignoring everyone darker than Desi Arnaz, an entire generation of urban blacks had been growing up angry. Although polls showed that ten times as many blacks supported Martin Luther King, Jr., as Stokely Carmichael, it was the militants who were getting the TV time. The culture that had worked so hard at placidity and "postideological" discussion just a few years before was suddenly showing a taste for confrontation, for sloganeering, for overstatement, and for blood.

More shocking than race conflict to most Americans was the rebellion of middle-class white college students. That revered first wave of baby boomers, those pioneer children of the suburbs, those Beavers and Wallys—they were casting themselves as "slaves" of the military-industrial complex, calling the educational system a "machine," referring to "society" as a hostile other. These were the kids who'd been raised to think the world revolved around them, and now they were discovering that the world expected them to fill a functional role, raised to believe the world was wholesome and benign and now discovering the lie of the cold war and the hidden shame of social inequity. As yet the actual number of rebels was small, but they were getting TV time. All the bored restlessness of suburban afternoons was about to boil over in a tantrum of idealism.

The enormous youth culture that was developing to serve the boomers' emotional wants made a point of distancing itself from the mainstream. The Beatles' huge success in 1964 had confirmed rock music as the common coin of the generation, and the innovations they began a year later with *Revolver* and *Rubber Soul* signaled a willful rejection of the adult world; with every quirky musical experiment and choice of oblique lyrics, they announced that they didn't need to have

182

their music understood except by the initiated. With the new wave of postteenybopper musicians in 1966 and 1967—Jimi Hendrix, the Doors, Jefferson Airplane—the boom generation announced itself culturally closed to its elders. The consumer society was entering its next phase: The parents had retreated from cities, extended families, and ethnicity, making a new world both homogenized and atomized; the children, hungering for both community and private gratification, turned to divisive politics and cultural esoterica.

Blacks and young adults were the most publicized cultural separatists of the time, but not the only ones. The women's movement and nonblack ethnic movements were gathering steam. Conservatives were drawing into defensive circles. Rural whites reacted to militant progressivism with self-conscious pride; country music, long concerned with humorous or wistful slices of life, began producing class identification anthems like Loretta Lynn's "Coal Miner's Daughter." Even the older generation of hipsters—the cool-jazz, martini, and *Playboy* set—finding themselves jeered at by the new youth, became pridefully defensive. The liner notes to Frank Sinatra's 1965 album *Strangers in the Night* said it all: "If the electric guitar were disinvented tonight, a few thousand singers would be out on their amps. But not Sinatra. . . . He's been a Stranger in the Night, and you have to be long rid of baby fat to be that Stranger. . . . [That's what's] allowed him to last through The Age of Anxiety and The Age of the Atom and The Age of Acne."

Sociologists had long been denying the reality of American cultural homogeneity, and now even the managers of the consumer culture were being forced to agree. The music and movie industries gave up on producing across-the-board hits and put all their energies into targeted products; Hollywood was in the process of scrapping the Motion Picture Code in favor of the ratings system, thus conceding for the first time that some movies should be allowed to exclude mass audiences and speak just to adults. The clothing business, for the first time since the '20s, promoted a range of fashions—unisex, miniskirt, denim—that simply couldn't be sold to the middle-aged, the conservative, the rural.

No wonder, then, that images of fragmentation dominated the sitcom. Ever since *Bachelor Father* the number of widowed parents and adopted orphans had been increasing, until by the second half of the decade they constituted the TV family norm. The sitcom success of 1966 was a *Bachelor Father* variant called *Family Affair*, about a globe-trotting engineer with an elegant Manhattan apartment and a perfect English butler who adopted his orphaned nephew and two nieces. Like its inspiration, *Family Affair* was about single men adjusting to domesticity, but it was cold at heart, in a way no '50s sitcom had been. The children were saccharine little dolls who never dreamed of challenging adult authority. Conflicts revolved around sibling squabbles and Uncle Bill's frequent business-related absences. Mr. French, the gentle but emotionally aloof butler, usually restored harmony by negotiating time-sharing plans for toys, trade-offs in parental and filial obligations. Despite hugs and smiles, *Family Affair* was more a lesson in peaceful coexistence than in family unity.

CBS even scheduled the show at nine-thirty on Monday nights, after most little kids were in bed, as if conceding that families could no longer be expected to gather before the tube and learn together from video lessons. *Family Affair* was for adults, adults who wished that they could have such perfect children, such manageable homes.

Sitcoms tried to grapple with the various divergent constituencies of the changing United States, but the need to maintain dead centerism, to reinforce domestic values, made that problematic. Workingwomen were popping up, although they remained dutiful, and somewhat scatter-brained, wives. In *He & She*, he was a cartoonist, creator of "Jetman" (a nod to the *Batman* craze), and she a social worker. In *Please Don't Eat the Daisies*, based on the book by Jean Kerr, wife of drama critic Walter Kerr, a suburban housewife tried to write books and raise her rambunctious kids while Dad was off being a New York intellectual. In *Love on a Rooftop*, dealing with newlywed baby boomers, she was a college art student and he a novice architect. The critics liked these shows— predictably, since all were sweet, quietly witty, and upper middle class in orientation—but none captured a big enough TV constituency to win the ratings wars.

ABC did have a solid success with the one sitcom aimed at independent young women: 1966's *That Girl*, in which Danny Thomas's daughter Marlo played a small-town girl trying to make it as an actress in New York. *That Girl* flirted with social realities, then backed away from them. Marlo's perky character may have been trying to establish a limited sort of independence, but she was all "Daddy's girl": She saw her father frequently and never offended his old-fashioned sexual morality; she desperately guarded her purity from flirtatious show biz men; she maintained a long, virginal engagement to a young publishing executive, her first and only heavy romance.

As safe as it was, *That Girl*'s image of independent womanhood was daring by sitcom standards. Its success helped inspire some other woman-on-her-own premises, like *The Doris Day Show*, about a widowed mom, but none featured a woman of Thomas's age. Sitcoms generally closed their eyes to unmarried youths in the late '60s, unless they were in religious orders (*The Flying Nun*) or living with their widowed dads (*Gidget* and *From Rome with Love*). As fascinated as mass culture was with young people, no one in television could find a way to make them universally inoffensive. TV tried to reflect the nation's fragmentation, but in its timidity produced even blander, safer comic visions than it had in the late 1950s.

Writers and producers of imagination and wit found it more fruitful to steer completely clear of reality and look for humor in the medium itself. The "camp" fad had been stirring in other media for a couple of years, inspired mainly by British models. Watching their own empire shrink as America's expanded, the British had developed an ironic fascination with the stuff of popular culture that struck Americans as excitingly sophisticated. From the art of Richard Hamilton and others who inspired American Pop Art to the Beatles, with their whimsical schoolboy approach to rhythm and blues, the British gave American mass culture back to us as detached, impudent drollery. James Bond did the same for the rusty icons of the cold war; John Kennedy, a new kind of cocky, witty cold warrior, listed the Bond books among his favorites, and they became an American fad.

Series like *The Avengers*, *Secret Agent*, and *The Saint*, meanwhile, brought the Bond style to British television, and as they began to circulate in American syndication, they inspired a passion for tongue-in-cheek espionage. *The Man from U.N.C.L.E.* and *I Spy* delivered the material in more or less straight form; in contrast was Mel Brooks and Buck Henry's broad spy spoof *Get Smart. F Troop* took camp's intentional badness into juvenilia, *Hogan's Heroes* played with its self-aware absurdity, and *The Monkees* gave it a teenybopper context, imitating the mock-suspense format of the Beatles' second movie, *Help!* In January 1966 camp became a brief national fad, thanks to *Batman*'s devious lampoon of cornball heroism.

The best of these were among the cleverest shows of the time. *Get Smart*'s gag writing far outshone every sitcom of the late '60s, and *Batman* has never been equaled in its full exploitation of the television medium, its synthesis of color, design, music, stilted acting, and baroque dialogue into a multilayered self-commentary. But this was the nervous cleverness of embarrassment. Prime-time camp was concerned almost entirely with the ironic lambasting of pop culture figures that had been admirable not many years before. When anti-Communist fever was running high, the government agent was a hero to the right and a terror to the left. His reduction to a self-conscious embodiment of male fantasies (the Bond clones) or a buffoon (*Get Smart*) revealed how embarrassed many Americans felt at the way they'd bought into the propaganda of the cold war. The ridiculing of juvenile heroes like Batman reflected a deeper unease with the fundamental American concepts of heroism. Postwar America was not working out as planned, so the heroes who stood for public conscience in its most primitive form had to be mocked to ease the sting. Camp was the humor of queasy disillusionment.

It was also the perfect humor for a time of fragmentation. Because it depended on double messages and internal references, it had the appearance of an in joke. Only those hip enough to understand *why* Batman was ridiculous could get it; the more culturally astute, more disillusioned members of the TV audience could thereby cut themselves off from the gullible masses.

For all their clever ridicule, however, the camp comedies steered well clear of the really meaty concerns of mass culture: sex roles, the family, social relations. One group of British programs the networks didn't emulate were the BBC's hostile, divisive new sitcoms, like *Till Death Do Us Part*, in which an aging cockney and his left-wing son-in-law argued violently about social politics, with words like *kikes* and *coons* punctuating the older man's speech. One American television cum movie producer, Norman Lear, was fascinated by the honesty of *Till Death* and bought the rights to adapt it for the U.S. But when he brought his pilot, renamed *All in the Family*, to ABC in 1968, the network turned it down flatly.

❏

Beyond the tube there was no such timidity in American comedy. A wave of fierce social satire was filling clubs, theaters, and record albums: Second City, the Committee, Dick Gregory, George Carlin, the successors of Lenny Bruce and Mort Sahl. In years past TV had been quick to gobble up new comedians, but the networks had no idea what to do with these.

CBS ventured to sign the least threatening of the lot, the Smothers Brothers, in 1965 and promptly wasted them in a "my brother the ghost" fantasy sitcom. When that bombed, CBS took the plunge and gave the brothers their own comedy-variety hour, even permitting them to take on topical subjects in a gently left-biased way. As the national debate heated up, however, the brothers became less gentle. First they offended the clergy, panicking the network; then, even worse, they went head to head with Johnson's Vietnam policy. CBS tried to stifle them, they wouldn't be stifled, and the network pulled the plug. Hiring the Smotherses was CBS's one bold move of the late '60s and the one it most quickly recanted.

Producer George Schlatter finally found the formula for incorporating topical comedy into a safely nonpolitical form and sold it to NBC as *Laugh-In*. This high-speed comedy hour barraged viewers with references to drugs, sex, and politics but was ultimately pure status quo, becoming so mainstream hip that Richard Nixon appeared on it. It provided a model for commercialized daring that was to serve TV well in the years ahead, but no one could immediately find a way to duplicate it or apply it to the sitcom. The pressure to do one or both of those things was increasing, however, as the priorities of broadcasting shifted.

As 1967 became 1968, American discord reached a shrill pitch. Johnson eliminated the draft deferment for college students, scaring hordes of middle-class kids into the antiwar movement, and student-police clashes blazed through the colleges, spilled to the streets. The Vietcong counter-attacked on Tet, Johnson fell, and the Democrats plunged into chaos. The melting pot was cracking, and unmelted constituents were hissing in the fire. Segregationists formed a new party around George Wallace; Black Panther membership swelled; King was murdered; Robert Kennedy was murdered. Trusted civic guardians went out on strike: cops, teachers, mailmen, garbagemen. The closest thing America could find to a unifying force that year was Richard Nixon, but even he, with his overt plea to the "Silent Majority," showed that he saw the nation in terms of competing factions to be separately wooed, not a mass to be brought together. Establishment and citizenry seemed ready to abandon the dream of a consensual, postideological world.

Still, prime-time entertainment might have been able to ignore even all this had it not been for a shift in the philosophy of sponsorship. Network TV had become the last big bastion of universal corporate culture, but under pressure from a new school of demographics-minded advertisers, it, too, was cracking.

Market researchers knew that America's most dedicated consumers were in the bracket defined as "18–34-year-olds." They knew that affluent people spent more than poor people, that suburbanites and urbanites spent more than country folk. In the mid-'60s sponsors began commissioning demographic surveys of TV viewers to supplement the Nielsen ratings, to determine, in the parlance of the moment, whether a show reached the "blue jeans" or the "Geritols." They found some radical differences in viewing preferences: Comparing the "top ten" lists for the South and Northeast in late 1967, Nielsen found they had only one show (*Lucy*) in common; comparing the under-five-grand-a-year set with the over-tens, they found only two in common (*Griffith* and *Family Affair*); comparing young adults with over-fifties, only *Dean Martin* made both lists. And the spooky thing for the network establishments was that the lists for the poor, the southern, and the old had a lot more in common with the overall national top ten than did those of the rich young northerners whom sponsors wanted to court. It appeared that TV advertising, as it was then sold, might be a big waste of money.

Frank Stanton, president of CBS, took the lead in defending the overall ratings system (not surprisingly, since CBS had become the top network largely on the strength of the least valued members of the consumer culture). He defended it on principle: "Rating television programs is the democratic way of counting votes and giving the public what it wants." This was the voice of the ideals that had shaped American political culture in the postwar years: one man, one vote, one tract house, one Nielsen point. It had been taken for granted in James Aubrey's day, such a short time before. Suddenly it seemed untenable in the fragmented America of 1968.

CBS may have resisted, but NBC and ABC began a push for young adult viewers, and in the light of current events, the element that executives thought the "blue jeans" wanted to see on TV was "relevance." NBC premiered *Julia* in 1968, the first sitcom about blacks since *Amos 'n' Andy*. The network played it safe, essentially just casting a black woman (Diahann Carroll) in a standard widowed mom role; her world, the aerospace corporation headquarters where she worked as a nurse, was white, middle-class, pro-government. Her race provided material for some mildly antiprejudice episodes and some cute banter with her enlightened boss, but little real conflict. The network nonetheless feared protests from both white segregationists and black radicals. None came—largely because *Julia* was masterfully inoffensive, partly because Americans were wearying of racial debate—and the next year NBC followed with *The Bill Cosby Show*. The comedian played a high school coach who helped his kids and peers through contemporary problems ranging from bigotry to an attempt to quit smoking. Both it and *Julia* enjoyed solid ratings at first, but once the novelty wore off, they were revealed as just two more bland sitcoms, and they perished in 1971.

ABC was, as usual, more aggressive in pursuing the baby boomers. *That Girl* had signaled a shift from early '60s kid-vid to late '60s youth-vid. The shift was completed in 1968 with *Mod Squad*, a crime drama about three young ex-criminals ("one black, one white, one blonde") who now go undercover for the cops to help "troubled" youngsters. More shows like it shortly followed, including *The New People*, about "blue jeans" stranded on a desert island with a chance to forge a perfect world, and NBC's *Then Came Bronson*, the prosocial wanderings of a sensitive biker.

All these played with "topical" issues (drug peddlers, go-go dancers, porno movies, bigotry) and were crowded with characters urging each other to "get involved," "be where it's at," and "tell it like it is." But not one of them dared challenge conventional assumptions of right and wrong, truth and deceit. All were clearly the products of committees of executives, playing to the young but afraid to alienate the old. When Nixon asked the networks to help him with his antidrug campaign in April 1970, the producers of every one of the "relevant" series rushed a "don't experiment with drugs" episode into production. TV historians Harry Castleman and Walter Podrazik have called the shows "rude and insulting . . . deliberately oversimplified . . . revolutionary fantasy . . . based on a philosophy that merely bringing together 'nice' people with 'nice' ideas could solve everything." *Variety*'s Les Brown wrote that to young viewers, "it was clear they were being seduced into a typical series of Establishment sermons."

Somewhat more effective was ABC's *Room 222*, a sitcom-drama synthesis about idealistic young teachers in an urban high school. It had some good writers—most notably the team of James L. Brooks and Allan Burns—who fleshed out the topical subjects with engaging human stories. But it, too, posited easy solutions to anger and alienation through enlightened liberal-centrist dialogues. The creators of prime-time entertainment still stood by the conviction that communication was all society needed to be whole. Another year or two of conflict was needed to make them see communication itself as a joke.

ABC used more than "relevance" to lure younger viewers. *Love, American Style*, an anthology of sitcomlike sketches, titillated with contemporary sexual situations (while always upholding traditional mores). *Mr.*

Deeds Goes to Town brought the Capra movie up-to-date, evidently to see if a class unity fable from the depression could pull Americans together yet again (it couldn't). *The Odd Couple*, based on Neil Simon's play, adapted by a clever writer-producer named Garry Marshall, went out on a limb with the first divorced protagonists in sitcom history (although they were men with older children and liberated wives and so not much threat to domestic ideals). *The Courtship of Eddie's Father*, a bit of smart sentimentality from young actor-producer James Komack, dealt more frankly with the isolation of modern life than any other sitcom; in it a lonely little boy spent most of his time in a city apartment with a reserved Japanese maid, vainly seeking ways to get his lonely widowed father a wife.

The network's daring was limited, however. Programmers took a second look at Norman Lear's *All in the Family*, to see if they were ready for such a dark vision of domestic life, but after a Hollywood preview audience reacted negatively to the pilot, they passed again.

In general the sitcom was fading. Boisterous comedy-variety hours and topical crime and doctor shows seemed better able to speak to the times. Most of ABC's new entries performed only modestly. Apart from *Julia* and *Cosby*, NBC had only one interesting new sitcom, a Thurber-in-the-suburbs experiment called *My World and Welcome to It* that lasted only a year.

As the decade ended, however, ABC found a way to bring the "hip" approach to bear on the sitcom family. *The Brady Bunch* and *The Partridge Family* were skillfully synthesized shows featuring bland, attractive parents (with a blond female singer as mom in each case) and five or six cute kids, carefully placed in age and type to bring in maximum preteen interest. In each show the oldest boy and oldest girl were groomed as teenybopper heartthrobs and hyped in the "teen" magazines. *The Partridge Family* was about an insipid family rock band, with a bubble gum pop song in every episode. The Brady kids added rock to their repertoire after a season or two. ABC knew its demographics; both shows netted their targeted juvenile market effectively.

The Brady Bunch was particularly noteworthy for its crassness—not just in the calculated cuteness of the kids or the contrived triviality of their problems, but right down to the theme song, the graphics, the expensive vulgarity of the Brady home, and the screaming polyester modness of the clothes. This was the L.A. suburban ideal of 1969. Gone were the genteel pretensions of the Andersons and the cultured veneer of the Petries. This was the Swingin' Sixties, which the Bradys would have us believe meant we were free to indulge in all our most flamboyant trash. Like Nixon's cameo on *Laugh-In*, this was the appropriation of counterculture values for the use of the mainstream. Under the cloaks of hipness and personal freedom, American consumer culture was celebrating its own ugliest aspects.

Buoyed by shows like these, ABC was moving up on the second-place network, which, in 1969, was for once not CBS but NBC. The fading of the sitcom meant the fading of Aubrey's empire: *Laugh-In* had knocked *Gomer Pyle* out of first place in the ratings; at the end of the first half of the 1969–70 season CBS still held six of the top ten spots, but NBC held the first and third (*Bonanza*) and was comfortably ahead in the overall numbers.

Compounding the ratings problem was the fact that some of CBS's biggest hits were failing to attract advertisers. Les Brown, the TV editor for *Variety*, reported that *The Red Skelton Hour* and *The Jackie Gleason Show* were among the last to sell their commercial time that season, although the former was rated seventh and the latter was respectably in the top thirty. "Conscious now of the quality of audience—on age, income, and education levels—the media buyers of advertising agencies considered the two CBS comedians overpriced for the kinds of people they delivered," wrote Brown. (Nielsen breakdowns released in 1968 showed *Red Skelton* to be the sixth most popular show in the South, fourth among viewers with incomes under five thousand dollars, and fourth among those with only grade-school educations; he didn't crack the top ten in the Northeast, among the ten-thousand-dollar-and-over set or among the college-educated.)

This state of affairs didn't sit well with the network patriarch, William S. Paley. As Brown wrote, "The chairman had always demanded that CBS be Number One. He liked to think of the network as the Tiffany of broadcasting, commanding the highest prices because of its leadership."

The new CBS-TV president, Robert D. Wood, knew this when he addressed Paley at a programming meeting in January 1970. He directed a particularly florid—and pointed—metaphor straight at the boss's vanities: "Mr. Paley, you can sit on your front porch on a rocking chair collecting your dividends on what you've created. A parade will be coming down the street and you may watch it from your rocking chair, collecting your dividends, and it will go by you. Or you might get up from that chair and get into the parade, so that when it goes by your house you won't just be watching it, you'll be leading it. Mr. Paley, CBS is falling behind the times, and we have to get back in step."

Wood's solution was to kick the rocking chair out from under the too comfortable network, canceling rural-oriented programs even if their ratings were still solid and replacing them with youth-oriented, more topical new shows. Gleason, Skelton, and *Petticoat Junction* would disappear immediately. Ed Sullivan, Jim Nabors, *Hee Haw*, *Gunsmoke*, and a spate of sitcoms—*Mayberry R.F.D.*, *Family Affair*, *Green Acres*, *Beverly Hillbillies*—soon followed. Replacing them would be "grittier, more realistic" programming; first on the dock were three "relevant" dramas: *Storefront Lawyers*, *The Interns*, and *The Headmaster*.

Programming chief Mike Dann protested the cancellations. He'd held his job since 1963, when James Aubrey was president and CBS sat on top of the world. He'd survived four network presidents, and he expected to survive his fifth, Wood. He stuck by the one-viewer, one-vote policy upon which network programming had been founded. He believed in the mass audience, the vast numbers agreeing on a single, multipurpose entertainment that was neither offensive nor inaccessible to anyone. This was the conceptual underpinning of postwar corporate culture, but Dann was its last major spokesman in network broadcasting.

Mike Dann fought, but Paley sided with Wood. *Petticoat Junction* was gone; *The Interns* was in. Within six months Dann quit the network, to be replaced by a young Wood protégé named Fred Silverman, who quickly gained a reputation for brilliance at strategic scheduling. Within two years CBS would be back on top of the heap, not only in profits but in overall ratings. And a new kind of show—confrontational, topical, often offensive to big chunks of the viewing audience—would be the norm.

It wasn't *Storefront Lawyers* that made it happen. All three of Wood's relevant dramas sank like stones. In classic CBS fashion, it was sitcoms that won back the audience.

14

Affirming the Worst

One sitcom on the 1970–71 schedule was expected to be a hit for the new-look CBS. It was called *Arnie*. It was a slight thing, about an ethnic blue-collar worker who is suddenly made an executive in his firm. Perhaps Bob Wood and his cohorts thought that by acknowledging ethnicity and physical labor after a decade of sitcoms centering on WASP professionals, *Arnie* would appear relevant. Quite the contrary, its genial treatment of assimilation and upward mobility in America-the-land-of-opportunity seemed plucked from the early '50s. *Arnie* flopped, but the show that followed it, at nine-thirty Saturday night, won its slot in the ratings, even with such a weak lead-in. The next year it followed *The New Dick Van Dyke Show*, a tepid family comedy, and outperformed it, too. CBS seemed hesitant to acknowledge it, but the fact was that *The Mary Tyler Moore Show* was a hit.

It was mainly a product of ratings analysis. Dick Van Dyke's star appeared to be descending in the late 1960s until his CBS special *Dick Van Dyke and the Other Woman*, reuniting him with Mary Tyler Moore, brought him a ratings hit in 1969. Moore got most of the credit from programmers, and the network invited her to create her own half hour sitcom to replace *Petticoat Junction* on Saturday nights. She and her husband, Grant Tinker—former adman, NBC programmer, and Universal Studios executive—formed MTM Enterprises to create a smart and funny and timely vehicle for the former Laura Petrie.

As head writers they hired James L. Brooks and Allan Burns, from *Room 222*. In forging the life and character of MTM's Mary Richards, they sought to be less calculatedly topical. "We dealt with problems, the day-to-day stuff that ordinary people go through as opposed to big themes," said Brooks. "Our timing was very fortunate, the way the women's movement started to evolve. So not only our ideas but what was happening in society began to appear in the show. But we did not espouse women's rights, we sought to show a woman from Mary Richards' background being in a world where women's rights were being talked about."

They made Mary's background reflective of women in the age, income, and educational bracket then being wooed by networks and advertisers. She was WASP, middle-class, thirty years old. Raised in an affluent northeastern suburb, she was well educated but undertrained for life in the working world. Sophisticated in knowledge but limited in experience, she was at once hip and sheltered. After a divorce from her physician husband, she was now truly on her own for the first time. Fleeing her sterile homeland, she—like millions of real suburban children then maturing—headed for the city. (But as if to keep the show from being too retrograde, it wasn't New York she chose but medium-size, low-key, liberal Minneapolis.)

The divorcée angle was to be the biggest break with sitcom tradition. It also quickly became a bone of contention. CBS flatly forbade it. Chris Bryars, in *The Real Mary Tyler Moore Show*, reports that Mike Dann had established through research—at least to his own satisfaction—that the American public wouldn't tolerate New Yorkers, divorced people, or mustachioed men in TV comedy. (TV historian Rick Mitz suggests that this was a PR-bowdlerized version of the actual CBS injunction: "Americans don't like New Yorkers, divorced people, and Jews.") Furthermore, writes Bryars, "A CBS official claimed that if Mary were a divorcée, people would think she'd divorced Dick Van Dyke, 'and nobody divorces Dick Van Dyke.' "

Moore, however, refused to play a wife. She wanted her character to be the sole center of her fictional world, a reflection of America's increasing number of once-married, not-yet-married, and never-married women. She also didn't want to be a widow, like the bland, backward-looking characters in *Here's Lucy* and *The Doris Day Show*. So Brooks and Burns substituted a broken engagement for the divorce. As the first episode opens, Mary has just left a long-term boyfriend who has reneged on his promise to marry her, and for the first time she is contemplating a future as something other than a wife.

The CBS veto of her divorce was a blow to MTM's effort to address a hot contemporary issue, but as David Marc suggests, "network censorship unwittingly served the muse. . . . A divorced Mary Richards would have advertised the show's hipness, raising the specter of sitcom pretense. But a single Mary simply placed the character in a familiar tradition of sitcom career girls." By playing off that tradition, Mary was able to seduce and surprise her viewers, to open TV to a new social epoch with the reassuring gentleness of wholesome family comedy.

The opening title sequence of the first (and every) episode contains all the clues. Mary is shown driving along a highway, away from the sprawling suburbs. The leaving-home motif suggests the rushing-railroad title shots of *That Girl*, the most prominent working-girl comedy of the years immediately preceding, but in traveling by train, *That Girl*'s Ann Marie signaled that she was still dependent, broke, little-girlish. Mary, alone behind the wheel of her car, provides a more mature and self-contained image (it was rare enough ever to see a sitcom woman in a car; as the first image of a new series it was almost shocking). A sensitive male voice croons the folky theme song: "How will you make it on your own? This world is awfully big. . . ."

Next a montage of Mary enjoying the sights of Minneapolis: downtown shopping (an affirmation of the city's superiority to the suburbs); a park (contentment in quiet and solitude); a couple of healthy male joggers (a shy assertion of female sexuality). Then a comic moment: Mary picks up a "single-size" portion of plastic-wrapped meat in a supermarket, rolls her eyes at the price, and tosses it disgustedly into her basket. A little moment, but a big departure for sitcoms. For perhaps the first time since radio days, a soothing, "nice" sitcom (as opposed to the harsh loser comedy of *The Honeymooners*) suggests that the consumer culture is *not* infallible, that basic goods are not always abundant, that the basic business of living in modern America can be stressful. Certainly there is no repudiation of the consumer culture here, but there is a wink at the audience, a reassurance that even though this is a sponsored, network, corporate product, the creators know about Vietnam-era inflation and the low wages of women and the difficulties of being single in family-oriented

America. As James Brooks later stated, "We didn't want to say that American life was perfect, trouble-free."

The theme song then turns upbeat, excited: "Love is all around, no need to waste it. . . ." Mary is seen entering her place of work, being greeted by her co-workers. This is where the love is; this is her home. The isolation of the opening car shot has been dissolved. For the final moment we cut back outside, downtown. Mary is alone but grinning. She flings her hat into the air in sheer exuberance. The shot freezes, with the hat suspended in upward flight, never to come down. She has found happiness as an individual in the big city, she has opened herself to the world, she has discovered emotional spontaneity, and she has discarded an item of clothing associated with '50s America and nonliberated women. The theme song answers its opening question: "You're gonna make it after all."

The emotional arc of the first show—and of the entire seven-year run of the series—is condensed into that sequence. But the first show itself plays the theme out in some surprising ways. Mary rents a room from her only contact in Minneapolis, an old friend named Phyllis. Phyllis is married to a doctor, the life Mary once anticipated for herself, and thus represents a traditional American female success story. But she is nervous, pretentious, insincere, social-climbing, desperate for approval yet destined to annoy and repel everyone she meets; she's clearly unfulfilled emotionally and—it is hinted—sexually as well. Mary herself, like Laura Petrie before her, is given to a certain nervous discontent, but compared with Phyllis, she is a Buddha. Unhappy wives had been a staple of sitcoms, of course, but their image had always been counterbalanced by that of the happy wife, either the protagonist or a loving spouse. With only a single woman as counterbalance, Phyllis came off as a mockery of that holiest of sitcom institutions, the middle-class marriage.

As she begins showing Mary the room she'll be renting, Phyllis whips back the curtains . . . and is appalled by an apparition of plump, dowdy, Semitic womanhood, outside washing the windows. Phyllis calls her "that dumb awful girl who lives upstairs," but she is, in fact, the sardonic, brash, eternally frustrated Rhoda Morgenstern, who left New York because she couldn't find an apartment, ended up in Minneapolis, and now intends to take over the apartment that Phyllis is saving for Mary. With urban cheek Rhoda intimidates the too polite Mary into agreeing to switch rooms with her. But then, taking pity on this poor goyische waif, she proves she's a good girl and gives in.

Rhoda is essentially Sally Rogers from *The Dick Van Dyke Show*: single and resenting it, complaining about dates, too quick to ask men if they're married, self-disgustedly wisecracking about her age and her weight ("I don't know why I'm bothering to put this chocolate in my mouth; I should just apply it directly to my thighs"). Her position in the drama, however, is significantly different. Sally always stood in contrast with the young, smug, gorgeous perfect wife Laura. Rhoda stands in contrast with the less young, insecure, pretty but shy, mixed-up single woman Mary. Sally would never have said an ill word about Laura, but Rhoda, upon discovering Mary in a ridiculously frilly nice-girl nightgown, challenges her taste, her sexuality, even her ethnic and social background in a single line: "Who'd you get that nightie from—Tricia Nixon?" Sally was a pitiable reminder of the rightness of married life. Rhoda is a wiser, tougher, more cynical veteran of the very same social struggles Mary is now taking on.

An odd alchemy has taken place between *Van Dyke* and *Moore*, as if Laura Petrie has aged badly into Phyllis Lindstrom and Sally Rogers has matured into Rhoda Morgenstern (and asserted her ethnicity in the process). Mary herself is like a might-have-been Laura, discovering that—in this atomized modern world—Sally might have had the best shot at happiness all along.

Once Mary's place in female and sexual culture is established—with Rhoda clearly set up as her friend and confidante and Phyllis as Rhoda's ineffectual nemesis—she ventures into the male-dominated economic world. Despite her economic and educational background, at age thirty she's qualified for little but secretarial work. A TV station is advertising for a secretary, but the job has been filled by the time she gets there. Newsroom chief Lou Grant is looking for an "associate producer" of the six o'clock news, however, and asks Mary if she'd be interested. Mary is flattered and impressed, until she learns that the job pays ten dollars a week less than the secretarial post. She takes it—what else can she do?—despite her suspicion that the male world has just taken advantage of her, as usual trading phony respect for economic means.

As associate producer Mary is a combination Girl Friday and newswriter. Her closest associate, perennially rooted in a desk right by hers, is Murray Slaughter, the main writer. A sadly genial, fading, balding little man, Murray is resigned to life's little inequities. His bête noire is Ted Baxter, the moronic, pompous, narcissistic anchorman. He rips Ted with wisecracks, but Ted never catches on; he feels infinitely superior to Ted, but Ted is the only fully confident, contented member of the WJM-TV staff; Ted doesn't understand the words that Murray struggles to write for him, but Ted is the one who gets credit.

Almost immediately Mary comes to trust Murray and his sad wisdom. What Rhoda is to the world of men and marriage, Murray is to the world of career dreams and professional success. When Mary asks him why Mr. Grant hired her for this job, Murray grins. "Don't you know? You're our token woman." So the modern world continues to push both for and against the baffled Mary. She can't get a man, but maybe she's better off without one. Feminist-inspired hiring pressures get her a fine-sounding position, but the pay is worse than in traditional female handmaiden work.

With work and home established, Mary's life is ready for a couple of big twists. Her boyfriend calls; he's in town and wants to see her. Mary, almost by reflex, finds herself hoping he'll propose to her, thus taking her back to the life she planned for and out of this challenging new reality. But when someone knocks at the door, it isn't the boyfriend. It's the inebriated Lou Grant. Grant starts mumbling about how his wife is out of town . . . and Mary thinks she understands everything now. It's the same old equation: job for a struggling single woman, sex for the boss. Maybe we're in a good old-fashioned pro-marriage sitcom morality play after all; it's Rob Petrie and the bohemian art teacher all over again. Mary's boyfriend will show up, rescue her from the predatory work world, stick around as a fiancé, and we'll have *That Girl* for thirty-year-olds.

But Mary's suspicions are wrong. Lou misses his wife and wants to write a letter to her, but he's too bombed. He wants Mary to type it for him. Now the boyfriend enters. Sitcom formula calls for a wacky misunderstanding or jealousy leading to a catharsis that brings them back together. But Mary clears the situation up quickly. She talks to her boyfriend. She realizes they have nothing to offer each other anymore. She wants to stay with Lou and Rhoda and the rest of her new family-of-strangers. He leaves, sad but resigned, telling her, "Take good care of yourself." Her response closes the episode and opens the series: "I think I just did."

The sense of ongoing change and uncertainty that this episode implied became the hallmark of the series. In contrast with the stasis of Rob-Buddy-Sally and Rob-Laura-Ritchie (and every other sitcom work and family group), Mary's world would always be a bit unstable. The personnel were generally the same, but they shifted their positions in relation to one another and to Mary. Lou Grant, the crusty and manipulative boss with seemingly very little personal life, got divorced and turned to Mary for support; father and daughter became mother and son. A period of tension followed, as they considered having an affair, only to have their attempt at a date dissolve into nervous, then liberating giggles. Murray finally revealed to Mary that he had a crush on her, although he had no intention of leaving his wife, who was on good terms with Mary; this added an edge of sexual tension that was only slowly eroded by affection. Rhoda lost weight, changed her hair, and boosted her self-image, becoming a role model—and even a rival—to Mary in the romance game. Rhoda and Phyllis then left the series, ushering in some major changes in the sexual politics of Mary's world. Even Ted finally revealed the insecurities behind his pomposity, found a ditzy woman to love him, and—in an ironic comment on the sitcom genre that managed to be sitcom-heartwarming at the same time—created the only stable nuclear family on the show.

MTM was a beautifully executed series and a huge critical hit. It won more Emmys than any other show in TV history—twenty-seven—including five writing awards in seven seasons. Critics dared call it "literature" and "the most important television show for women ever." Robert Bianco of the *Pittsburgh Courier* wrote that "you really could live your life by episodes of *The Mary Tyler Moore Show*, if you selected them carefully." MTM Enterprises picked writers for their subtlety and literacy and directors (most notably Jay Sandrich) for their soft touch and sensitivity to characters. The cast was delightful and except for Moore herself owed little to the Hollywood sitcom factory: New York stage actor Ed Asner as Lou; Second City alumna Valerie Harper as Rhoda; serious movie actress Cloris Leachman as Phyllis; voice-over actor Ted Knight as Ted Baxter. Only Gavin McLeod was a veteran of bland TV, and as Murray he showed a humanity that none of his other roles had hinted at. Moore, remembering her *Van Dyke* days, insisted upon working in front of an audience, to energize everyone's performance (and she made it a point of pride as well, reminding us in a taped voice-over in every episode that "This show was filmed in front of a live audience"). *MTM* gave the critics all those little things that critics like: verbal wit, character subtlety, irony, gentleness, poignancy. It defined what has been known as quality television ever since.

It was a popular hit as well. CBS finally gave it the nine o'clock time slot in its third season, leading into MTM Enterprises' own creation *The Bob Newhart Show*, and it rose into the top ten. Typically, independent producers and writers had intuited the national consciousness far better than the networks.

Perhaps most important for networks and advertisers, *MTM* soothed the anxieties of its targeted viewers: the huge new army of single baby boomers (from 1960 to 1978—or, roughly, from the end of *Father Knows Best* to the end of *Mary Tyler Moore*—the number of under-twenty-four-year-olds living alone soared from less than a quarter of a million to over a million and a half); the increasing numbers of women choosing to remain single (nearly twice as many as a decade before) or finding themselves suddenly single (the divorce rate in 1960 was 2.2 per thousand marriages; it more than doubled by 1973 and hit 5.1 by 1979); and all those who felt the American family dissolving, the neighborhood becoming meaningless, relations between the sexes growing too complex to comprehend.

In the early 1970s the mass media made clear what psychologists and social workers had been noting for several years: that under the political hysteria of the late '60s lay a deep anxiety about the family. Generational disputes, the stresses on lower-income families caused by the slowing of the economy, the fear of a future with diminished resources, the rising divorce rate, the new sexual and living arrangements of the young, the increasing number of working women—all were tearing at the domestic ideal, turning the family into a battleground.

MTM, in fine sitcom tradition, dealt with none of this directly but offered a sweeping reassurance. It had no ideology. As Brooks pointed out, it was no feminist vehicle. Mary could never be called liberated. It engaged the scariest emotional issues of the time with a nervous uncertainty—Mary's own nervous uncertainty—and offered only the awkward affection of the characters as a salve. Mary and Rhoda valued themselves too highly to settle for just any man, yet they were desperate enough for a partner that they'd *date* just about any man. Rhoda's cynical comments played with an ironic tension between worldly wisdom and received platitudes. When a man dumps Mary because she won't go to bed with him, Rhoda tells her that the guy just wants to find out what kind of girl she is, and now that he knows, he'll call her. "Do you think so?" asks Mary. "No," says Rhoda, "but my mother does."

Mary accepted her Girl Friday position and her meager pay, called her boss Mr. Grant even though he and everyone else told her to call him Lou, allowed his masculine energy and greater life experience to overawe her. Yet she was the figure of strength when he crumbled, she gradually won his respect as a producer, and in the end it was her affection and emotional moderation that held the workplace together.

MTM spoke not to the New Woman, not to the self-conscious feminist, but to the woman in between—the nice girl, groomed to be June Cleaver or Samantha Stevens and then suddenly required to be an independent adult. (Although it was very popular in its first run, it is in rerun that *MTM* has taken on "cult" status and earned a passionate following among bright but baffled young urbanites; late-night *MTM* viewings by pairs or groups of single women became an East Coast phenomenon in the '80s. It is to the younger baby boom women, who came of age after women's liberation had lost its idealistic heat and the "sexual revolution" of the '60s had become the stressful reality of the '70s, that Mary speaks most poignantly.)

MTM challenged very little in American culture. Its emphasis on quiet tolerance placed it within a safe liberal-centrist position; it allowed itself some modest anticorporate humor (as in the final episode of the series, when a large company buys the station and fires everyone—except the imbecilic Ted). Ultimately, though, it taught that the modern commercial world can save us. When the family is shattered and sexual love lets us down and our individual resources are not enough, there will always be the family of the workplace to carry us through.

From the first episode it was clear that Mary's office mates would function as a sort of secondary family. (After Rhoda and Phyllis were spun off into their own series, and Mary moved into a stressful new phase of female relationships, they would be her *only* family, and Lou and Murray would become the centers of her emotional life.) Mary's last words of the last episode finally made the point explicit: "I thought about something last night. What is a family? And I think I know. A family is people who make you feel less alone and really loved. Thank you for being my family."

What a family apparently is not, however, is permanent. Mary gives this speech as she and her friends are about to leave the newsroom from which they are forever barred by an arbitrary business decision, presumably to go their separate ways and try to forge new work families (indeed, MTM produced a follow-up series, *Lou Grant*, in which Mary's father figure worked on a newspaper in Los Angeles and had nothing but a nostalgic connection to his old gang). Such a fate could not have befallen any biological sitcom family, and past sitcom "work families," like Bilko's army, were never shown to be so emotionally dependent on one another.

MTM's message was ultimately one of bleak and incomplete consolation, but it may have been the only consolation that its audience could believe. Even in a world devoted entirely to commerce, even when we are reduced purely to economic units, it whispered, we need never be completely alone. Corporate culture may take away, but it will also—at least temporarily—provide.

15

Enduring the Worst

In 1971 American sitcoms were finally able to go head to head with family anxieties, but they managed it only because of the British. Popular culture in Britain had long shown a greater tolerance for cynicism and human misery than in the United States. Having suffered longer and more severely through the Industrial Revolution than Americans, Britons were far more skeptical about progress and technological culture even before World War II. While the U.S. came out of the war cocky and rich and dreaming of a postwar consumer paradise, the battered, financially depleted U.K. hung its hopes on Labour party socialization. When that turned into a fiasco of depression, bureaucracy, and continuing class conflict, British movies and television took a swing toward bleak social comment and dark satire. Where American "problem dramas" showed the instruments of the corporate-therapeutic world solving individual troubles, their British equivalents left their protagonists trapped by poverty and social immobility.

Till Death Do Us Part wasn't the only tough sitcom made possible by Britain's nonsponsored television; among others was *Steptoe and Son*, about two generations of junk dealers, bound by blood, futility, and class limitations. The strength of these shows lay not in neat resolutions, as in American comedies, but in eternally, comically unresolved conflicts.

By the time Norman Lear bought the American rights for *Till Death*, he had spent years writing and producing TV variety shows. In the early 1960s he'd teamed up with another TV producer, Bud Yorkin, to make movies under the name Tandem Productions. Their specialty was saucy comedy that took advantage of Hollywood's loosening censorship restrictions, marked by slick, titillating wit and a safe dose of social comment: *Come Blow Your Horn*, *Divorce American Style*, *The Night They Raided Minsky's*. Lear was interested in reentering television, but only if he could shatter the networks' blandness and fear of controversy; *All in the Family* was the hammer he wanted to use.

Lear turned *Death*'s xenophobic old Brit into Archie Bunker, a warehouse worker in Queens, a blue-collar union man but also an unreconstructed racist and social conservative. The Labour-leftist son-in-law became Mike Stivic, Polish-American sociology grad student and knee-jerk liberal. Tying them together in running verbal combat was Archie's cute, dopey daughter, Gloria Stivic, who loved her father but swallowed her husband's worldview whole. Archie's wife, Edith, was the ineffectual conciliator of the group: timid, tolerant, politically naive, a sweet-tempered Christian, a Pollyanna, a "dingbat" in Archie's parlance.

When ABC ordered a pilot, Lear had a chance to assemble a superb cast. His first choice for Archie had been Mickey Rooney, but Rooney told him, "If you go on the air with that, they're going to kill you dead in the streets." Lear turned to Carroll O'Connor, a lesser-known Broadway and film actor, who was able to bring Archie to life in all his anger and vulnerability and life weariness, to make him both ridiculous and lovable. Another stage veteran, Jean Stapleton, brought the same combination of laughability and cuteness to the character of Edith. Lear cast Carl Reiner's son, Rob, as the mooching, self-important Mike and young stage actress Sally Struthers as the naive, emotionally charged Gloria. The chemistry among them—shouting, weeping, insulting, hugging, dithering, wise-assing—was explosive.

After ABC's second rejection the pilot caught the eye of Bob Wood. CBS already had a show in development called *Man in the Middle*, a safer variation of *Till Death Do Us Part* (Van Johnson as a neutral, likable middle-class dad, with a wacky daughter, wife, and mother-in-law representing political extremes). Wood—showing an uncommon nerve for a network executive—preferred the gutsier *All in the Family*, which declined to give viewers a safe middleman. He had Lear's pilot tested in New York in March 1970. This time the test audience loved it.

Variety's Les Brown speculated that the difference between the ABC and CBS tests might have been due to the different outlooks of New Yorkers and Angelenos but even more likely to the six months that had passed between tests. As the Nixon administration wore on and the Vietnam War showed no signs of ending, as ethnic movements grew more militant, as Spiro Agnew began sounding off, as feminism hit mainstream America, the national debate kept getting louder. "ABC tested the pilot," Brown said, "when there was still some disbelief in the national rift; CBS when the national anxiety over it became serious."

Wood became Lear's biggest backer. (And an inadvertent helper in other ways, too; Lear so loved Wood's habitual use of mangled metaphors and clichés that he imitated them for Archie's speech pattern. Lines like "It smells like a house of ill refute" became some of Archie's most endearing moments.) The show was slated for a January 1971 premiere. But the network was nervous. The censor pressured Lear into withdrawing a sly sexual reference and the word *Goddam* from the first script. A disclaimer was scrolled across the screen before the first episode, assuring viewers that its intention was to "throw a humorous spotlight on our frailties, prejudices and concerns." Executives feared an explosion from the watchdogs of public morals and did what they could to soften the blow.

The first episode opened with generational and religious conflicts on full display: Archie and Edith go to church; Mike and Gloria stay home (with an implication that they do so in order to have sex). A scatological TV taboo is defied when living-room arguments are disrupted by the loudly flushing upstairs toilet. Archie speaks the forbidden word *terlet* on prime-time TV. Race quickly enters the picture as Archie taunts Mike: "You are the laziest white boy I ever met." Mike: "Meaning that the blacks are even lazier." Archie: "Wait a second, wise guy . . . I never said that at all. Of course, their systems are geared a little slower than ours, that's all." Archie then gets into a conflict with black neighbor Lionel Jefferson, in which Lionel amusedly—and affectionately—makes a fool of Archie. Ultimately Lionel, with that condescending grin reserved for harmless idiots, tells Archie that they can still be friends, "in spite of racial differences."

Later episodes continued to air racial, sexual, and religious laundry in the nation's living rooms. Archie regularly paraded his archaic, provincial attitudes, filling the airwaves with words formerly taboo: *hebe, mick, spic, fag, polack, jungle bunny*. He regularly defended himself in transparent stupidity: "Look, Archie Bunker ain't no bigot. I'm the first to say that it ain't your fault you're colored." Just as regularly he got his comeuppance from the world or his smug son-in-law.

Network, producers, and advertisers braced themselves for protests from the Bible Belt, from the self-appointed guardians of good taste, from conservatives offended at being ridiculed. But the only serious protests came instead from old-line liberals. Laura Z. Hobson, author of the anti–anti-Semitic *Gentleman's Agreement*, took the show to task in *The New York Times* for making racism acceptable by placing it within an affectionately humorous context. She thought the scripts were particularly dishonest in playing at racial epithets without going all the way: *Hebe* and *jungle bunny* were quaint, almost funny; *kike* and *nigger* never passed Archie's lips. (Network censorship was partly responsible for the absence of such words, but even had standards been looser, it's hard to imagine Lear and his fellow writers putting such vicious epithets into the mouth of their ostensibly harmless little antihero.)

A snowstorm of letters agreed with Hobson. The debate spread through the country's newspapers and magazines, the biggest debate ever engendered by a piece of TV entertainment: Did *All in the Family* ridicule racist behavior or make it seem permissible? Lear presented himself as a misunderstood liberal, maintaining that Archie was purely a negative example, and the plot structure of the episodes seemed to bear him out, at least to many viewers' satisfaction. Most liberal critics praised the show as antiracist propaganda. Schoolteachers across the country assigned their students to watch it and requested *All in the Family* study guides from CBS. The TV professionals who voted for the Emmy awards—who in those years were very supportive of liberal-centrist messages—endorsed it enthusiastically, giving it nearly every comedy award not won by *Mary Tyler Moore* in the early '70s.

There was just one problem with this liberal morality play scenario: Archie was simply too damned lovable. He was ignorant but never mean-spirited. All he wanted was to sit in his easy chair in front of the TV, pay his bills and take care of his wife and family, enjoy his cigars and cups of coffee. When, after each new intrusion and humiliation by the outside world, he glowered at us with weary chagrin, our hearts inevitably went out to him. He was the focus of viewer empathy and affection.

Second only to Archie in emotional appeal was Edith, so well intentioned but so befuddled. And Edith loved Archie. He might not respect her mind, he might tell her to "stifle" herself, he might demand to be served, but he dragged himself to work every day to support her, and he once passed up a flirtatious divorcée to remain faithful to her. Gloria was nearly as likable as Edith, and she, too, loved Archie. The show's most touching moments came when she bridged the gap of generations and politics and hugged her daddy.

Archie's only constant opponent was Mike, and Mike was the least likable of the four. He did have some good lines and some fine ideals, but he also took himself too seriously, he couldn't drop his political position to establish a personal link with Archie, and he was a parasite. He and Gloria lived rent-free with the Bunkers while he worked his way through grad school, a situation that Archie grudgingly endured out of paternal love but that Mike seemed to take as his due. He hogged Archie's food, took over his living room, and provoked him needlessly into argument.

He was also a hypocrite. When Archie cut down people who moved to communes, Mike got up on his high horse: "It's a question of each man doing his own thing. Your thing is grubbing for a living in this polluted, crime-ridden city." Archie responded, "And your thing is sponging off my thing." As Archie became a better-rounded, more understandable character, Mike's immutable hostility made of him an insensitive ingrate. Once he complained to Edith that Archie wouldn't stop riding him, and Edith flashed an uncharacteristic indignation: "Do you wanna know why Archie yells at you? Archie yells at you because Archie is jealous of you. You're going to college. Archie had to quit school to support his family. He ain't never going to be any more than he is right now. Now you think that over."

Despite all the conscious plot strategies to create a liberal impression, the emotional reality of the show was clear: Archie Bunker was the hero of *All in the Family*.

Even the look and feel of the show reflected Archie's nature. The compressed verticality of the set, the bright videotaped look, the restriction of action to a single artificial-looking living room with adjoining kitchen—all suggested the live comedy shows of the '50s. Lear did, in fact, use a live audience and made sure his actors played to it; *MTM* may have reintroduced the live audience to the sitcom, but it was *All in the Family* that buried the laugh track forever. The show's pace, volume, and humor—funky, abrasive, and confrontational—was straight out of *The Honeymooners* and *Bilko*. As with Ralph Kramden, the audience was invited to cheer at Archie's weekly humiliation. Even the acting was a little too broad, too theatrical for the modern TV norm. Lear stripped away a decade-plus of quiet, spacious, multilocaled, upper-middle-class gloss to place his Archie in the precorporate world of primitive sitcoms. In a '60s TV aesthetic Archie would have been a grotesquerie. In *All in the Family* he made sense (while, in Archie's world, Rob Petrie and Samantha Stevens would have been pale nonentities).

There seemed to be a war going on between Lear's plots and his characters or perhaps between his conscious and unconscious. Lear, as David Marc makes clear, based Archie largely on his own father; just as Carl Reiner had transformed a bridge-and-tunnel Jew into the white-collar WASP Rob Petrie, so, Marc notes, Lear transformed a depression era working-class Jew into a recession era working-class WASP. And just as Reiner was able to bring both amused distance and a deep, poignant connection to the character of Rob, so Lear did the same with Archie. In that context Mike Stivic's arguments with Archie might have reflected the long-ago arguments of young, assimilating, cosmopolitan Norman Lear with his father. But the undercurrent instilled by the older, wiser, more sentimental Norman was one of forgiveness of his father's shortcomings, sympathy with the forces that shaped him, and disgusted embarrassment at the insensitivity of youth.

All in the Family contained a deep strain of sentimentality—not too obvious in the earliest shows but more and more dominant as the Bunker household was repeatedly split and then glued back together by Edith and Gloria—that set it sharply apart from its British inspiration. In part this reflected the compulsion of American popular culture always to soften and sweeten; in part, too, it reflected the imperative of commercial TV that the audience always be sent away associating the sponsor's products with warmth and joy. But that sentimentality also supported the strongest message that Archie brought mass America: that the world is insane and destructive but that somehow, with the support of our families, we will endure.

Lear once said that he had "had a strong conviction for some time that you can discuss national issues and deliver a large audience if it's done just right. . . . I want to do SALT and nuclear energy and right-to-life and other issues that trouble people. . . . People will watch. And they will learn." Lear did indeed parade a lot of "national issues" through the Bunker living room: street crime, Jewish and anti-Jewish violence, mixed marriage, Watergate. He put even more sexual issues on parade, that being the easiest way of breaking TV taboos, getting instant press coverage, and drawing a huge, curious audience: Archie is impotent, Mike gets a vasectomy, Edith goes through menopause, Gloria has a miscarriage, someone they know turns out to be lesbian, Edith befriends a drag queen, Archie nearly cheats on Edith, Edith is nearly raped, and on and on. But for all this parading, very little of political substance was really said.

In one episode Archie endures a personal nightmare: He's trapped in an elevator with a bunch of "ethnic types." Most vocal among them is an extremely articulate and confident black man. The subject of military service comes up, and Archie—rather implausibly—assumes that the black must have been on "latrine duty" during the war. The black man reveals that he was an intelligence officer, Archie looks chagrined, and the studio audience laughs in appreciation of Archie's embarrassment. Archie is effectively humbled, however, and by episode's end he respects the black man and the black man lets him off the social hook with a noble courtesy.

This interchange has the look of being about racism, but what does it say? Only that Archie is so naive in his stereotyping that he can't conceive of intelligent, responsible black people. The fact that nearly all blacks were given lousy duty in the military in World War II—and in 1971, for that matter—is not addressed. Nor is the possibility that preconceptions like Archie's might be preventing other blacks from rising above the bottom of the social totem pole; Archie's folly is shown to be harmful only to Archie himself. Nor is the likelihood that such preconceptions might be so deep that an Archie Bunker couldn't respect a successful black man even after learning of his accomplishments. Archie's idiocy and social incompetence are the only issues at stake, and those issues really aren't national ones; they're personal and at most familial.

In this way *All in the Family* fit the patterns of the early ethnic sitcoms. Archie was an archaic figure, lovable but unprepared for the brave new world, being trained by those more assimilated than he. Lear, however, broke from *Amos 'n' Andy* and *The Goldbergs* in an important respect: The brave new world into which Archie was being forced was not an altogether happy one. Archie, therefore, never internalized its lessons. He merely learned to keep his mouth shut, to endure. And his viewers loved him for it.

The world of "issues" that Archie had to confront wasn't so much the world of new family realities as the world of TV news. For a few years the news had been blasting the American living room with hyped-up, decontextualized snippets of horror: dryly reported body counts; burning cities;

well-heeled kids bloodied by cops; angry young black men with machine guns; naked young people painting their bodies under the influence of some futuristic-sounding chemical compound. The direct impact of these social realities on actual families was usually pretty slight, but the impact of the images on the national imagination was huge. For older viewers, it was enough to make the entire course of American life from depression through war through Age of Prosperity seem utterly meaningless.

TV dramas had started incorporating the news images into issue-of-the-week dramas like *Marcus Welby, M.D.* Lear had now done the same with the sitcom. But where *Welby* and its ilk tried to lend a sense of seriousness to their "issues" and propped up cardboard cutouts of wisdom and responsibility to deal with them, Lear allowed those mass media nightmares to remain just as insane as they must have seemed to Archie Bunker, and he left his hero a confused, inarticulate victim of it all.

This tendency of Lear's came clearest in the episode in which Edith falls ill and her cousin Maude—played brilliantly by the big, deep-voiced, forceful Beatrice Arthur—comes to take care of her. Feminist, liberal, thrice-divorced, assertive, and combative, Maude is Archie's nemesis and Edith's opposite. She seems to represent everything that mass media feminists want modern women to be. She is, as she herself suggests, what Edith could blossom into if she were free of Archie's tyranny. But she's also ridiculous. And she's miserable. Behind every one of her insults lies a bitter, pressing dissatisfaction with life (later, when she was spun off into her own sitcom, she would say with painful frustration, "I just want everything"). Edith's occasional discontent and emotional emptiness can, at least, be dispelled by the love of her family and a few simple joys; even Maude's abrasive presence cheers her. Maude apparently doesn't even have that capacity.

Archie is helpless to get Maude out of his house. She will be dug in there as long as she believes Edith needs her. At the end of a full episode of insults, wisecracks, and sociosexual clichés, she glowers at Archie while speaking to Edith and intones, "Don't worry, dear. Maudie's here." All Archie can do is grimace in chagrin and turn to the cheering studio audience for compassion. It is a defining moment for *All in the Family*: funny, tense, pathetic, ridiculous, topical, endearing. Its implications are profoundly pessimistic about the course of the greater world. Yet it somehow reassures us of our ability to survive the madness.

Like so many mass audience successes—*The Beverly Hillbillies*, radio's *Amos 'n' Andy*—*All in the Family* could be viewed on different levels. Liberals, intellectuals, the upper middle class, the "New Youth" could see their beliefs vindicated, if they wished. At the same time old white conservatives found a new hero and felt that the world had acknowledged them.

Perhaps more important, Archie spoke to the anxieties of those confused masses in between. When he spoke of "jungle bunnies," he released a little internal pressure for millions of Americans who felt socially unacceptable hostilities bubbling within themselves. When he subsequently got his comeuppance, he vicariously soothed the guilt of those same millions. Archie was a sacrificial lamb for an angry, frightened, would-be progressive America.

There was such an electric tension to the first couple of years of *All in the Family* that it is difficult to believe this duality was calculated. It seemed to spring, rather, from a duality within Norman Lear himself, a common split within sensitive middle-aged progressives in those challenging times: He was an intellectual liberal but an emotional conservative. Whatever he may have *thought* about social revolution, he seemed to yearn for continuity and family.

Ultimately it is the emotional content, not the intellectual, that bonds an audience with a TV show. City folk may have wearied of the humorous conceits of *Beverly Hillbillies*, but country folk stayed true to the befuddled Clampetts. Liberals welcomed the overt messages of *All in the Family* at first, but it was the Archie Bunkers of America who stayed with the character once the novelty had worn off.

CBS's new programming chief, Fred Silverman, must have intuited that. The network had originally dropped it into a dead time slot— Tuesday at nine-thirty, up against ABC's top-rated *Movie of the Week*— perhaps to minimize the amount of trouble it could cause. It came in at fifty-eighth in the ratings and was considered for cancellation, but the building media storm encouraged Wood to give it a push with the start of its first full season. Silverman moved it to eight on Saturday. This was not a viewing time associated with the "blue jeans"; it was little kid and old folks time, with a good chunk of the tired middle-aged (for years it had been home to *The Jackie Gleason Show*). That put Archie squarely in the face of the mass TV audience, and that audience made him a tremendous hit. *All in the Family* topped the Nielsens that season with a 34 rating, solidly above the 29.6 that had made *Marcus Welby* the top-rated show of the previous year. Ratings slipped a little thereafter, but for five straight years Archie sat on top of the list.

The degree to which the Bunkers touched their audience was revealed by the products that sprang up in their name. A tongue-in-cheek but affectionate book called *The Wit and Wisdom of Archie Bunker*. A more serious collection of Edith's little homilies, compiled by a Christian publisher. A record of O'Connor and Stapleton singing the show's theme, which asserted that in the good old days we "didn't need no welfare state, everybody pulled his weight. . . . Mister, we could use a man like Herbert Hoover again." T-shirts, mugs, and stickers advocating "Archie Bunker for President." They continued to sell long after teachers stopped asking for study guides.

Advertisers knew what was happening. In the beginning *All in the Family* pulled a broad assortment of commercials, including some blue jean–targeted spots. For the most hyped, and therefore most expensive, episode of the 1974–75 season (Gloria's announcement of her pregnancy), the sponsors were Geritol and Preparation H.

The success of *All in the Family* guaranteed a flood of more shows to come: more shows breaking taboos, playing with topical issues, pitting family member loudly against family member, featuring political misfits and working-class louts. Along with *Mary Tyler Moore*, it taught TV entertainment how to grapple humorously—and profitably—with the anxieties of the time; along with *MTM* it unleashed waves of sappiness, hostility, preachiness, and vulgarity that have been battering the prime-time airwaves for more than twenty years; along with *MTM*, in short, it laid the foundation for nearly every sitcom since.

Yet the nature of its success also hinted at a tendency that became increasingly obvious during the '70s: Sitcoms, no matter how conceived, have a hard time reaching the prime advertising market. Some sitcom producers would try to change that tendency, with varying results. Most would flow with it, gunning for the less affluent, the less educated, the suburban, the old, and the very young. The sitcoms that followed *All in the Family* put steadily less emphasis on political dialogue and generational dynamics and steadily more on sex, shock value, sentimentality, and lovable buffoons.

After a few years *All in the Family* itself fell prey to its own sentimentality and repetition. But in its moment of gutsy, self-contradictory glory it had changed American mass culture. It was the first postcorporate sitcom. It dared state that the culture of assimilation and consensus wasn't working, that communication—that most sacred process in the creation of the postwar, postideological commercial utopia—did not dissolve our differences. In the Bunker household communication didn't create Pat Weaver's "cybernetic civilization." It just created a lot of yelling.

Yet as pessimistic as it was about the systems of the modern world, it was optimistic about the basic natures of people and families. It asked viewers to believe an almost Kierkegaardian absurdity about the family. Without offering any dramatic, systemic demonstration of the family's ability to survive our times, it showed the Bunkers holding together, episode after episode, by foolish love alone.

The Mary Tyler Moore Show suggested that when the family is gone, the commercial world can replace it. *All in the Family* countered that the greater world is insane, but the family will abide. One was tentatively progressive; one, embarrassedly conservative. But both turned their backs on the promises of postwar optimism. Both gave up on the ideal of a mass culture, a fully integrated society. They were the twin, small comforts of the American TV audience in a time of deep anxiety. They were just dark enough, just sad enough, to ring true.

16

Take Your Flies with You

*M**ary Tyler Moore* and *All in the Family* returned to sit-comland constituents who had been missing for years: grown-up single women, Jews, bickering families, the working classes. The last might have been the biggest breakthrough. According to Lear's partner, Bud Yorkin, "For years TV networks and ad agencies said, 'We don't want to show anybody poor,' the theory being that people will be depressed if they see anyone lower down the economic ladder than themselves." The whole point of sponsored TV, after all, is to make viewers feel that consumer goods are within their grasp and will make them happy, but the Bunkers scarcely did that, and with the door thrown open to them, the nonwhite working class could not be far behind.

Early reaction to *All in the Family* convinced NBC that Lear and Yorkin were hot. When Lear reworked the British *Steptoe and Son* into *Sanford and Son*, about a widowed black junkyard owner, the network snapped it up and shoved it onto the schedule as a mid-season replacement in January 1972. At the end of the previous season NBC had canceled *Julia*, the integrated sitcom that had seemed so daring in 1968; *Sanford* was not so much a replacement for it as a repudiation.

There were no clean, modern settings for Fred Sanford, no kindly, liberal white bosses. Fred lived in a cluttered, shabby, funky junkyard in Watts. The only regular authority figures were the cops who dropped by to check into neighborhood crimes and make sure Fred wasn't fencing stolen goods. Fred's world wasn't integrated; his peers were lazy, loudmouthed, overweight black ne'er-do-wells with names like Bubba, Rollo, and Skillet. The only prominent nonblack was Julio, the Puerto Rican neighbor who kept a goat in his yard. Fred felt no politically correct solidarity with his fellow oppressed; when his son, Lamont, lent Julio their pickup, Fred yelled, "Now you gone got Puerto Rican all over our truck!"

Fred was a black Archie Bunker: racist, provincial, ignorant, trapped in his economic and cultural stratum and afraid to move out of it. Even more than Archie, though, he tried to hold his limited world together. Archie seemed to understand that Gloria should be allowed to marry a grad student and move out of the working class, even if he resented Mike's mooching, but Fred used every trick in the book (browbeating, insulting, faking heart attacks) to force the restless Lamont to stay in the junk business. "If it wasn't for you holding me back," Lamont said, "I could be in an office." "Yeah, the welfare office," snapped Fred. Lamont complained that Fred had forced him to quit high school; Fred called him a dropout and a dummy. Lamont asserted that he wanted a job "where I can use my head as well as my hands." "That's easy," said Fred. "They'll put a cap on your head and a broom in your hands."

Fred and Lamont waged an endless, screaming, guilt-laden debate between separatism and integrationism. It was a debate with few intellectual underpinnings, however. Fred's separatism was born of a simple, deep suspicion of the white world, a conviction that if Lamont ever tried to raise his head above the color line, the whites would knock him down. His black-supported independent business, however modest, was his security against that world. Lamont's integrationism was driven by desire for the comfort and prestige of middle-class affluence and by a rather naive belief that success was just one clever idea away.

Fred and Lamont also shared the most abusive family dynamic in sitcom history. Fred constantly hurled the word *dummy* at Lamont; it was a spin on Archie Bunker's *meathead* epithet, but *meathead* was a goofy word with little bite, and Archie reserved it for his son-in-law. Fred systematically undermined his own son's self-esteem and had presumably been doing so all of Lamont's life. No wonder Lamont was unable to break away from him, unable to sustain a relationship with a girl, unable to make any of his success schemes work.

Like the Bunkers, the Sanfords were always together at the end of each show. But few episodes ended with Lamont affirming his love for Fred, as Gloria and Edith often did for Archie. Usually it was Lamont who ended up trapped and chagrined, as Fred threw himself into another histrionic "heart attack." Fred was an Archie-like character, but in terms of dramatic structure, Lamont was the Archie of this show, the long-suffering victim of unbeatable social forces. In the case of *Sanford*, those forces weren't modernity but archaism. Fred represented all the cultural and racial baggage that held Lamont back. This was the same conflict as the ethnic sitcoms of the '40s and early '50s, except back then archaism always yielded to modernity. Fred Sanford didn't yield to anything.

Sanford and Son was a huge ratings hit, ranking second or third in each of its first three years. Much of the reason was simply that it was funny. Fred was played by Redd Foxx, a vulgar and vital comedian who had cut forty-nine raunchy comedy albums for a largely black audience and made a black-targeted comedy movie called *Cotton Comes to Harlem*. The gags poured out by Lear's writers were tight, caustic, and racially edged (a white man thinks Fred has been hurt and asks if he wants to go to the hospital. "I can't waste three days," says Fred. "It only takes a few minutes," says the honky. "It only takes you a few minutes. It takes us three days in the waiting room"). Foxx delivered them loud and hard and well.

Much of its success, though, must also have been due to its sociological bluntness: *Sanford* acknowledged that there are people locked out of the American consensus, living off its scraps (specifically, in this case, by reselling its goods as junk), and defensively resisting all efforts to pull them in, even sabotaging one another when they try to climb over the wall. Millions of Americans could see their own plight, fears, and despair in that; millions could see themselves in Lamont, denied access to the affluent society, not by the social mainstream itself but by their own class and ethnic burdens, their own personal Freds.

And there was another element feeding into the show's success, one that alarmed black commentators. Fred was a stereotype of the petit bourgeois black, a throwback to Amos and Andy and the Fresh Air Taxi Company of the radio days. His ugly, prissy, appearance-obsessed sister-in-law, Esther, was a redux of Kingfish's wife, Sapphire. And Fred's laughin', jivin', drinkin', gamblin', schemin' cronies were the Kingfish times three. Fred and Lamont, wrote one black critic, were "conceived by white minds and based upon a white value system." They were "not black men capable of achieving—or even understanding—liberation. They are merely two more American child-men."

The producers responded by hiring black writers, but the tone didn't change. Foxx responded defensively that "the success is what matters, not the color," that doing a black-cast show with a broad appeal was a step forward in itself, an echo of the arguments black entertainers had used in support of *Amos 'n' Andy*. He resorted to token gestures, like changing a "sapphire" ring in one script to a "ruby" to avoid evoking the name of the *Amos 'n' Andy* character. Black viewers defended the show in letters to newspapers and the network, but *Sanford* never enjoyed the broad and articulate defense that *Amos* had, twenty years before.

At the same time the criticism had almost no effect. No boycotts were organized; no advertisers quaked in fear. By the early 1970s, after all, American racial debates were a nightmare. Moderate civil rights leadership had been swept away after the assassination of King. Bloody prison riots and a murderous escape from a California courthouse were being presented by many radicals as the next legitimate step in the black revolution. Whites fled the cities faster than ever as crime rates soared. Nixon had won the presidency by calling out to the silent (white) majority; in 1972 he won a landslide reelection after the Democratic Convention broke down into a battle of special-interest groups, many of them ethnic and radical. Young black men haunted the nightmares of middle-class whites. When a black gang called the Death Angels started to shoot whites at random and the mainly black Symbionese Liberation Army kidnapped white heiress Patty Hearst, too many whites imagined those nightmares coming true. Busing and affirmative action seemed to do nothing but aggravate the conflicts.

By the time *Sanford and Son* premiered, all sides of the racial conflict were becoming exhausted by the leaderless struggle. It was easier for blacks and whites just to accept the impermeability of the racial membrane for a while. Negrophobic whites could laugh at the harmless Fred. Frustrated blacks (and browns and many poor whites) could enjoy a sad, sympathetic chuckle over Lamont. No one seemed to want to fight over it. NBC ran with its hit, sponsors fought for spots, and only liberal producers and black actors felt the need to defend what they were doing.

The relatively unchallenged success of *All in the Family* and *Sanford and Son* shattered the timidity of advertisers and network programmers. By late 1973 it seemed that anything went on prime time; any loud, insult-filled, topical show—especially by Norman Lear—seemed worth a shot.

When Lear proposed a spin-off featuring Florida, the black maid from *Maude*, as a mid-season replacement, the network jumped on it. The show, *Good Times*, was a revelation of the dangers inherent in the Lear approach to television.

At the start *Good Times* was intended to portray a believable and admirable black family in a ghetto housing project, struggling to get by but always sticking together out of love and pride. The mother, Florida (played by Esther Rolle), had won over black and white viewers alike as a proud, no-nonsense maid dealing caustically with Maude's liberal conde-scension (Maude wanted Florida to enter through the front door; Florida insisted on using the back because it was closer to the garage). As a housewife with three kids she would be the good-natured, earthy, emo-tional heart of the family. Her husband, James (John Amos), was a hardworking traditionalist, a bit of a disciplinarian who had to be occa-sionally softened by his wife. The teenage daughter, Thelma, was an average kid, concerned with boys and her appearance, a bad house-keeper trying to learn. The younger son, Michael, was serious, studious, political, proudly black.

And then there was the older son, J.J. He was intended to be the screw-up, the one who thinks he can get rich by hustling and jiving, who has to be taught the importance of education and work and family in most episodes. The trouble was, J.J. was played by a young stand-up comedian named Jimmie Walker, part of a new wave of depoliticized ethnic humor. During the debates of the '50s and '60s a polite chill had frozen public humor; only satirists like Dick Gregory could get away with joking about race. In the exhaustion of the early '70s white and nonwhite audiences alike found themselves responding to young comics who made fun of their own ethnic traits.

Walker was a skinny kid with a huge, toothy grin, rubbery lips, and big, rolling eyes. He played off his blackness with self-loathing glee, tossing out jokes about watermelon eating and "the ghet-to" that were guaranteed to provoke shocked, nervous—and occasionally liberating—laughter. He had an electric effect on kids and teenagers, the segment of the public that created media crazes, often made early-evening TV-viewing deci-sions for the family, and made the most noise in studio audiences. He had a catchphrase, hollered with a huge flash of teeth: "Dyn-O-Mite!" Every time he yelled it, the studio audience exploded into whoops and cheers.

Blending commerce and art is always dangerous—more to the latter than the former—but never more so than on television, where the pressure to deliver a huge audience by any means is instant and intense. Ironically the use of a live audience—of which Tandem and MTM were so proud—only compounded the problem, as writers and actors played for loud crowd response. J.J. was clearly the show's laugh getter, and Lear and his writers responded by centering more and more episodes on him. The plots continued to try to teach him lessons, but the denouements got smaller and the J.J. bits got bigger. He never learned his lesson anyway. He became the emotional focus of the show, its Archie Bunker.

The older members of the cast were unhappy. Said Esther Rolle: "I resent the imagery that says to black kids that you can make it by standing on the corner saying 'Dyn-O-Mite!' He's eighteen and he doesn't work. He can't read or write. He doesn't think. . . . Negative images have been quietly slipped in on us through the character."

John Amos complained along with Rolle, in an article in *Ebony*. Lear, reportedly, was incensed. Florida was too central to the sitcom dynamic to be cut, but James was not. Amos was released from his contract, and James was killed off camera in a car accident. Now the stable black family had become a fatherless black family, the very image of black cultural dysfunction, a stereotype that incensed black male critics (and Amos himself). J.J. was now the head of the family, and his parts got even bigger.

Before the next season Esther Rolle quit the show. "It's a matter of black pride," she said. She expected that Florida, too, would be killed by the writers; instead, they had her go to the South for health reasons and stay there with her new husband, leaving her children to fend for themselves. "A mother just wouldn't do that," said Rolle. "It's wrong, terribly wrong." Now J.J. became almost the entire show, and the writing devolved to incredibly primitive insult humor.

Sex was another big source of cheap laughs on *Good Times*. It had begun with frequent intimations of James and Florida's sexual enthusiasms for each other. (The idea of middle-aged parents enjoying sex must have seemed like a liberating one in 1974. Lear wanted Florida to enjoy the fruits of loosening TV standards and the national obsession with female sexual satisfaction.) Then Ja'net DuBois, who played Willona, the neighbor, insisted that her character be changed from a mother to a swinging single. Her main function became delivering lines like "I like my coffee like I like my men: hot, black, and strong." Those lines invariably provoked explosive whoops from the studio audience and no doubt made much of the TV audience feel it was seeing something bold, forbidden, and new. Finally, there was J.J.'s shtick of playing himself as an operator, a ladies' man. It was somewhat funny simply because it was so improbable, but in script terms it just translated itself into more sexual innuendos. More whoops. More shock value.

All put together, these elements laid another stereotype on top of the pile: Blacks are oversexed. Black mamas are big earthy tubs of desire. Single black women are easy. Young black men are penises on the make.

It was hard to believe this was a Norman Lear program. Norman Lear, the liberal, Norman Lear, the fearless opponent of conservative broadcast standards, Norman Lear, who put sitcom arguments about Watergate in American living rooms, was projecting an image of blacks as horny, eye-rolling, unemployed, hustling, hollering clowns. And this a quarter century after the NAACP had fought to keep the Kingfish off the air. But people watched it: a lot of blacks, a lot of nonblack minorities, a lot of kids, a lot of lower-income whites.

Lear and Yorkin followed with a third black sitcom, a spin-off of *All in the Family* called *The Jeffersons*, in 1975. Not nearly as offensive as *Good Times*, this was a variation of the comic strip *Bringing Up Father*. George Jefferson was a small-time dry cleaner (and neighbor of Archie Bunker) who hit it big with a dry cleaning chain and bought a co-op on Manhattan's Upper East Side. He was a retrograde bigot, a domestic tyrant, a social idiot, a more frenetic version of Archie. His wife, Louise, was an expansive, tolerant lady, trying to become elegant, trying to remain friends with the white neighbors and the black domestic helper whom George consistently alienated.

This was a liberal-consensus show in the old mold, with an archaic individualist being dragged into the future. It had blustery conflicts but sentimental endings. It had an intelligent, modern protagonist in Louise. George learned valuable lessons: on the first show, to tolerate a black-white mixed couple living in the building; later, to continue loving his son after he marries the same couple's mulatto daughter.

Yet in its tone it was nothing like the old ethnicoms. Nearly every episode was just thirty minutes of "zingers," vaudevillian insults: George tells Louise to be careful with a mirror because "you don't need any more bad luck"; "I know," she says, "I already got you." George's mother shows Louise a picture of herself as a young lady. "Oh?" says Louise. "Is this the one taken during the Civil War?" Loud deliveries and long reaction takes increasingly took the place of wit. Embarrassing slapstick filled in when insults ran dry.

Lear had torn away the phony gentility of '60s TV, increased the speed and force of humor, allowed people who loved each other to fight, as people really do. But the emotional honesty and tension that marked the early *All in the Family* could not sustain itself. Each new laugh had to be louder, each new topic more sensational, each sexual reference more daring, each insult more extreme. Within five years Lear had gone from giving new meaning to prime-time entertainment to overseeing some of the most brutishly offensive and moronic shows on the air.

Lear never acknowledged the change. In 1979 he was still talking about doing national issues on TV. He did come to show a certain defeatism, however: In 1983 he was quoted as saying, in response to questions about the possible negative effect of *All in the Family*, "I don't believe at all that it reinforces anything bad in society. But again, I don't see that it has changed anything for the good, either. I would be a horse's ass if I thought that one little situation comedy would accomplish something the entire Judeo-Christian ethic hasn't managed in two thousand years." He had learned some hard lessons about television. He had, at least, learned how to make people watch. Neither *Good Times* nor *The Jeffersons* was a huge hit, but both held audiences well enough to last for six and eleven years, respectively.

Other sitcoms followed Lear's lead onto ethnic turf: *Bridget Loves Bernie*, about a mixed Irish-Jewish marriage; *Love Thy Neighbor*, about the first black resident of an exclusive neighborhood; *The Cop and the Kid*, in which an Irish policeman gets custody of a ghetto youth; *Roll Out*, a sort of black *Mr. Roberts*, about a transport unit in World War II. They were all too polite, too old-fashioned, too middle-class for TV tastes in the age of Lear.

The one producer who seemed to have a clear grasp of what the Lear comedies indicated about viewing preferences—perhaps clearer than Lear's own—was actor-producer James Komack. His *Courtship of Eddie's Father* had been as cute and well mannered as any show on late '60s TV. What he came up with in 1974 was a radical change: *Chico and the Man*.

This was a vehicle for Freddie Prinze, another ethnic comic of the new school. He was a "Hungarican," he said: half Puerto Rican, half Hungarian. He was a likable, vulnerable-seeming kid, with a routine built around quaint ghetto stereotypes and funny-accent catchphrases ("Ees no my chob, mon"). Komack decided to build a sitcom around him that would do for Latin Americans what *Sanford and Son* did for (or to) blacks.

Chico, however, had a massive dose of sentimentality built into its very structure. Komack sensed that viewers wanted not just funny ethnic conflict but funny ethnic conflict erased at episode's end by *awww*-inspiring tugs at the heartstrings. Prinze's Chico was a Mexican-American mechanic in search of a job. The Man was Ed Brown—played in the "cantankerous but lovable" mold by Jack Albertson—a lonely and hostile old white man who owns a garage in an L.A. neighborhood that had gradually gone nonwhite. (The incomprehension of Latino culture by WASP and Jewish TV show creators is painfully evident here and in *Sanford*: Fred's neighbor in Watts is a Puerto Rican, not impossible but far less likely than a Mexican; here the character is an L.A. Mexican, but he's played by a New York Puerto Rican.)

In the first episode the Man is openly hostile to Chico, yelling: "Get out of here and take your flies with you!" The lovable, vulnerable Chico is hurt by this raw racial slur, nastier than anything uttered by Archie Bunker. But more important, he isn't really *angry*. He doesn't belt Ed in the jaw; he doesn't organize a neighborhood boycott of his garage. Rather he comes *back*: to find the vulnerable center of Ed's bitter heart, to make him acknowledge that he needs help, to turn this old coot into a loving, tolerant man. Finally Ed gives in. He really is an old softie after all. He graciously allows Chico to sweep his floor and move into an abandoned truck in his garage.

Chico walked a comedic tightwire. It fed the audience shocking lines like "take your flies" (but were we to laugh at the bigot's ignorance or at the stinking greaser?). It diverted viewers with cartoony supporting characters, played by the likes of Scatman Crothers, Della Reese, and Charo, who sang and did self-contained comedy bits. Then it turned around and delivered hugs and sighs.

The only thing that kept it from falling apart was its extreme simplification of human motivation: Chico had no reason in hell to love Ed, except that he was a naive innocent who loved all those who needed loving. The dialogue was primitive; the situations were stripped down and obvious. The ritual emotional play of the two appealing lead actors—Chico loves Ed, Ed spurns him, Chico is hurt, Ed reveals that he loves Chico—was its one strong selling point. In its first year it took third in the Nielsens, trailing only *All in the Family* and *Sanford and Son*.

Komack and his writers and actors had burrowed into *All in the Family* and come out with the emotional core that Lear buried under subtle characterization and topical argument. *All in the Family* acknowledged that the world was made ugly by racial and generational conflicts; *Chico* acknowledged it, too, in simple, repetitive form. *All in the Family* suggested that we could survive this if we just loved one another; *Chico* stated it, in the easiest, most condescending, yet most unembarrassed terms. *All in the Family* suggested that hatemongers might be decent people who are trapped by ignorance and fear; *Chico* reduced that to "He's only mean because he's lonely." This was sixth-grade psychologizing applied to a national anxiety. And the audience—because a lot of them were sixth graders and a lot of others found it pleasant to regress into that simpler worldview—ate it up.

Chico took the Bunkers' conflicts a long step further from reality; families really did fight, like the Bunkers, but how often does a lonely old racist end up living with a young Chicano? Yet in the context of sitcoms it managed to pass for "realism"; escapist shows were associated with all-WASP casts, nebulous suburban locales, canned laughter, sleek production, nice sets. *Chico* had the taped look, the shabby settings, the ethnic presence, the "hip" references of the Lear shows. It simultaneously satisfied the audience's self-congratulatory desire for "relevance" and its deeper yearning for a feel-good solution to its fears.

Chico had one more element to bring to the sitcom, one that was not part of Komack's plan. During the third season Freddie Prinze—long given to depression and suicidal fantasies—killed himself. Komack decided to press on with the series, despite cries of "bad taste" from critics and industry insiders. A new "Chico" was found: a twelve-year-old Mexican-American orphan whom Ed adopted, proving just what an old unprejudiced softie he had become. The chemistry wasn't there, and the show was soon canceled, but sitcoms had been brought back to one of their time-tested formulas—the patched-together family—with unsettling new racial and class overtones.

The very next season found a white millionaire adopting two black ghetto kids on a new NBC series, *Diff'rent Strokes*. This premise had been played with on *The Cop and the Kid*, but *Chico* and *Strokes* bypassed crime-oriented "relevance." They found a strategy to invoke a lump-in-throat optimism for the fate of a divided humankind: the infantilization of minority males (and thus the removal of physical threat), enabling the "adult" world, the white mainstream, to extend a paternal hand. Lyndon Johnson had tried to play a similar parental role in reality with his Great Society; '60s radicals may have spurned him, but in the sweet confines of the sitcom one could be sure that *these* little ethnics would be grateful.

On *Diff'rent Strokes*, revealingly, it was the undersize, precocious younger boy—played by Gary Coleman, an actor locked in chubby, prepubescent cuteness by health problems—who stole the show. His big brother, more street, more "black," and threateningly normal-size, was shoved into the background. For timid whites the message seemed to be: "We don't hate these people; it's just the way they're raised that we hate" (or, below the level of consciousness, "Black children would be fine if they didn't have the misfortune to be raised by niggers"). For nonwhites (many of whom did, according to surveys, actually watch these shows) they spoke to the embarrassed, unspoken dream of a white bailout from misery.

These multiethnic families worked on another, perhaps more potent emotional level as well. The racial differences of parents and kids was a strong metaphor for the alienation of generations, and images of cross-cultural living-room harmony indirectly addressed viewers' anxieties about family rifts.

Komack played more extensively with these multiple dynamics in his next sitcom, which he sold to ABC in 1975, after *Chico's* instant success. This was another vehicle for another rising New York comedian, Gabe Kaplan, whom one of Komack's associates, Alan Sacks, saw when he opened for Freddie Prinze at L.A.'s Comedy Store. The centerpiece of Kaplan's act was a long routine about his old high school classmates: the Puerto Rican troublemaker, the Jewish nerd, the Italian ladies' man, the tough slut, and so on. It was a clever routine, rich in funny names and details (the troublemaker was actually half Jewish and so was named Juan Luis Pedro Phillipo de Huevos Epstein; he peppered his speech with Spanish-accented Yiddishisms). Like Prinze and Walker, Kaplan played off young Americans' pent-up desire to laugh about race after years of liberal-minded silence, but he used his stereotypes with greater complexity and intelligence.

Sacks wanted to develop the routine into a sitcom. Since Kaplan was too old to play a high school kid, he was cast as a permissive teacher, Gabe Kotter, trying to ride herd on a class full of "sweathogs"—troublemaking, ignorant, but ultimately good-hearted kids of diverse types and ethnicities. Kotter himself was an alumnus of the school, coming back as an adult to teach the kids whatever he could about the big world outside, especially about overcoming conflicts and functioning together. Hence the title: *Welcome Back, Kotter*.

Kotter was a sharply written show, using Kaplan material and a staff of bright young writers who could deliver the same stand-up style of rapid comedy. Says Vinnie Barbarino, the Italian stud: "A woman's place is in the car." And Juan Epstein, the animal: "Tie yourself up with some chick and pretty soon she's gonna have you eating with a knife and fork." The plots were in the shocking but sentimental mold: A girl gets pregnant and won't reveal who the father is, figuring he should be noble enough to admit it himself. Horshack, the nerd, confesses, to be nice, even though no one can believe he's been with the girl. The guys ridicule him, but the girl is so touched that she decides he's the only real man in the group. The other guys are abashed, stop picking on poor Horshack, repent their machismo. The assorted guys who've had sex with the girl agree to take responsibility for her and the kid, but it turns out she isn't pregnant after all.

Like *Chico*, it used the real-seeming tone and style of Norman Lear. But the use of an ensemble cast of eccentrics, a familial emotional support group created not by the family but by a public institution, owed more to *Mary Tyler Moore*. In many cases, in fact, the families of the sweathogs were shown to be broken or dysfunctional. High school *was* family for them, as WJM-TV was family for Mary.

Kotter also ran Lear's beloved ethnic elements through an MTM filter and came up with a new use for stereotypes. Instead of these characters being *about* Italianness or Jewishness or blackness, their Italianness, Jewishness, blackness was merely used to create character eccentricities. Barbarino's "Heeeey," his primping, and his idolization of his mother weren't cultural issues; they were comic shticks. "Boom Boom" Washington's cool-black manner was no more socially "relevant" than Horshack's nerdiness.

A new synthesis of sitcom elements was being forged here: *Kotter* blended farcical situations with juvenile life lessons just like *Father Knows Best*, but in a "postfamily" context and with the racy '70s elements of ethnic stereotypes and sexual humor. It all held together because the show made no bones about being synthetic. The writing was a little too wise-ass to be real. The actors overplayed their characters with self-conscious cuteness. And then there was John Travolta as Barbarino. He became, almost instantly, a marketable heartthrob to teenage girls everywhere, on his way to becoming the Sex-God of the Disco Era. The way he played to the pubescent squeals from the studio audience left TV viewers with no doubt that they were watching a show, not participating vicariously in the lives of others.

Kotter seemed to be saying: "We've had our national debate, we've had our reality TV, and none of it amounted to anything. Now let's just wink at one another and play the game." Yet even with that tone—and maybe partly because of it—the show was able to give its viewers a sense of family, a fragmented and parentless family, but an easy one to belong to. It was a solid hit with kids, generating a flurry of comic books, stickers, and character dolls.

Like *Chico*, *Kotter* was an ill-fated show. After a solid start, various personnel conflicts split the crew, led to the firing of several writers and directors, and finally pushed Kaplan himself into appearing only occasionally. It was canceled after four years. Its lessons for the sitcom would have to be picked up by other producers, including the same ones who concocted *Diff'rent Strokes*. *The Facts of Life* was a *Strokes* spin-off about a white housemother at a girls' school with an assortment of charges: affluent WASP, tough ethnic white, sassy black, middle-class cutie, and dumb fat girl. It extended the white-parenting model into the ensemble cast, institutional family genre, as *Kotter* had begun to do.

By the end of the 1970s the conflicts of Norman Lear's ethnic sitcoms had been submerged in a new, synthetic domesticity. In the ragged aftermath of national division, viewers were eager to buy it. American culture was returning to themes of harmony and family, by whatever contrivances it could muster.

17

Sex and the Sitcom Girl

Ethnics weren't the only groups being pulled into the sitcom coalition in the early '70s. MTM Enterprises tried bringing rural southerners back to sitcoms, in a more dignified manner than Paul Henning had, with *The Texas Wheelers*, but it died almost instantly in the ratings. Just as doomed was *Paul Sand in Friends and Lovers*, MTM's look at a sensitive classical musician. Lear tried for some controversy in 1975 with *Hot L Baltimore*, featuring prostitutes, gays, and derelicts, but controversy was fatiguing by then, and the show fizzled. His company also tried out fat people (*The Dumplings*) and a May-December couple (*All's Fair*). From other producers came shows about with-it couples (*Bob & Carol & Ted & Alice*), old folks (*A Touch of Grace*), and irreverent medical professionals (*Temperatures Rising*). All vanished without a trace.

Even neurotics were welcome. MTM's second most successful series was *The Bob Newhart Show*, a sort of sitcom outpatient program about a psychologist who, as Ella Taylor writes, "is blessed with the kind of success attributed to some psychotherapists; he has a steady cadre of patients, none of whom are ever cured." He had a loving but assertive wife, an idiot neighbor, a sassy secretary, and various other hangers-on who blurred the line between healthy and neurotic. The writers played ingeniously with the role of jargon in a therapy-obsessed society. Playing off the daffiness of the supporting characters with his flat, halting manner, Newhart captured the befuddlement of a mediocre man in a changing, loony world. This was the first sitcom to grapple with the increasing self-absorption of American culture, although it kept its satire fairly safe by avoiding normal domestic life. When other series flirted with the same theme in more familiar settings, the results were far more volatile, far less satisfying.

Feminism was everywhere in mass culture in the early '70s. No longer just equal pay feminism or reproductive rights feminism or overthrow patriarchy feminism, but family room and bedroom feminism, the feminism of personal fulfillment and self-esteem and orgasms and freedom of wardrobe. That, plus the eternal preference of advertisers for females, guaranteed that no demographic group would inspire more sitcoms in those years than single, professional women. On top of that, ratings analyses were beginning to show that women watched more prime-time entertainment than men; specifically, women were more likely to be faithful followers of particular sitcoms.

Many "women's programs" were just vehicles for using new or old stars in whom the networks saw potential: Shirley MacLaine (*Shirley's World*), Debbie Reynolds (*The Debbie Reynolds Show*), Diana Rigg (*Diana*), Julie Harris (*Thicker than Water*), Sandy Duncan (*Funny Face, The Sandy Duncan Show*). But some—the Lear and MTM creations, at least—tried to grapple with the realities of womanhood during the sexual revolution and the liberation movement.

Lear led the way with *Maude*. She was a wife and mother—that much about her was consistent with sitcom tradition—but she was on her fourth marriage, and her daughter was an adult divorcée with a child of her own, living with her mother and stepfather for financial reasons. The series was intended to be an exploration of current issues, but with a woman's twist. Unfortunately—but inevitably—it broke down into a series of "shock" shows. Maude got pregnant. She had an abortion. She went through menopause. She had a face-lift. She went to a psychiatrist. The neighbors tried to talk her and her husband into wife swapping. Her husband had a nervous breakdown. He was revealed as an alcoholic. One week much of the audience tuned in because word had been leaked that Maude would say "son of a bitch" on the air. She said it all right.

Maude struck an uneasy balance between coarse humor and heavy drama. The studio audience whooped in shocked delight, then fell utterly silent as an emotional bombshell was dropped. The no-laughter, no-applause cliff-hanger fade-out became a staple. But the sources of both drama and humor grew cheaper and cheaper as the writers had to top each old shock with a new one. Maude herself became a victim of her own modernity.

A different set of problems ruined Mary Richards's best pal, after she was spun off into *Rhoda* in 1974. On *MTM's* third season Rhoda had already begun to change: losing weight, dressing better, fretting less about men, becoming a "today" kind of woman. When her own show started, she moved back to New York, took her dumpy kid sister under her wing, and began a series of good-natured battles with her "unliberated" mother. Almost immediately she met a man—a rugged but sensitive self-made Italian with a big, hairy chest, a *Cosmopolitan* magazine ideal for the time—and married him in the eighth show of the season. From a kvetching Sally Rogers, Rhoda was being transformed into the liberated working wife, satisfied financially, sexually, creatively, politically.

The trouble was, there was no conflict. Even the arguments with her mother diminished after the wedding. The "liberated" woman apparently didn't fight. She didn't provoke laughs either. MTM's writers made her too precious a figure to satirize. *Rhoda* opened to tremendous ratings, indicating the popularity of the character and the audience's desire for strong female sitcom protagonists. But after the marriage the audience slipped rapidly away. The producers doubled back on themselves, having Rhoda and her husband separate and then divorce, but that seemed only to alienate those viewers who had stuck around after the wedding.

Phyllis, spun off the next year, was an even bigger mess. As the first episode opened, Phyllis's husband had died; she moved in with her mother-in-law and found a job as a photographer's assistant. Also in the household were her teenage daughter and ancient, cantankerous Mother Dexter, creating one of those daffy recombinant sitcom families. The main source of conflict was Phyllis's self-absorption, and most of the jokes were insults directed at her, especially by Mother Dexter. Like a bad Norman Lear comedy, *Phyllis* became a one-dimensional running conflict with shock humor to perk things up. It, too, opened to strong ratings and then plummeted. (It should be said that strong opening ratings were a phenomenon of the times, since the sensation surrounding *All in the Family* had trained the TV audience to feel as though every new over-hyped sitcom was a cultural event not to be missed; the audience was generally disappointed.)

The national confusion over women's roles seemed to afflict sitcom creators worst of all. Rhoda the cynical single gal became Rhoda the "together" wife. Phyllis the nervously frustrated middle-class wife became Phyllis the dizzy sitcom widow. Maude, meanwhile, was apparently being made to suffer every week for being affluent, educated, and independent.

The female dynamic on *The Mary Tyler Moore Show* changed drastically after Rhoda and Phyllis were spun off. Mary was left without her sisterly support group, and the character who moved to the forefront in Rhoda's absence was a very different kind of female image: Sue Ann Nivens, WJM's "Happy Homemaker," an aging, manipulative, competitive man-eater.

Sex among the middle-aged and elderly was an increasingly popular theme in both Lear and MTM comedies. (Maude and her husband engaged in innuendos as well as unwanted pregnancies. Edith got giggly, and Archie turned smug at the mention of "last night." Rhoda's mother issued heavy-handed injunctions against being disturbed by the kids on Saturday morning.) As sexual references on TV got steadily bolder and more titillating, geriatric sex became an easy crowd pleaser, less socially threatening than sex between young people, comically incongruous with the sexless American stereotype of the aged. The audience could thus enjoy a depoliticized bawdy thrill while patting itself on the back for its hipness. Sue Ann crystallized the trend. She was a truly funny character, played with a masterful blend of white bread innocence and sneaky raunchiness by Betty White (who until then was known to TV audiences mainly as a motherly commercial spokeswoman). Her lines were the best written of their type: "You know, I was lying in bed last night and all of a sudden I had a great idea for the show. So I went right home and wrote it down!" Delivered with White's ingenuous sweetness, they were disarming and effective.

What gave Sue Ann's character real force was the fact that she was not just a horny broad but a pernicious, destructive female type. Mary's "nice girl" image annoyed her, and she played cattily on Mary's sexual insecurities. "Mary, what do you think turns on a man?" she asked. Mary, tired of Sue Ann's obsession, blustered back, "Sue Ann, I haven't the slightest idea." Sue Ann, smiling as her trap snaps shut, said in her sweetest voice, "I know that, dear. I was just trying to make your day."

Sue Ann enjoyed the sexual freedom of the '70s but was completely trapped in prefeminist sexual politics. She had a desperate hunger for Lou Grant, the virile father figure, the only power center on the WJM staff; she tried sexual come-ons, cooking, old-time feminine wiles, but all of it just scared Lou away. Whereas Mary and Rhoda had stood together to protect their dignities from male rejection, Sue Ann only resented Mary's easy, nonsexual rapport with the boss. And unlike the bitchy women in past sitcoms (Samantha's cousin, Serena, for one), Sue Ann never got her comeuppance. Her single-minded devotion to manipulating men and competing with women made her far stronger than the confused, good-hearted Mary. For Sue Ann, sexual freedom was only a weapon to wage an archaic war.

Mary did gain a female friend after Rhoda left, but sweet, dizzy little Georgette—utterly devoted to her man, Ted Baxter—was no help at all in sexual politics. Perhaps there was, in this, a foreshadowing of the collapse of mainstream feminism. Where Sue Ann was a predator unleashed by liberation, Georgette was an eternal child for whom liberation would have been an alien concept. Mary's only allies against the sexual destruction of woman by woman, it turned out, would have to be her sexless male friends Murray and Lou. It was indeed a lonely world for the modern woman.

It was during this period that Mary's ratings began to slip. In 1975–76, when *Phyllis* sat in sixth place (thanks to its strong start) and *Rhoda* was still holding in seventh, *MTM* fell to nineteenth. By the next season all of them had dropped out of the top twenty-five, and Moore had decided it was time to pull the plug.

Most women's sitcoms were proving to be badly ineffectual. They did, however, succeed in bringing more women into TV writing and production. Into the early '70s sitcom writing had been an almost entirely male concern, but by 1977 half the scripts bought for *The Mary Tyler Moore Show* were written by women. Among them was Treva Silverman, who won a "Writer of the Year" Emmy for her script about Lou Grant's divorce in 1974. Then, in 1975, Norman Lear's company developed a new sitcom created by a woman, a veteran actress named Whitney Blake (who had once played a bland sitcom mom on *Hazel*). Her *One Day at a Time* became the longest-lived, the most lifelike—and the most traditional—of all the women's comedies.

Its protagonist was a divorced mother of two teenaged girls, which was something of another Lear breakthrough (Maude had been divorced but was currently married; *The Odd Couple*'s Felix and Oscar were divorced, but they didn't function as parents; Rhoda's divorce was another season hence). Played by Bonnie Franklin, an appealing but not

231

glamorous Everywoman, Ann Romano was a housewife of seventeen years who found her stable, conventional life suddenly gone. Finding a job, trying to steer her kids through their most rebellious years, dating men in a time of sexual confusion, she discovered that all the rules by which she'd lived her life were no longer applicable. She and her daughters had to invent guidelines for modern American life as they went along, "one day at a time."

It was, in its subject matter, a "relevant" show, although it focused on continuing sexual and parental conflicts, rather than headline issues. At the same time it was a throwback, a semidramatic exploration of life lessons in the tradition that started with *Father Knows Best* and decayed into *The Brady Bunch*. The comedy bits were rarely as loud and broad as on the usual Lear shows, and the jokes frequently gave way to laughless fights, hugs, and message statements. This blend of comedy and drama derived most directly from *Maude*, but it went back ultimately to *Father Knows Best*. *One Day* also borrowed from the soap opera, traditionally the most female-directed of all entertainment genres, in its use of two- and three-part continued story lines. (Other sitcoms, particularly *Maude*, had used occasional cliff-hangers, but *One Day* made them part of its normal structure.)

One three-part comedy-drama follows Ann's romance with Neal, a "terrific guy" who turns out to be married. Traditional sitcom proprieties would have demanded that she dump him right there, but at the end of the first episode Ann decides to keep seeing him. Says she to her daughters: "It may not be proper, but you can't tell me what's right. I don't expect you to understand. I only hope that you will." The older daughter (representing worldly sophistication) does understand; the younger (idealism) does not.

In the second episode the illicit couple go to a restaurant and see an old friend of Neal's. Ann wants to be honest, but Neal lets the friend assume Ann is his wife. It's her "safe" male friend Schneider (representing a more mature, less self-consciously hip level of worldly wisdom than Ann's daughter) who makes Ann see that not only is Neal being unfaithful to his wife, but he's being dishonest with her as well. Conventional ethics may not be enough to make Ann end the relationship, but dishonesty is. She decides to break. But before she can, Neal announces that he's leaving his wife.

Ann and Neal's relationship now seems to meet the requirements of all the advisory characters, but in the final episode it comes clear that

Neal is driven more by a desire to do what's right than by a real readiness to commit to Ann. They both agree that the water under the bridge has rendered their relationship impossible. Ann (as a mature woman, with a newfound wisdom that transcends and synthesizes one daughter's conventional idealism, the other's hipness, and Schneider's modern relationship ethics) tells him good-bye with the line "There is something that matters more than you do: my self-respect." Thus the causes of moral relativism, personal satisfaction, and conventional decorum all are served.

Rick Mitz notes contrasts and parallels between a story line from *One Day* and another from *Father Knows Best*. Bud Anderson runs away from home because he feels unappreciated. Ann's older daughter, Julie, runs away with her boyfriend because her mother's household rules are too restrictive. Jim Anderson is concerned but confident. Ann goes through agonies of self-doubt: "I don't think this whole thing would have happened without the divorce. I'm the one who's always talking about finding myself, leading an independent life. Why the hell *should* Julie act differently?" Bud is brought back by nothing more than his sister's pretending to need him to fix her radio. Julie has to be tracked down, confronted in anger and tears. Bud immediately becomes the perfect son again. But Julie says she won't come home unless her mother erases all the rules. Ann draws the line at that. She gives Julie a tough speech about how much she wants her home but only if she'll obey the rules of the family. The applause track claps politely for Jim and Bud and Betty. The studio audience hoots and thunders in support of Ann. After a frozen moment Julie—touched, humbled, and welcomed home—embraces her mother.

In the corporate-suburban instructional plays of the '50s, no deep, angry conflicts were allowed to rise, and the contrived conflicts that were substituted were easily dispelled by rationality and conventional systems. In the wake of the despairing, combative sitcoms of the '70s Ann had to rely on her own selfishness, aggression, and "tough love" (to use a family therapy term becoming common in those years). But the result was the same: Julie, just like Bud, was back in the family.

One Day incorporated some of the trendiest elements of '70s sitcoms into its neotraditionalist vision. Schneider, the super of Ann's building, was a self-proclaimed stud ("Why do you think the women in the building call me super?") who hit on Ann in the first episode but, upon being put in his place, instantly dropped his sexual pretense. Ella Taylor describes him as "part of a long line of castrated males in television entertainment, men who make themselves absurd with tough macho talk, who are safe because they have been stripped of the sexual challenge that complicates relations between men and women, and who melt into vulnerability and loving support when the chips are down." He was also a source of safe, easy sex jokes to juice up flat scenes.

Another common element of successful late-'70s sitcoms appeared in the body of Valerie Bertinelli, playing the wholesomely sexy younger daughter. She became a teenybopper heartthrob, female equivalent of *Kotter*'s John Travolta, but she was a family girl, not a sexually potent troublemaker. She was an update of *Donna Reed*'s Shelley Fabares, an essential tool in selling the sitcom to kids but a role model acceptable to adults. (Fabares herself later joined the cast, as did Elinor ["Princess"] Donahue, in an explicit linkage with the old family comedies.)

One Day at a Time had reinvented the sitcom in the images of both *All in the Family* and *Father Knows Best*. In doing so, it helped lay a pop culture basis for America's self-conscious reinstatement of "traditional values" in the late 1970s.

Although Norman Lear's company produced it, *One Day* was more Whitney Blake's vision than Lear's. Lear himself continued being pessimistic and confrontational, and that was getting him in trouble with the resurgent Christian conservative movement (many members of which no doubt saw *One Day* as a step in the right direction). The right-wing backlash against the "tastelessness" of *All in the Family* and its successors finally came, and by mid-decade all three networks were feeling intense pressure to clean up their acts. In 1976 they agreed to institute Family Viewing Hour Practices, under which every show aired from 8:00 to 9:00 P.M. would fit standards of language and subject matter akin to those that had prevailed on prime time before Lear came along. Lear opposed the idea, even moving *All in the Family* to a later time slot to keep it unadulterated (which no doubt contributed to its immediate drop from first to twelfth in the ratings). That fight—plus the disputes over *Good Times*, plus fading ratings—fed into his growing dissatisfaction with the networks. That dissatisfaction became nearly complete after *Mary Hartman, Mary Hartman*.

This was Lear's darkest and most genuinely satiric vision, his comment on American womanhood, the consumer culture, and mass entertainment. A parody of soap operas, it aped their form and their story lines: Mary's daughter is taken hostage by a killer, her country singer friend is paralyzed, Mary's husband is impotent, and she has an affair with a police officer. But instead of being set among the beautiful and glamorous, it wallowed in the dreariness of Fernwood, Ohio. Mary herself, played by Louise Lasser, was dowdy and stupid, with that blankness that psychologists call flat affect. Despite all the horrors orbiting her, her greatest concerns were "waxy yellow buildup" and other fears induced by TV commercials. Ultimately her zombie state was shattered, and she had a nervous breakdown.

The networks wouldn't touch it. Some execs found its format unwieldy; others couldn't see who would care about a satire of soaps; still others said it was just "too controversial" (a testament to its satiric bite; it was the least "tasteless" of all of Lear's creations). In 1976 Lear sold it through syndication to individual stations, where it enjoyed relatively impressive success, enough to engender a spin-off (the talk show satire *Fernwood 2-Night*). But it never had the mass market impact Lear would have liked.

He followed with *All That Glitters*, a daffy satire produced by Stephanie Stills and Viva Knight that postulated a future in which male and female roles have been reversed (women execs value a male secretary for having "the cutest little buns in the corporation"). This one didn't find many takers even in syndication. Despite all of Lear's "breakthroughs," there was clearly a limit to the kinds of satire TV would support.

It was about this time that Lear withdrew from television. Troubled by the New Right's censorship campaigns, in 1980 he helped form People for the American Way, a political action group dedicated to free press issues. By that time the only Lear programs still on the air were *Archie Bunker's Place*, a pale shadow of *All in the Family*, a very tired *Jeffersons*, and *One Day at a Time*, his company's last top ten hit. But the Lear legacy was not dead. Rather, it had taken television by storm in 1977—although in a mutated form that enraged the critics and sickened sensitive industry insiders.

In 1973 Michael Ross, Bernie West, and Lee Kalcheim won an Emmy for an episode of *All in the Family* called "The Bunkers and the Swingers," which threw Archie and Edith's prudery into conflict with a couple of middle-aged sexual liberationists. Ross and West were the show's most influential writers, after Lear himself, and had great success pushing the boundaries of prime-time sexual permissiveness. In collaboration with Don Nicholl, *All in the Family*'s executive producer, they created and produced *The Jeffersons* for Lear. Then, again with Nicholl, they branched into independent production.

Following Lear's example, they picked up a controversial British comedy called *A Man About the House* and Americanized it. The British show was a raunchy vehicle about two dowdy working-class women and a man who rooms with them, silencing the landlady's suspicions by pretending to be homosexual. It was raw, loud, and sometimes effectively satirical of conventional mores. Nicholl, Ross, and West made it less raunchy, relying instead on juvenile, winking double entendres ("Jack's doing a project in the kitchen with this girl?" "Yeah, and they're in there right now, *making it* . . . oops!" Wide eyes, covered mouth, big laughs from audience). They made one of the women cute (Joyce DeWitt) and the other a dizzy sexpot (Suzanne Somers). They renamed the man Jack Tripper and cast John Ritter to deliver some frenetic, overplayed slapstick. They gutted the satire, leaving only the gripings of a sexually impotent old landlord to oppose the trivial, apolitical hipness of the youngsters.

The critics railed against *Three's Company*, but fifty million people watched it. With an audience buoyed by kids and young teens, it started third in the ratings and rose to second. In retrospect, it was probably inevitable. By late 1976, when a minority of Americans dragged themselves to the polls and yawned as they chose between Carter and Ford, the national political energy seemed badly depleted. "Relevant" sitcoms were being pulled back toward sentimentality and conservatism. Nicholl, Ross, and West realized what most critics didn't: that much of the appeal of the Norman Lear shows had always been simple titillation. Now they took advantage of TV's new hipness to give the public that titillation in completely undemanding form. This was an ingenious trivialization of the agonies of the early '70s, a trivialization that the public was waiting for.

For the anxieties of national debate and personal revolution, the sitcom demonstrated two tranquilizing alternatives. *One Day at a Time* showed how we could cling to what little we had left and perhaps approximate what we'd lost. *Three's Company* showed that the energy of rebellion can be channeled to less stressful ends, that "liberation" is fine, as long as it sets us free to have fun.

18

Manly Retreats

The TV sitcom was mainly a creation of the 1950s. The form came from radio, but *I Love Lucy*, *Father Knows Best*, and *Sergeant Bilko* defined its content, conflicts, limits, and variations ever after. In the '60s sitcoms pulled slowly away from those models, but then *All in the Family* went right back to them in search of a style and a tone, and a few years later *One Day at a Time* returned to them for content. Between the debuts of those series a couple of oddball sitcoms returned to the '50s in search of new ways to reflect their own times. What they came back with were to be the last two components in the sitcom synthesis of the 1980s.

M*A*S*H began as a novel by Richard Hornberger (*Richard Hooker*), a doctor who'd served with a Mobile Army Surgical Hospital during the Korean War. His book was a funny, cutting look at the means men find to deal with the ugliness of war and the idiocies of the military, like drinking, sex, black humor, boyish camaraderie, and the ingenious undermining of officers. In 1970, as Nixon's promised end to the Vietnam War was being replaced by new escalation, a hot young director (Robert Altman) and a once-blacklisted screenwriter (Ring Lardner, Jr.) turned the book into a darkly funny, antiauthoritarian movie that audiences welcomed as an antiwar statement. William Self of 20th Century-Fox

237

thought he saw a TV series in it and commissioned producer Gene Reynolds to make it.

Reynolds, like James Brooks and Allan Burns, had been involved with *Room 222*. But for his *M*A*S*H* writer he picked not a young TV Turk but a veteran he admired: Larry Gelbart, who had written good ensemble comedy for radio's *Duffy's Tavern*, had visited wartime Korea as one of Bob Hope's writers, had written a great deal of TV in the '50s, and had then broken through to Broadway with *A Funny Thing Happened on the Way to the Forum*. Reynolds persuaded Gelbart to return to television by holding up the new Lear and MTM shows as examples of the quality now possible in the medium. Gelbart seized it as an opportunity to refract the '70s through the '50s and reach a vast public with an antiwar message.

CBS programmers saw *M*A*S*H* as a gamble, politically and commercially; that may be why they slipped it into a dead Sunday night slot, against the unbeatable *Disney*, on the 1972 schedule. By the time it hit the air, however, much of the political danger was removed, as Nixon was obviously hurrying to get out of the war before election time. No hawks rose in protest of this cynical look at U.S. involvement in an Asian war. By the time the next season was scheduled, Vietnam was already becoming something to contemplate from a distance, to recover from. CBS moved *M*A*S*H* to its hottest time slot, directly following *All in the Family*, and it began a run of nine years in ten as a top ten hit.

It was a show like no other: wise guy ensemble comedy over the shredded bodies of wounded GIs. A group of lovable eccentrics sits around bitching and teasing, and then the helicopters are heard in the distance, and the eccentrics turn grim and they go to the bodies. They joke while they cut and sew, but the jokes are dark ("Do you realize what time it is? It's quarter to dead"). Then they stagger out and they drink and the doctors try crudely to score with the nurses and they talk about going to a whorehouse called the Pink Pagoda. Plots run through this— romances, fights, combat crises—but the real substance is the repetition of smart-assing, operating, smart-assing.

It was an antiwar show, but antiwar in the way Hollywood had been in the early '30s. With an ugly war past and no new one on the horizon, everyone could agree that war is dehumanizing, that it should be avoided, that enthusiastic militarists are crazy. It was a bold show in its willingness to present the bloody realities of war at all; no sitcom ever had, and during the most painful Vietnam years even dramas about war disappeared. But it never really did take a political stand.

A liberal bias was apparent in the frequent jabs at MacArthur and McCarthy, two deceased, disgraced heroes of the right. When on more controversial ground, the writing became guarded. In one of the show's most often quoted speeches, "Hawkeye" Pierce reflects on Communist aggression: "I don't know why they're shooting at us. All we want to do is bring them democracy and white bread, to transplant the American dream: freedom, achievement, hyperacidity, affluence, flatulence, technology, tension, the inalienable right to a coronary at your desk while plotting to stab your boss in the back."

At a certain cautious level this does cast some doubt on the rightness of the American cause in wars like the Korean and Vietnamese. But the question doesn't cut very deep. It is wistful, like the sigh of the harried executive that poor folks really know how to live. Hawkeye's crack presumes that an American victory might truly bring affluence to these people, that communism is opposed not to poverty and degradation but to white-collar anxiety. He questions whether the "American dream" is altogether good—far more than a sitcom could have questioned in years past—but never the assumption that that dream is attainable, even inevitable. Given the skeptical spirit of the times, this was a position quite acceptable to corporate America.

Despite a certain level of political engagement, *M*A*S*H*'s appeal was largely escapist. The Korean War functioned as a safe haven; it was long ago, and we'd survived. Even when it brought to mind Vietnam, it evoked an episode already behind us for almost its entire run. *M*A*S*H* helped TV viewers integrate the horrific media memories of Vietnam in human terms, but the horrors it presented were more sad than scary; they generally evoked less anxiety than the arguments in the Bunker household, which addressed ongoing problems.

*M*A*S*H*'s most seductive charm may have been the escape it offered from modern sexual politics. Even before feminism polarized sexual attitudes, a rigid politeness had descended over man-woman relations. On TV, male sexual predators were being tamed as far back as *Bachelor Father*, and husbands had been made more fragile and sensitive since the time of *Dick Van Dyke*. With the arrival of Gloria Bunker, Mary Richards, and cousin Maude, TV's sexual dialogues became tense and confused. But the *M*A*S*H* docs, at least in the beginning, were indefatigable in their pursuit of tail. And when they encountered an attractive but rigid nurse—Major Houlihan—they nicknamed her Hot Lips and taunted her ceaselessly. No character could have done that to Mary, or even Phyllis, without requiring some sitcom retribution. In *M*A*S*H*'s historical context, though, our heroes could engage in the most archaic, misogynistic male bonding and still get laughs.

The mass media fascination with sex during those years made men and women alike curious about the ways men do, and should, interact. *M*A*S*H* provided a dramatic laboratory in male relations under highly emotional circumstances, with an appealing cast of eccentrics: Klinger, the malcontent who dresses in drag in hopes of a discharge; Radar, the mousy clerk; Frank, the vain neurotic in love with Hot Lips; Colonel Blake, the goofy but likable commander; the gentle chaplain, Father Mulcahy; Trapper John, the nice-guy rebel. And, at the center, Hawkeye (Alan Alda), a Bilko-like conniver and joker but with a dark side: a streak of pain and outrage, a craving for alcohol.

They played with many questions of vulnerability and toughness, masculinity and femininity, in contexts ranging from jokes about Klinger's new purse to the death of an old friend in Hawkeye's arms. Most of all, they demonstrated the dynamics of smart-ass emotional support, survival through wise guy humor; this was a study, as Gelbart said, "of grace under pressure." *M*A*S*H* gained early attention with its subject matter and politics, but its importance in the long run lay in its character work.

It also broke new ground in structure, tone, and technique. It often abandoned the neat patterns and rhythms of sitcoms in favor of a choppier, shorter-scened, movielike pace. Some episodes were narrated by a single character, usually through the device of a letter to the home folks. One story brought a reporter onto the scene, so that the cast could be observed from a "cooler" dramatic distance. Another blurred reality and hallucination, as Hawkeye talked to a psychiatrist. Another took the form of a documentary, with grainy black-and-white film and head-on interviews of the characters.

This was a self-conscious show. It presented itself *as* a show, as a piece of the past, as a calculated dramatic statement. It willfully blurred comedy and tragedy. When other sitcoms were boasting of their use of live studio audiences to prove their genuineness, *M*A*S*H* had a laugh track chuckling through outdoor long shots. It was intelligent, but also self-important, precious, and phony. It was always aware of itself.

About the same time that *M*A*S*H* was in development, Garry Marshall was taking his own sitcom look at the 1950s. Marshall had passed through adolescence in that decade, before graduating to TV writing (including work on that first pointedly post-'50s sitcom, *Dick Van Dyke*).

By 1970 he was the principal writer of ABC's *The Odd Couple* and wanted to create his own pilot; given the revival of interest in early rock music and the camp mystique then being bestowed on old sitcom reruns, he thought a comedy about horny, naive teenage boys in the '50s might find an audience. ABC thought otherwise and turned the pilot into just one more episode of *Love, American Style*. A young filmmaker named George Lucas saw it, however, and was inspired to create his own music-filled reminiscence of pre-Vietnam heartland adolescence, *American Graffiti*. It became a huge youth hit in 1973, setting off a '50s craze. Marshall dusted off the pilot that started it all, and in 1974 *Happy Days* premiered on ABC.

At first glance it would be hard to find two shows more dissimilar than *M*A*S*H* and *Happy Days*. Where *M*A*S*H* was dark, *Happy Days* was bright. Where *M*A*S*H* was witty, *Happy Days* was dopey. Where *M*A*S*H* was grainy and naturalistic, *Happy Days* was a colorized version of the glossiest '50s sitcoms. Their only point of correspondence would seem to be the decade in which they were set. Yet there were some interesting similarities: acute self-consciousness, prefeminist sex games, masculine ensemble comedy, and an oddly twisted escapism that reflected ironically on the present.

The self-reference that *M*A*S*H* achieved through structural gimmicks, *Happy Days* achieved by placing itself squarely in the context of old sitcoms: The soda fountain with the dry-witted Asian proprietor was straight out of *Dobie Gillis*; characters compared themselves with TV personages, making explicit references to *Ozzie and Harriet*; the lead actor was Ron Howard, the former Opie of *Andy Griffith*. What didn't come from sitcoms came from other familiar pop culture: Fonzie, the local tough guy, was a self-amused imitator of Brando's *Wild One*; the opening credit sequence focused not on the characters but on a spinning record, Bill Haley's "Rock Around the Clock." Where *M*A*S*H* tried to obscure its own nature as television and sitcom, *Happy Days* jumped up and screamed, "I'm a sitcom! Not modern, not daring, not sophisticated! I'm a sitcom, just like *Beaver*!" (which was, of course, a pretty modern, daring, sophisticated position to take—aesthetically, if not politically).

To say *Happy Days* trivialized history, as some critics did, misses the point. *Happy Days* ignored history. It constructed a picture of teenage life in mid-'50s Milwaukee from the most available images in mass entertainment, then—almost jokingly—strung in some references to Eisenhower and old TV shows to give it a sense of existing outside rerun reality. It created a fantasyland '50s where all "relevant" anxieties were unheard of.

Then, by acknowledging its own falsity, it made itself hipper than the reruns it imitated. Hipper, in a jaded, postpolitical way, than even *All in the Family* and *MTM*.

As part of that hipness and part of the '70s cultural continuum, it dwelt on one aspect of adolescent behavior that the old sitcoms had glossed over: the pursuit of sex. The protagonists, Richie, Potsie, and Ralph, were three high school guys constantly looking for a way to get girls to let them feel them up, yet they were more cloddish and virginal than Bud Anderson. Only Fonzie, the "cool" guy in the leather jacket, appeared to be able to handle women. He could bring hot, cheap-looking chicks swaying toward him with the snap of a finger. Richie and the guys were awestruck but helpless to imitate.

Through Fonzie, "the guys" entered into an inarticulate dialogue on masculinity and sexual power; like the Korean War, '50s puberty was a historical crucible that tried men's souls. He tried to instruct them in controlling women and looking out for one another. He was impatient with Richie's feminized, good-boy devotion to his boring nuclear family. For him, life was riding a motorcycle, getting laid, being cool. He lived in a prefeminist, preadult paradise of his own making, which, the show suggested, was possible and permissible in those "happy days." The plots, of course, stayed jokingly true to their cornball sitcom antecedents: Richie always did end up loyal to his mother, his sister, the nice girl, not to Fonzie or the cheap girl.

The fact was, most Americans still felt pretty much the same about sex as they had before the "revolution" but in the sexual self-consciousness of those years were embarrassed to admit it. Kids saw their elders engaged in sexual struggles that were far from "liberated." For those men, women, and kids, the sitcom retreat into the '50s allowed for humorous exploration of such struggles without the complexity of contemporary dialogue.

Happy Days, however, was a show that found its audience only after it had lost its way. From the start its goofy-guy humor and simple plots appealed mainly to kids. And the kids knew what they liked best: Of fifteen thousand fan letters received in the show's first two years, ten thousand were addressed to Fonzie. He was a kid's ideal. Older than the guys but not a parental figure, he was the untouchable, independent child-adult. Played with affection and poise by Henry Winkler, he had power but no menace. Suddenly eight-year-olds all across America were jabbing their thumbs back toward their shoulders and saying, "Aaaaay."

Marshall and his crew moved Fonz to the center of their plots, eclipsing Richie. He moved in over Richie's family's garage, and, as Marshall said, "I knew that if I could get him over the garage I could get him into the kitchen. He could become a member of the family." Ratings rose and rose and rose; in its third season *Happy Days* hit the top spot in the Nielsens, ending *All in the Family*'s five-year reign.

But in joining a '50s sitcom family, Fonzie fell prey to dread responsibility. Parents and teachers by the thousand, troubled to find their charges emulating an apparent hoodlum, urged the producers to make the Fonz a positive role model. Norman Lear might have ignored them, but Marshall felt responsible for his kid audience and complied (thus falling victim to what pop culture historians Steven and Joseph Filice have called the Chico Marx Syndrome, the almost inevitable softening of rebellious comic figures—Mickey Mouse, Lucy Ricardo, the Marx Brothers—through the timidity of commercial entertainment). Suddenly Fonzie was helping Richie with his "relationships," demonstrating the importance of a library card, and even helping Richie's mother around the house.

From offering an alternative to modern sex roles he had come full circle and was now proving that even "cool" guys can be part of the domestic coalition. Unlike past cool cats, like Eddie Haskell, he didn't need to be humiliated. As an archaic stereotype in an admittedly phony show, he could be molded into whatever form parents demanded.

Kids and cultural conservatives may have been vaguely disappointed, but ABC was thrilled. The network had been skidding badly. In 1974–75, CBS had ten of the top fifteen shows; NBC had the other five. In a desperation move in 1975 ABC hired away Fred Silverman, the master programmer who had gotten most of the credit for CBS's resurgence. Silverman had a reputation for spotting a network's strong points and structuring schedules around them, hooking viewers at the start of prime time and then "feeding" them from show to show to show.

He saw ABC's strengths immediately; its biggest hits were action shows, like *S.W.A.T* and *The Six Million Dollar Man*, and the rising *Happy Days*. All of them appealed to kids. He also understood that mid-'70s viewers wanted to laugh; the top seven shows in 1974–75 were sitcoms, an unprecedented dominance for the genre (four were Lears, one an MTM, one a Komack, and one was *M*A*S*H*). Silverman built a new ABC around kid-vid and sexual titillation. He pushed *Happy Days* heavily and encouraged Marshall to spin off two goofy female characters into *Laverne and Shirley*. He used *Welcome Back, Kotter* to anchor Thursday night and followed it with another ensemble show, *Barney Miller*. He seized upon *Three's Company*, using it to bridge *Laverne and Shirley* and a raunchy new sitcom, *Soap*. He brought in *Charlie's Angels*, a female cop show that introduced the word *jiggle* to discussions of TV. By the end of his first full season ABC had the top three shows, four of the top five, ten of the top fourteen.

In the intoxication over these leaping ratings, not many people mentioned demographics. The buzzword of 1970 was already becoming a secondary concern by 1975. Audience surveys were finding that no matter what was on television, it was simply difficult to keep those affluent, educated young people at home in front of the set. A few shows could always sustain "good demographic" markets: *Mary Tyler Moore*, *M*A*S*H*, and more recently *Cheers* (along with several "quality" dramas in the 1980s). But most such targeted shows failed. Advertisers generally found more reliable markets in "Bill and Mary Six-Pack," and raw ratings continued to translate into revenue. Fred Silverman of ABC was a rerun of Jim Aubrey of CBS: offending critics; driving sensitive creators into other fields; amusing the millions in front of their tubes.

Garry Marshall summed up the ABC philosophy when justifying his top-rated spin-off *Laverne and Shirley*: "You have to do something silly to get their attention. Then I like to knock them off their chairs with laughter. I go for the gut. I want them to laugh *hard*. I don't want them quietly staring at a bright, witty show."

The huge success of the Garry Marshall shows proved to be a bubble. In 1979 both *Happy Days* and *Laverne and Shirley* plummeted from their pinnacles. Maybe kids got sick of the softening that parents nodded at in approval. *Happy Days* had certainly lost its ironic distance, succumbing to late-'70s sentimentalism, blurring its position in time (Fonzie's cousin Chachi, with a disco era haircut and some Travolta-like shticks, was added for heartthrob appeal), dumping '70s psychobabble into juvenile plot structures (at Fonzie's urging, Richie tells his girl, "I should have had more faith in our relationship"). Maybe the pop culture journey to the '50s had completed its task; after all, the host of *Death Valley Days* was about to be elected president. Or maybe the limited characters and situations had simply become too repetitive.

M*A*S*H, by contrast, stayed high in the ratings well into the '80s, its well-developed ensemble comedy enabling it to survive the shifts in public concerns and a change in its own tone. Larry Gelbart left the show after four seasons. A younger touch, clearly influenced by the character sensitivity of MTM, began to be felt. Alan Alda, an outspoken feminist and a popular example of the '70s "New Man," became a stronger creative force in scripting and direction. About the same time two principal actors left: Wayne Rogers, who played devil-may-care Trapper John, and McLean Stevenson, the self-interested Colonel Blake. Their replacements were Mike Farrell, as B. J. Hunnicutt, a softer, more thoughtful presence (critic Tom Jicha called him "Mr. Sensitive, Mr. Phil Donahue in 1950"), and Harry Morgan as Colonel Potter, a dedicated, gruff-with-a-heart-of-gold type. Soon after, the nasty Frank Burns (Larry Linville) gave way to the annoying but much more sympathetic Charles Winchester (David Ogden Stiers). That left Hot Lips without a lover and shoved her inevitably toward Alda's Hawkeye. In a watershed episode, they are trapped together in a farmhouse during combat and discover their mutual vulnerabilities and needs. The characters called Hot Lips Margaret thenceforth.

By the end of the decade the caustic, anachronistic guy show had become an emotionally sensitive, modern coalition comedy. It lost some of its earlier audience but added new viewers, mostly female; even in its eleventh and last season it was the top-rated sitcom. The humor declined as writers tried to sustain its wisecracking style even as the characters pulled against it; silly lines ("She's a North Korean guerrilla!" "Then let's frisk her for bananas!") replaced dark ones. But it held its fans with steadily developing characters, shifting relationships, a blend of soap opera continuity and sitcom reassurance. It emerged as a more serious *Mary Tyler Moore Show* or a nonfamilial, more liberal *One Day at a Time*. With its own internal dynamic, *M*A*S*H* had broken down the throwback sexual politics that fascinated viewers in the early '70s and carried those viewers into the inevitable sitcom consensus.

A new subgenre grew up in the shadow of this transforming *M*A*S*H*. The first and best of the type was *Barney Miller*, which writer-producer Danny Arnold created for ABC in 1975. Arnold had been involved with *The Real McCoys*, *Bewitched*, *My World and Welcome to It*, and others, but had never done much with a really personal touch. In the energized atmosphere of early-'70s TV, he was able to. His first plan was for a more conventional comedy about the domestic life of a New York cop, but as other producers opened up the sitcom form, he felt emboldened to jettison that idea in favor of an all-male ensemble comedy about an ethnically mixed group of desk cops in a decaying Greenwich Village precinct.

Like *M*A*S*H*, *Barney Miller* was about survival at the edge of combat. But this was contemporary urban combat: emotional, psychological, legal, and ideological assaults on old-fashioned middle-aged men. The cops shuffled an endless series of petty thieves, perverts, streetwalkers, lunatics, political activists, and complaining citizens from desk to desk to desk. The cops themselves were all incomplete humans, but they used their personal idiosyncrasies and obsessions to carry them through: Harris, the cultured black, with his Wambaughesque literary dreams; Yemana, the dry Japanese, with his racehorses; Fish, the tired, impotent old Jew, with his eternal gripes; Dietrich, the would-be psychiatrist, always making bogus sense of nonsense; Wojo, the thick-headed Pole, with the loony romanticism that led him into crush after crush on arrested prostitutes.

As in *M*A*S*H*, the men's individual resources are never quite enough to save them, and male peer support is needed. Usually the source of that support is Captain Miller himself, genial, befuddled, perceptive, engagingly played by Hal Linden. In the privacy of his office the other guys can drop their wisecracking defenses, stretch out on his couch like therapy patients, and unload. Miller never makes speeches. He may toss off a commonsense suggestion; he may just listen and try vainly to understand. Then he sends the guys back out, a little calmer, to continue the bureaucratic flow of madness.

To capture the sense of lunacy better, Arnold developed a multiple story line structure for his episodes. As many as three different cases may come into the office at once: A religious nut is thrown in the holding cell; a victim is complaining to Miller; one of the other cops is trying to talk sense into a young purse snatcher. Often the plot lines intersect or create a thematic counterpoint; sometimes one clever solution is found to two problems. (This would be adapted into a sitcom convention in the 1980s, although not so much to create texture as to prevent slight plots from having to sustain a half hour's tension alone.)

Barney Miller offered few social lessons or triumphant resolutions. It wittily affirmed our suspicions that the world is, in fact, collapsing. As a solution it offered only survival, showing how unsentimental unity and an emotional remove can help beleaguered males keep their heads just barely above the swirling seas.

As *Happy Days* called forth a female equivalent, so did *Barney Miller*: *Alice*, starring Linda Lavin, who'd played a female detective on *Barney*'s first season. Loosely based on the Martin Scorsese movie *Alice Doesn't Live Here Anymore*, this was the story of a New Jersey widow who heads for L.A. but ends up working in a roadside diner in Arizona.

What futile bureaucratic service was to the men of *Barney*, bottom-rung food service was to the tough, weathered gals of *Alice*. Bizarre customers and frustrating boyfriends drifted through, straining relations between the women and aggravating conflicts between them and their exploitative male boss. Ultimately sisterly affection and crass humor held them together. Unlike *Barney*, *Alice* was a predictable show, full of obvious gags. But it built a big following, lasted a decade, and guaranteed a place for groups of discontented but mutually supportive women in the sitcoms of the '80s.

A couple of years later four MTM alumni—James Brooks, Ed Weinberger, Stan Daniels, and David Davis—followed *Barney Miller*'s lead with *Taxi*. This was a major leap for the MTM crowd, dropping from their middle-class plateau into the realm of grease and sweat, a New York taxi garage. The humor was broader and the characters were nuttier than on *Barney*. There was Andy Kaufman as a spacey immigrant from an unspecified Slavic country, Christopher Lloyd as a mad acid burnout cum preacher, and Danny DeVito as a pint-size screaming Italian-American. There was a more sensitive tone and a stronger female presence (an independent woman driving cabs to support her artistic dreams), as might be expected from MTM veterans. But there was the same joking unity against lunacy and the same unassumingly wise emotional axis, this time played by Judd Hirsch. There was the same intelligent scripting and compassion for character. *Taxi* moved *Barney*'s subject matter into the new sitcom center, right where *M*A*S*H* was moving by itself.

That same fall, 1978, MTM itself brought out its last sitcom, *WKRP in Cincinnati*. This was a young adult–oriented show constructed around rock music. A hip, unpretentious young drifter turns a stodgy old "easy-listening" radio station into a freewheeling rock station. Although sometimes a bit too self-consciously "with it" for comfort, it was a funny show, and it did make some interesting comments on its times. One of the DJs was Dr. Johnny Fever, a drug culture carryover feeling left behind and out of place, played with painful conviction by Howard Hesseman, who had once been prominent in the San Francisco radio and comedy counterculture of the '60s. The other was Venus Flytrap (Tim Reid), a shy, very mainstream black man who switched to the role of a jiving soul brother on the air for purely commercial reasons. Fever and Flytrap were only a little less ridiculous than the baffled holdovers from the easy-listening days.

Flytrap was an important creation for a different reason as well: MTM's vision of "quality TV" was so strongly determined by the affluent main-stream that for years it seemed to shun ethnic diversity. While Lear and others were bringing blacks and browns and yellows into sitcomland, MTM had given us only WASPs, a few not too ethnic Jews, and one boring Italian, Rhoda's husband. *Taxi* added more Italians and a Slav, but still no blacks, Latinos, Asians, Arabs (one wonders how long it had been since any of the creators had ridden in a New York cab). Finally, in *WKRP*, MTM brought a black into its middle-class family.

Inspired largely by the comedy-drama blending of *M*A*S*H*, Mary Tyler Moore and company eased away from sitcoms in the late 1970s, with the drama series *Lou Grant* and *The White Shadow*, the latter about a white gym teacher in a largely black school. That led them deeper into urban, race-conscious drama, specifically to *Hill Street Blues* in 1981, which kicked off a new phase in "quality television."

By then MTM and its alumni had made their conclusive sitcom state-ment, their epitaph for the '70s: "Relevance" is dead. Finding a bearable way to make a living and watching out for our fellow flotsam and jetsam: that's all we can do now. And most important, we have to see that we're all in the same boat: black and white, old and young, hip and square, taxi driver and disc jockey.

The sitcom coalition of the '50s had been shattered, but a new one had been forged. This one would help carry mass culture into the '80s and straight to the present.

19

Believing Because We Want to Believe

Todd Gitlin has called television "recombinant culture." No group of programs bears him out better than the sitcoms of the 1980s and early 1990s. By the end of the 1970s all the present elements of the genre had been developed and market-tested, and structures had been created that could combine them all. Some sitcoms are clever, most are not; some are funny, most just obnoxious; but nearly all use the same recipe.

There are ceaseless insults à la Norman Lear but divested of political weight in the manner of *Kotter*. There are titillating sexual references, also from Lear, but by way of *Three's Company*: all innuendo, no activity. Also from Lear come "issue-of-the-week" shows, but now avoiding controversy in favor of generally recognized ills: child abuse, drug abuse, deaths in the family, pornography, environmental destruction, or, at the bolder end of the spectrum, South African apartheid. Along with them come speeches, straight out of *M*A*S*H* but not as well written. There are great globs of sentiment, as sticky as *Chico and the Man*, and those no-audience-sound serious moments from *One Day at a Time*. There are continued stories and soap opera character progressions (*One Day*, *M*A*S*H*). Nearly every show has the Norman Lear look: small, overlit sets and few of them, living rooms with stairs coming down in the background and kitchens adjoining. But the furnishings are more attractive, more consumer-friendly, more Brady Bunch than Bunker.

Most sitcom folks belong to mixed-up, patched-together families, some crossing ethnic lines. (Single-parent households are nearly gone; even *One Day*'s Ann Romano remarried in 1982.) Others are members of eccentric work ensembles. Sometimes work and family are combined. Certain character types appear again and again: the horny old lady; the sassy black woman; the uptight yuppie woman; the buffoonish child-man; the impish teen heartthrob; the cynical toddler; the sarcastic wife; the housewife with a hippie past; the nerdy pal; the secretly insecure stud. And in nearly every last one there is the same tone: a little loud, a little gag-heavy, mock-hostile, and superficially smart-ass; a little too conscious of the studio audience and of the show's own artificiality.

Since the late 1970s TV-viewing demographics have settled into dependable patterns that help lock the sitcom into these forms. The primary watchers of sitcoms are kids and young teens. Their parents often end up watching, too, making it important that the shows avoid pure childishness and toss the adults a little something (targeting the material at about a thirteen-year-old mentality covers both bases). Old folks watch a great deal of television but tend to prefer dramas to sitcoms. Since the 1970s, however, women, including many single women, especially widows and divorcées in middle age, have come to constitute a larger and larger part of the sitcom audience. Young adults are always open to being lured to the TV set, and advertisers love to lure them, but since the disintegration of the relevant comedies it's been hard to sell them on sitcoms. As a rule, less educated, lower-income adults are most likely to take the bait. Those educated young adults of the middle class, those sponsors' dreams, can show fierce loyalty to a series once hooked on it—witness *M*A*S*H* and *Cheers*—but they, too, prefer dramas (*Hill Street, Thirtysomething*), and few are the sitcoms that can hook them.

If any show can cut across constituencies—as *The Cosby Show* did in 1984—it can become a huge hit. But since the exhausting public debates of the '70s Americans have been far less inclined to be electrified by anything in mass culture. Corporate logic dictates that product be geared to reliable markets, to minimize loss. In these days of buyouts, rapid executive turnover, and control by accountants, the pressure to maintain quarterly profits has made audience-targeted predictability more important than ever.

Yet another concern of sitcom producers is rerun potential. Syndication has been a solid source of additional profit since the early 1960s, but the shifting TV marketplace has raised its importance. Cable TV, home video, and alternatives like the Fox Network have cut sharply into the audience size of the three networks (a top-rated show might only pull a rating of 25 now, whereas 30 or more was standard in the '70s); at the same time cable has considerably increased the market for reruns. Sitcoms, with their lightness and their half hour length, are far more profitable in rerun than dramas. The standard production logic now is to keep a series alive for five years, even if costs are high and profits narrow, thereby generating enough episodes for a syndicatable package.

Since the money is made down the road, it's wise to keep new sitcoms from being too timely, too idiosyncratic, too dependent on novelty or shock. (Demographics come into play again; the biggest watchers of early-evening and weekend TV, the big rerun hours, are kids, joined by sizable numbers of unemployed adults and old people.) *The Cosby Show*, with its quirky, ephemeral appeal, scored an astounding 34.7 rating at its peak but has fared unspectacularly in rerun. *Who's the Boss?*, a standard, well-tooled show that never topped 22, plays regularly in every sizable regional market, in some places two or three times a day.

Under these conditions it's difficult for any sitcom writer or producer to develop a new comic vision that captures his social moment. Adding to the difficulty is the creators' own self-consciousness about being cultural commentators. Ever since the early MTM and Lear "breakthrough" comedies generated so much publicity, a premium has been placed on shows that can appear to be making a progressive social statement: This is the first sitcom to make older women sympathetic; this one reverses the white-father-black-kid pattern; this one shows how the '60s generation has sired the Reagan generation.

Yet truly pointed commentary invites controversy, and controversy is no longer considered a boon to family TV shows. The career of Susan Harris is revealing. Controversy surrounded her work since 1972, when she wrote the "Maude Gets an Abortion" episodes for Norman Lear. Advertisers pulled out; Christian groups protested; some stations refused to show the episodes. In 1975 she created the short-lived *Fay* for NBC, about a divorcée who becomes a swinging single. Then, in 1977, when Fred Silverman felt ABC needed a good shot of controversy, she gave him *Soap*.

Picking up the lead of Lear's *Mary Hartman*, this was ostensibly a satire of soap operas, but unlike *Mary*, it was loud and wacky and weekly. It featured a rich family, headed by a philandering man and a ditzy, sexy older woman; one daughter was a teenage sexpot, acutely conscious of her breasts; the butler was a caustic, uppity black man named Benson. Their in-laws included a mafioso and a homosexual. Plots turned on the murder of a womanizing tennis pro, amnesia, sex with a Latin American revolutionary, and, eventually, extraterrestrials and clones.

Every plot seemed to involve sex: flirtation, innuendo, adultery, prostitution, gay jokes, everything. Even when a character is cloned by aliens, it becomes an excuse for gags about how much the guy's wife prefers the clone in the sack. Harry Castleman and Walter Podrazik spoke for many observers when they called it "a series of silly slapstick scenes and sophomoric one-liners . . . a tiresomely childish program." *Sic transit* "breakthrough television."

ABC promoted it fiercely. "The summer of 1977 may well go down in television history," said Fred Silverman, "as the summer of *Soap*." Conservative Christians helped with the promotion; mere descriptions of the still-unseen show were enough to inspire a protest campaign that showered thirty-two thousand "no *Soap*" letters on the network. *Soap* became the focus of years of pent-up outrage against the advance of shock TV. As the Reverend Everett Parker said, "Who else beside the churches is going to stand against the effort of television to tear down our moral values and make all of us into mere consumers?"

A couple of years earlier this would have been great news for the network, but the public was apparently tiring of TV tempests. Only nine letters dribbled in to encourage ABC to go ahead with the show. When ratings finally came in, they were good but not amazing. *Three's Company*, just preceding *Soap* on the schedule, drew a 28.3 rating for the season; *Soap* drew 22. In contrast, CBS ran *M*A*S*H* and *One Day at a Time* back to back during that same hour, and their ratings were nearly identical (23.2 and 23). *M*A*S*H*'s audience hung in for *One Day*, but a lot of *Three's Company*'s viewers tuned out when *Soap* came on.

To shore up their crumbling audience, Harris and her cohorts softened the show, added dramatic pauses to make viewers care more about the characters. They also backed off some of the politically touchy matters: The gay man discovered he liked women, too, then women exclusively; he fathered a child and became involved in a seriocomic custody fight. On those terms the show lasted four years. Controversy proved to be more trouble than it was worth.

There was a new mood in the country as well. When *Soap* was developed, a Democrat had just won the presidency, disco was in full flower, and pop culture watchers were trumpeting hedonism as the movement of the moment. Within a couple of years Jimmy Carter was feeling the national malaise and the conservative phoenix was rising to devour him. Aleksandr Solzhenitsyn had seized the national spotlight with his Harvard speech against "destructive and irresponsible freedom . . . the abyss of human decadence," including "TV stupor." Reagan was coming, borne on Christian wings. There were rumbled fears in the broadcast industry that his FCC wouldn't be as laissez-faire as Nixon's, Ford's, and Carter's had been.

When Susan Harris and her partners—Paul Junger Witt and Tony (son of Danny) Thomas—decided to spin off a new series from *Soap*, they took a radical departure. Benson, the churlish black butler (played by Robert Guillaume, a veteran of Broadway musical comedy), was given a new employer: spacey, naive Governor James Gatling of an unnamed state. Gatling was a widower with a cute, precocious little daughter, an icy German housekeeper, and assorted bumbling and bitchy assistants. Benson, now less caustic and more quietly competent, became a mother hen to the governor and a surrogate father to little Katie. He became increasingly indispensable until in the third season he was appointed state budget director and in the fifth elected lieutenant governor.

Benson, quite in contrast with its parent program, played for the "family" audience. It presented an apolitical model of black progress (from domestic service to bureaucracy to elected officialdom, with no mention of black political machines or race politics) that played to liberal-centrist sentiments with no danger of worrying conservatives. It constructed a dignified image of a black male but channeled his energy into helping white domestic and political systems function. In the person of Kraus, the Aryan housekeeper implacably hostile to Benson, it hinted at the persistence of racism but removed it to a foolish, female, foreign presence (and even Kraus never made an explicitly racial remark; that would have been controversial). In Katie it created an image of innocence, the sense of a fresh start; she loved Benson regardless of race and class, free of the emotional baggage of the Age of Hostility, now implicitly past.

Benson replaced the mockery of *Soap* with heart-tugging messages. Most of them were domestic: Kids need to be honest with their parents; parents need to make their kids a higher priority than work. Some were political. In one episode the governor and his gang withdraw to a bomb shelter for a computer-planned simulation of a nuclear strike. Initially businesslike, the characters become increasingly thoughtful as the computer describes new horrors. Finally, when the computer designates that Katie has contracted radiation sickness, the governor and Benson realize that the world must get rid of its nuclear weapons before it's too late.

"How?" wonders the governor's cynical assistant. "We've been asking that question for forty years." Close-up on Benson: "Just because we don't have the answers doesn't mean we should avoid the question. Maybe some young person will hear us ask it, and in his desire for an answer he'll find what none of the rest of us have been able to." The governor: "One thing we'll always have is hope." Benson: "And if we approach the dilemma with humanity and morality, we may find the solution." Katie: "Dad? Would it be okay if I went outside? I just want to look at the stars . . . and walk in the grass . . . and breathe." The others leave, but Benson stays behind to turn off the computer. He says: "The war we have been conducting has been temporarily disconnected." Fade-out on a close-up of the computer and the echo of Benson's departing steps; no studio audience applause.

The sight of an actor as good as Guillaume struggling, with head bobs and hesitations and changes of cadence, to make his lines sound like human speech is a painful one. But it's a familiar pain in modern sitcoms. The speech, the silence, the patronizing play for childish idealism are parts of the form. So is the deft use of an "issue" without debate. No character takes a side, as the Bunkers would have. None advocates the nuclear freeze or SALT II or the dismantling of the military-industrial complex; none raises the threat of the USSR or the role of nuclear weapons in maintaining peace between the superpowers. In fact, by asking some "young person" to find a new answer, the show as much as declares that all current efforts to disarm are hopeless. While striking a liberal-sounding "nukes are bad for children" pose, it tacitly supports the status quo.

Benson debuted during a time when sitcoms in general were suffering from viewer boredom (an unprecedented twenty-nine new sitcoms premiered in 1978–79, but most of them flopped; two years later only ten were launched). More daring shows like *Love, Sidney* (Tony Randall as a homosexual) fared poorly. The survivors were the likes of *Facts of Life* and *House Calls* (a cute blending of work group and young couple comedy, about a surgeon and a hospital administrator). *Benson* survived, for seven years, and thrives in rerun. It laid the foundation for a Junger Witt–Thomas–Harris stable of sitcoms. From Maude's abortion to an alien clone stud to a black bureaucrat and a little white girl fretting about war: so the '70s became the '80s.

Who's the Boss? may be the most complete example of the sitcom synthesis. Created for an early-evening ABC time slot in 1984, it consistently dominated its competition by offering something for every big component of the sitcom audience. In standard form, it's built around an actor of proven sitcom appeal, Tony Danza, a boyishly charming, expansively emotional TV-Italian who played a naive athlete on *Taxi*. As the series begins, Tony Micelli (Danza), a widowed ex–baseball player with an eleven-year-old daughter, is seeking a new career. His daughter, Sam, is played by Alyssa Milano, who became one of the teen dreams of the decade, selling magazines, calendars, and her own *Teen Steam* exercise video (Milano is the kind of sitcom gold mine producers would kill for, having passed from little-girl cute to teenage sexy-cute to grown-up pretty with no gawky interludes). Tony answers an ad for a live-in housekeeper placed by a divorced advertising executive, Angela Bower. Hers is the sitcom house: the living room, the stairs, the couch facing the studio audience, the front door, the swinging door to the kitchen. After some comic awkwardness (Angela expected a woman), Tony gets the job and moves in.

Immediately we have the show's self-justification, its "relevant" original twist: sex role reversal. Tony is an old-fashioned macho guy, but he has to adopt a feminine role in serving Angela, Today's Woman. But this cuts too close to real American anxieties—to male fears that break up families and turn to violence—and so is never allowed to become a conflict. Angela remains self-doubting and deferential enough never to threaten Tony's manly authority, and Tony is so boyishly simple and secure that he never thinks about the ironies of his life. Sex roles are a hook, not an issue.

We also have a class conflict with vaguely ethnic overtones. Angela is Connecticut WASP, uptight and professional, progressive in matters like child rearing but personally conservative. Tony is blue-collar Brooklyn Italian-American, loose and gregarious, tradition-minded but easygoing. The palpable affection between the principals, however, keeps this as nothing more than a source of running, well-intentioned verbal digs.

Angela's eight-year-old, Jonathan, and Tony's kid, Samantha, instantly begin to function as TV brother and sister. Sam is streetwise and tomboyish, Jonathan sheltered and wide-eyed; she gets an open field for smart-alecky put-downs, and he countless opportunities for self-conscious cuteness. Since Angela is often away at her agency, Tony becomes a surrogate father to Jonathan, and since Angela can relate to Samantha's pubescent female concerns, she takes on a nonauthoritarian mother–big sister role. Though not spouses or even lovers, Tony and Angela become coparents in a patched-together family.

This is all very wholesome, too wholesome for "hip" '80s comedy. So Angela's divorced mother, Mona, turns out to be a neighbor and constant visitor. Played by Katherine Helmond, the sexy older wife from *Soap*, she functions as our horny geriatric. She dyes her hair bright red, dresses to emphasize her breasts, lusts after younger men, goes out on all-night dates. She encourages Angela to hire Tony in the first place because of his well-toned chest and buttocks, embarrassing her repressed daughter. To sex role reversal is thus added an equally hip generational reversal: old woman as swinger, young woman as prude. This acknowledges America's new conservativism, counterbalancing and neutralizing the progressivism of the gender switch.

Most of all, though, Mona provides a source of titillating sex jokes. Her one-liners are constant and vulgar, but because they come from the "harmless" figure of a postchildbearing woman with no remaining social function, they are prime time safe.

Many Mona lines are constructed—ostensibly—to sail over the heads of children, while in fact being fairly obvious; preteen audience members can thus congratulate themselves on their savvy as they join in the dirty laughter. (Jonathan breaks his leg and worries that it will handicap him forever. Tony says: "Hey, I broke my nose twice, and I can still smell." Sam, the teenage phone hound, adds: "I broke my finger, and I can still dial." Then Mona: "And I once broke my pelvis." She smiles smugly, the others—including Sam, who at twelve is "old enough"—roll their eyes in disgust, Jonathan stares blankly, and the studio audience roars. Tony finally breaks the tension: "And she can still dance!" But Mona won't let him pull her out of the gutter, smiling and purring, "All night long.")

When Mona's lewdness isn't providing sex jokes, childish innocence itself comes through. Jonathan asks questions laden with sexual implications, then stares wide-eyed as the adults react with leers and snickers. Tony makes sex-related jokes but only cutesy allusions to his past successes with the ladies, which mock masculine pride and remind us of his basic sensitivity. Two characters almost never initiate sexual humor: Angela, the household's breadwinner and foundation of respectability, and Sam, the boy-crazy, nubile woman-in-process. In shows where men hold equivalent positions the restrictions are shifted accordingly. Kirk Cameron, the teen idol of *Growing Pains*, can be as girl-crazy as he wants, but he never alludes to carnality per se, nor does his sage psychiatrist father. That's the job of his innocent tyke brother or, at times, his caustic mother. The more fertile, the more socially important the character, the more dangerous sex becomes.

Producers have found that they need no longer fly in the face of critics and protesters as in the days of *Soap* and *Three's Company*. They can now provide the same kind of mindless stimulation in a politically and socially neutral guise with the right conceptual gimmicks.

In addition to innuendo, the insult remains the other de rigueur source of sitcom one-liners. In *Who's the Boss?* Mona provides most of these, too; the with-it geriatric of '80s TV is never just horny but is sharp-tongued besides. Mona engages in a running assault on her daughter, reminding her sharply of her uneventful adolescence, her prolonged virginity, her ineptitude with men. Angela goes rigid as the lines strike home, but her only defense is a tense "Motherrrrr!" The others laugh affectionately.

This is another almost ubiquitous element of the genre: a house full of love but with one member who smart-asses the others or one relationship built on funny hostility (or, as in *Family Ties*, one member who is the designated jerk, the deserving target of everyone else's one-line zingers). But this apparent domestic viciousness lacks the punch of Fred and Lamont Sanford's or Maude and Walter Findlay's battles. The backdrop of reality has been carefully peeled away from behind contemporary sitcoms, so these insults feel like harmless wisecracks.

By numerous internal clues, today's sitcoms wink at us and remind us not to believe. The mere absurdity of a woman as sexually obsessed as Mona raising a daughter as virginal as Angela announces itself as a contrivance. (In *Family Ties* the jerk-victim Alex is made an acceptable target when he is presented as a cartoon of the young Reaganite, by far the least realistic member of the family.) This is not a dramatic failure: it's a way of disengaging comic hostility so that it can be endlessly recycled.

The conflicts that demand resolution are of a different nature. Sam wants to do some modeling for Angela's agency, but Tony has old-fashioned ideas about modeling; he has to learn to support his daughter in her maturation. Sam wants to impress some rich friends at school and lies about Tony's job, hurting his feelings; she has to learn to accept herself and her father for what they are. In one drama-heavy two-episode story, Angela's ex-husband wants custody of the boy, and Jonathan agrees because his father lives a fun life on the California coast. Angela clings and fights but finally has to learn to let go, to respect her son's wishes. Others have learning to do, too, however. Jonathan's father realizes he wants the boy as a prize and isn't really prepared to raise him. Jonathan, simultaneously, is shown by Sam how much his mother needs him. The father withdraws, Jonathan stays, and we end on hugs, hugs, hugs.

The easy solution has always been part of domestic sitcom structure, but a certain amount of compromise and sad, wise acceptance used to be a common part of such solutions. In the '80s the preference shifted toward solutions of convenience that left all parties perfectly content. This is the keynote of the '80s TV family: Everyone gets to be everything. Change is inevitable these days, but it is always for the best (Angela is fired, then forms her own agency and does splendidly; Tony and Angela become lovers, break up, then become better friends than ever). Tony and Angela, to borrow a phrase, are always better off than they were four years ago.

The joyous resolutions of sitcoms have always relied upon slight dramatic support, but even the Andersons' easy life lessons and Chico and the Man's hugs demanded stronger support than these '80s denouements. But then, the logical support for electing a president who promised to balance the budget and build up the military without raising taxes or seriously cutting social programs was pretty slight, too. A Hollywood actor paraded images of middle-class heartland contentment before our eyes, and we chose him resoundingly as our national representative. His opponents, meanwhile, settled on the dullest, most ideologically fatigued bureaucrats to run against him and his successor.

When postwar dreams fell short, an exhausting intellectual war followed. Radicals rejected the dreams, and liberals retreated to disparate issues. Only corporate conservatives, by masquerading as precorporate individualists, were able to present the same dreams in a form new enough, cynical enough, to enable the public to seize upon them again. Most of us, we were told, could still enjoy the technological consumer paradise we'd been promised, but now we had to accept that a certain large chunk of citizens would get screwed. The restored middle-class coalition would have to be based on mutual greed. The government would pretend to withdraw from its union with the corporate world, while, in fact, shifting its energies from aiding consumers to aiding producers. And from all this, we wished to believe, would come a kinder, gentler America.

Similarly, in sitcoms the optimistic consensus of the '50s collapsed and a period of intelligent conflict followed. Then, slowly, producers, networks, sponsors, and viewers worked together to sift out the elements the public could accept and recombine them into a compromised version of the same old consensual ideal. Now sitcoms accept broken and patched-together families, accept verbal violence, accept moral confusion and racial and generational rifts. Yet within all this, they hasten to reassure us, we will be happier than ever before. In sitcoms, as in life, we believe because we want to believe.

It's fitting, then, that the only show to cut across all viewer groups and become, briefly, a national fad featured that long-extinct standby of the domestic comedy: the harmonious middle-class nuclear family.

The nuclear family crept back into sitcoms in 1982 with *Family Ties*. In promoting the show, most attention was paid to the relevance gimmick of the premise, that two former counterculture types have spawned three very '80s children: money-hungry yuppie son; airhead consumer daughter; punky-precocious younger daughter. The creator, a self-proclaimed old hippie named Gary David Goldberg, presented it as a personal statement on our times. Once the novelty wore off, however, the emphasis of the stories shifted to the functioning of the family, which fitted most of the patterns of '80s sitcoms except that both parents had created and raised all three children. And there were no sassy black maids or horny old grandmothers thrown in. It was a smarter and subtler show than most, with a family dynamic enlivened by Michael J. Fox as the son, Alex. Through the interactions and reminiscences of parents and children, *Family Ties* gained a textural richness that drew in viewers who had little interest in its gimmick. It became a modest success.

Then, in 1984, came Bill Cosby's return to the screen. He had done only moderately well in a relevant schoolteacher show in the '60s, then flopped with a variety show in the '70s. He was, however, doing extremely well goofing around with little kids in a popular series of commercials, and his stand-up comedy act was gaining a big new following as he shifted his material toward fatherhood. NBC's Brandon Tartikoff saw him dishing out his warm, funny reflections on middle-class family life on *The Tonight Show* and knew he wanted to turn that into a sitcom.

The Cosby Show turned the comedian into Dr. Heathcliff Huxtable, an obstetrician with an office in the New York town house he shares with his lawyer wife, teenage son, and daughters of assorted ages. "Cliff" is warm, he is funny, he is hip to the ways of the kids, but he is also a traditionalist. He believes in parental authority, male primacy, old-fashioned sexual morals, monetary caution, respect for elders. He is proud of his position as part of the black middle class: He reminds his kids that everything they have is due to their grandfather's hard work as a Pullman porter; he insists that they go to old-guard black universities; he is an aficionado of Harlem Renaissance painting and modern jazz. Yet he is miles away from the sitcom blacks of the '70s, those jolly ghetto dwellers. Cliff is rich, richer than most TV whites.

Cosby made Cliff one of the most appealing characters on television. His bits of comic business with the kids, his rambling diatribes, his face-bending takes created humorous moments that transcended their setting. He and his writers avoided insult and innuendo; affectionate teasing between wife and husband was as tart as the dialogue got. Cosby and his supporting cast created a sense of abiding love—as opposed to the sentimental outpourings of other shows—that made their unshakable unity plausible.

The conflicts—and plots—were slight. Some were pure '50s suburban stuff; the Denise-makes-Theo-a-shirt episode was Wally-gives-Beaver-a-haircut redux. The writers played loosely with sitcom structure, running multiple plots back and forth, resolving them with a simple twist or a few words from Cliff. Much of the show's appeal, in fact, was its low-pressure, spontaneous storylines. Anything could happen: a Cosby routine; a guest appearance by Dizzy Gillespie; a troupe of toddlers in the living room. That it became a huge hit is no surprise.

A hollowness began to show, however. As the novelty of the comedy riffs began to wear off, the stories had to lean on character developments and life lessons. But the characters were too good, too lacking in areas of conflict, to be very interesting. And the life lessons failed to convince.

Like *Father Knows Best*, *Cosby* made its lessons easy to demonstrate by keeping its conflicts tiny and its characters virtually without vices. But *Cosby* lacked a cultural context to make its little world plausible or relevant. The Huxtables couldn't venture too far into contemporary urban America—or even the America of the TV imagination—without encountering problems too big for Cliff's little remarks to solve.

This was old wine in a new skin, and once we got used to the skin, we realized the wine had turned. Critics who had glowed about the show in the beginning began to assail it for falsity. Ratings began to drop. Then, through fatigue or worry or force of genre, it began to pick up all the traits of standard '80s sitcoms.

Cosby was a too easy exercise in wish fulfillment. It showed the nuclear family flowering in the heart of present-day New York. It showed a father exerting traditional control over his world without ever resorting to force or even anger. It showed blacks living the American dream, with no residual racial rage. In an episode timed to coincide with Martin Luther King, Jr.'s birthday, Cliff, his wife, and her parents reminisce about the 1963 March on Washington for the benefit of the kids. They talk about riding down to Washington in time for the speeches (evidently they didn't participate in the march itself) and glow about the feeling of togetherness and joy that filled the crowd. One waits for some mention of the substance of King's work or his dream, but they continue to talk about the feeling in the crowd, only the feeling. Like Ronald Reagan, Cliff Huxtable projected an appealing image of things as they should be, without much concern for how they were. *Cosby* was a feel-good show, and it faded as fewer and fewer Americans found the strength to feel good.

Cosby inspired a great renewal of interest in situation comedy (the year before it premiered, three of the top twenty-two shows were sitcoms; by its third year, the peak of its ratings, sitcoms accounted for twelve of twenty-two). But it only increased the volume, didn't change the form. A few more nuclear family shows popped up (*Growing Pains*, *Valerie*), and a few black shows (*Amen*, *227*), but the former were just like the usual recombinant family shows, and the latter were derivative of *The Jeffersons* more than of *Cosby*. As the '80s closed, the sitcom scene was about the same as when it opened.

There were *Kotter*-style kid ensembles, like *Head of the Class* with Howard Hesseman, who had gone from *WKRP* to marrying Ann Romano on *One Day at a Time* and had come out a reprocessed establishment-friendly hipster. There were nutty workplace comedies, like *Night Court*, which built sex jokes, gushing sentimentality, and family-style character dynamics into the milieu of *Barney Miller*.

There were plenty of women's sitcoms, with more adult-targeted scripting but the same elements. *Kate & Allie* was about two thirty-something divorcées with kids, combining their families. Susan Harris ventured back into more adult realms with *Golden Girls*, one of the best performed and most energetic of recent sitcoms, in which three women in their sixties and one sharp-tongued octogenarian support one another sentimentally, insult one another ceaselessly, and talk a great deal about sex. In *Designing Women*, a workplace-family-women's-racial combination, four women inclined toward bitchery and innuendo open their own business and hire a black assistant. The critical favorite is *Murphy Brown*, coming at the tail end of the decade and gaining popularity into the '90s, which stars Candice Bergen as a TV newscaster. Murphy is a ballsy version of Mary Richards, a living comment on changing sex roles; hers is a witty show, but its social viewpoint seems frozen, like the rest of the women's comedies, in the sex conflicts of the '70s.

Even the fantasy genre has been pulled into the same union of elements. Remembering the hits of the '60s, networks continued to try launching fantasy and gimmick sitcoms during the '70s: *Me and the Chimp*, *Nanny and the Professor*, *Far Out Space Nuts*, *Good Heavens*, *The Ghost Busters*. The only one to do well was Garry Marshall's *Mork and Mindy* in 1978–79, which succeeded because of comedian Robin Williams, in his first national exposure. When cheap sitcoms began to be produced directly for syndication, many of them (expecting juvenile audiences) opted for variations on *Bewitched* and *Mr. Ed*. But fantasy did not click on the networks.

Then, in 1986, soon after the huge success of the movie *E.T.*, actors Paul Fusco and Tom Patchett found a way to bring an extraterrestrial into a uniform '80s sitcom. *ALF* (for Alien Life Form) crashes his spaceship into a suburban garage and moves in with a nuclear family. Thereafter he camps in the kitchen (or adjoining living room), tries to understand the ways of earthlings, talks them through domestic problems, and makes smart-aleck remarks. (He doesn't, however, say much about sex; *ALF* is too obviously for kids.) He recombines Alex-the-jerk from *Family Ties*, Mona-the-heckler from *Who's the Boss?*, and the helpful black tykes from *Diff'rent Strokes* and *Webster*. In his own silly way he says what all the others do, in the new domestic coalition: that from our modern alienation, weirdness, and hostility will come a happy family.

Exceptions to the sitcom norm have not done very well in the last decade. In pursuit of an irreverent baby boomer audience, NBC tried a couple of screwball, media-oriented comedies in 1983 and 1984: *Buffalo Bill*, about a singularly unsympathetic talk show host, and *The Duck Factory*, about a failing animation studio. ABC later tried *Buffalo Bill's* star, Dabney Coleman, in a vehicle about an abrasive TV sports commentator, *The Slap Maxwell Story*. All of them won loyal followings, but small followings, and died quickly. The same happened to a later round of intelligent, laugh-trackless "dramedies": *Frank's Place*, a fresh, rich look at black urban culture, was canceled over the protests of its scarce but loyal fans; *The Days and Nights of Molly Dodd*, a self-consciously hip look at a single woman bouncing from job to job, hung on by the skin of its teeth.

One successful exception was *Newhart*, an absurd and ingenious show that played perversely with the middle-class fantasies of its times. Bob was an '80s man in this reworking of his '70s hit. No longer a representative of the therapeutic establishment, he became an author of do-it-yourself books who bought a country inn and ended up hosting a local TV talk show. Newhart played it all with flat befuddlement, just as he dealt with the bizarre hicks and '80s cultural stereotypes who passed through his inn and his show, a man adrift in a world of insane change. Yet even he, in '80s fashion, had a stable marriage to retreat to. (In the final moments of its final episode *Newhart* even acknowledged the falsity and self-consciousness of the modern sitcom: A dark bedroom; Bob wakes up in a sweat; he babbles to his wife about the strange dream he had, in which he ran a country inn and hosted a ridiculous talk show. Then his wife raises her head and tells him to go to sleep; the wife is Suzanne Pleshette, his costar from the original *Bob Newhart Show*.)

One sitcom has enjoyed great success by questioning the familial model of its rivals. Alone among network sitcoms, *Cheers* has suggested that the ways in which we bond in this atomized world may be more destructive than nurturing.

Cheers was created by James Burrows and the brothers Glen and Les Charles, some of the principal writers of *Taxi*, and it almost single-handedly continues the MTM ensemble style. Like MTM's best creations, it places multifaceted characters in a web of crisscrossing relationships, but this is a more barbed, more hostile ensemble than any of MTM's. The characters are the habitués of a Boston bar: white, middle-class, slouching gracelessly into middle age. Ex-baseball player Sam Malone runs the place; he's a recovering alcoholic and a self-advertising stud (after first meeting his attractive new employer, he says wistfully, "I wonder what she'll cook me for breakfast"). Unlike most sitcom studs, however, Sam actually scores with a procession of sexy women, and his braggadocio masks not a sensitive vulnerability but a crippling ineptness with emotional relations.

Sam's nemesis is his barmaid, Diane Chambers, a repressed collegiate intellectual who fancies herself a sensitive aesthete in a world of clods. Sam and Diane hate each other instantly. Unfortunately they also lust for each other instantly. They have nothing in common except sex, but that is enough to pull them into a seven-year hell of a romance, alternately pursuing and rejecting, breaking up and reconciling, insulting each other and falling into bed. ("Sam," says Diane, "that's the stupidest thing I ever heard." "I thought you weren't going to call me stupid now that we're being intimate." "No, I said I wasn't going to call you stupid *while* we were being intimate.")

The other residents of Cheers are similarly broken people: Carla, bitter and combative in her role as a barmaid but a sucker for crude, exploitative men; Coach, the senile bartender; Woody, his replacement, a stupid Iowa farm boy; Norm, a constant barfly, a likable but self-loathing refugee from a sterile marriage; Cliff, a figure of general ridicule, an inept pretender to intelligence and cocksmanship; and Frasier, a lonely, emotionally thwarted psychologist, hopelessly stuck on Diane.

The bar is a refuge for these cripples of the modern world. They bring in their pain from the wounds inflicted by the world outside, armor themselves with their assorted postures, and blow off their rage in an endless round of insults and practical jokes. Their time at the bar leaves them no better prepared for grappling with the real world, but as the theme song has it, "Sometimes you want to go where everybody knows your name . . . and they're always glad you came."

Cheers the bar and *Cheers* the show are clubhouses for the alienated. Most sitcoms try to make themselves accessible to any viewer who happens to show up in front of the tube, but *Cheers* pointedly woos those who feel isolated by intelligence from the TV-watching mainstream. The character of Diane provides for cultural references that let better-educated viewers know they are on friendly turf here. When Woody is ordered by his father to leave the corrupting influence of Boston and return to Iowa, the gang decides to make a home movie of themselves to convince the old man that they're good influences; Diane takes over the project and converts it into a pretentious film school exercise in "meaningful" imagery. After Woody's father sees the film, he becomes more insistent than ever. Sam asks Diane what she expected; her fancy imagery wouldn't mean anything to an old Iowa farmer. "Yeah," agrees Woody. "Besides, he said it was too derivative of Godard."

These references create a sense of audience solidarity, but they work the other side of the fence as well. Diane fits the classic sitcom mold of the intellectual as social failure, emotional cripple, sexual icebox, and pest. She is a better-written version of those countless nerdy pals and failed suitors on the mainstream comedies. (The references, too, are constructed so as to be universally comprehensible; even a viewer who knows nothing of cinematic clichés will recognize that Woody is using an incongruously fancy word and foreign name in quoting his father's "derivative of Godard.") Like most successful sitcoms, *Cheers* is a meeting area with doors on both sides of the cultural divide. While speaking to different audience members on different levels, it touches the nerves of loneliness in all of them.

Although the quality of its writing is far higher than that of most sitcoms, *Cheers* relies on the standard '80s patterns of insult humor and cartooned characters. It breaks from the pack with its central drama, the mutually destructive relationship of Sam and Diane. (Now that Shelley Long, who played Diane, has left the show, this has been replaced by a similar love-hate tension between Sam and his yuppette sometime boss.) Feelings of love, it says, cannot be trusted. The desire for union that, on other sitcoms, patches together so many happy unions of dissimilar people leaves Sam and Diane more damaged and alone than ever. As the '80s dragged on, as *The Cosby Show* faded, *Cheers* rose slowly, steadily from its initial modest ratings. In early 1991 it was still the most popular TV series of all.

Another alternative to the prime-time norm has been provided by the Fox Network, a collection of independent stations—mostly in urban markets—assembled by 20th Century-Fox and its corporate affiliates. With limited broadcasting hours, a citified audience, and lower advertising rates, Fox has aired high-impact, youth-oriented programs that defy some network truisms about what will and will not sell to a mass audience. Most of Fox's sitcoms have not done well, but *Married . . . with Children* immediately found an audience when it started in the summer of 1987.

Following Frank Sinatra's cheerful rendition of "Love and Marriage," we cut into the living room of the Bundy family: Al, a life-sick shoe salesman; Peggy, his bored, cheap, sex-hungry wife; Kelly, their idiot sexpot daughter; Bud, their bright but uncooperative son. They are fighting, sabotaging one another's small efforts at happiness, cutting the others down behind their backs. We realize quickly that "Love and Marriage" is an ironic counterpoint. These are people who don't love one another, or anything else for that matter. They are trapped in their lives by the consequences of long-ago moments of passion, by economic deprivation, by a resentful observance of convention.

Married takes the insult and sex humor of conventional sitcoms and pushes it out until it becomes a self-parody. The insults aren't witty because the characters are too stupid. The sex references aren't titillating because they've been stripped of all coyness. The characters are unlovably cynical (Kelly, after seeing her father reduced to a wreck by overwork: "Work is such a bummer. I'm glad I'm a pretty girl and I'll never have to worry about it"). The only triumphant resolution ever allowed to Al is the freedom to sit on the couch, spread his legs, and jam a hand under his pants waist; it's a pathetic gesture of privacy, but precisely because it's so small and sad, it brings huge whoops from the studio audience.

The creators of *Married* have said more than once that they see it as a reflection of working-class family life, a line so patronizing that one hopes they aren't serious. It seems, rather, to be a reflection of its fellow sitcoms, a revelation of the real desperation and disappointment that might lie behind the funny hostility of Alex's family, and Mona, and the Cheers gang. *Married* strips the sentiment from sitcoms and lets the bile pour out. It wins its audience over by shouting, in sitcom form, that sitcoms are a lie.

Married helped turn Fox into a workable concern. (It also seems to have emboldened the big three networks to shift into darker brands of humor. ABC's *Roseanne*, a vehicle for the abrasive comedienne Roseanne Barr, presents another slobby lower-middle-class family battling in the decaying heartland. *Roseanne* is more attached to its happy resolutions, but it does show the optimism of the genre beginning to crack.) Fox's one undisputed success, however, is also one of the great oddities of the form. Matt Groening, a cartoonist whose acute satiric eye made his *Life in Hell* comic strip a fixture in alternative newspapers, developed a series of animated cartoons for Fox's *Tracey Ullman Show* in 1987. These sharp one-minute spots illuminated painful moments in the life of an American family and became the hit of the series. In 1989

Groening and some of the most innovative people in the animation field (backed by James L. Brooks, one of the architects of *Mary Tyler Moore*) developed this family into the stars of a sharp, cynical cartoon sitcom, *The Simpsons*.

For the name of the Simpsons' town, Groening chose an ironic reference to *Father Knows Best*: Springfield. In a sharp bit of contrast, he took the family name from a character in Nathanael West's *Day of the Locust*, Homer Simpson, West's embodiment of emotionally crippled Protestant American manhood, destroying himself in his ignorant gropings toward contentment. Groening's Homer was less grotesque but not much nobler, a paunchy slob, not yet forty but already skidding downhill, slaving away in Springfield's nuclear power plant. His spirit has been worn to a dull sheen by existence. In one show he thinks he's terminally ill and, upon discovering that he isn't, vows to "live every moment to the fullest"; the episode ends on a long, long take of Homer sitting blank and alone, drinking beer and eating fried pork skins in front of the TV, from which issue the sounds of a bowling tournament.

His son, Bart, is the liveliest creation of the show: a bratty, skateboarding wise guy, brought to life by Groening's amazing ear for kid talk. Bart tries, at times, to obey the rules, please his father, succeed in school. But he is damned. His father sees him as either an extension of his own vanity or a threat to his fragile respect in the community. And school is a nightmare of boredom, useless information, and capricious justice. Bart withdraws defensively into a loser's pose, flamboyant and stupid; once he uses herbicide to spell "Bart" in forty-foot letters on the school lawn. His rebellion even spills beyond the show, into real life; Bart's face, with his line "underachiever and proud of it," briefly became the T-shirt image of choice among pubescent Americans, sparking the ire of school administrators nationwide.

The rest of the family is equally hopeless: mother Marge, with her tiny worldview; sister Lisa, the ineffective intellectual, using dead pop psych clichés to make sense of her sterile life; baby Maggie, agitatedly sucking her pacifier, staring wide-eyed and mute at the world as if in horror at what she's destined to become.

One brilliant episode, written by John Schwartzwelder, nearly allowed them to escape their patterns. Bart and Lisa are addicted to violent TV cartoons. Maggie, excited by them, hits Homer on the head with a hammer. Marge is driven to her first act of social commitment, organizing a parents' campaign against the cartoons. She finally wins, and Bart and Lisa lose their *Itchy and Scratchy*. They step outside. Other children step out at the same moment. They blink; they rub their eyes. They see the sun, the sky, the trees, as if for the first time. Beethoven's Pastoral Symphony swells. The kids run, play, swing, swim, laugh; for the first time in their stunted existences they are free of the consumer society's traps and they are *alive*.

It's an absurd, ironic, mock-glorious happy ending. And it's false. Before the episode ends, Marge discovers a problem: Her moral watch-dog group now wants to forbid Michelangelo's *David* from touring Springfield. She realizes that if great art is to be protected from censorship, then popular culture must be protected, too. She turns against the campaign, and it collapses. As the show ends, Bart and Lisa are back in the living room, laughing insanely at *Itchy and Scratchy*. Homer laughs with them. Maggie sucks madly on her pacifier. Marge sighs, quietly wondering if she's done the right thing.

A small point is made here about censorship, but its effectiveness is shattered by the deep, queasy ambivalence it evokes about the value of television, the impoverishment of life, the effectiveness of social action, and the nature of childhood in America. This is no true sitcom, to be entered vicariously. This is bitter, self-conscious, self-dissecting satire.

Satire, cartoons, and truly dark humor have always done poorly in prime time, but *The Simpsons* has been a huge hit. On top of the predictable audience of astute young adults it has piled a vast number of kids, who have made Bart a spokesman of bored, insolent resistance ("Don't have a cow, dude"). When Fox decided to pull the show out of its safe Sunday night slot and put it head to head with *The Cosby Show* on Thursday nights, many industry observers thought the upstart network was committing suicide. But in nearly every major urban market, the Simpsons clobbered the Huxtables.

The newest, most cutting sitcoms are about the sitcom form itself as much as about life. The sharpest humor on these shows is not character comedy but detached irony. *Seinfeld* follows the misadventures of a stand-up comic, cutting back and forth between snippets of his perfor-mances and related comedy plots. Even the newest network "dramedy" hit, *The Wonder Years*, distances itself from its viewers' emotions with the device of a wisecracking, self-conscious narration running through every scene. It purports to be the story of a boy's coming of age in the late 1960s, prime baby boom time. It is more the story of the unseen adult narrator, trying to make sense of his boyhood memories. His conclusion seems to be that those years of anxiety—personal and public—weren't so bad after all. Then, at least, he was fully alive and experience was immediate. Now he is only an observing eye, a smart-assing voice, without human context.

It may be that the sitcoms have lost their alchemical power to transform social reality into fictional reality, now that the fictional reality itself has been revealed as socially conscious calculation. The mask of illusion has been stripped away by creator and audience alike. The TV viewers who once stared into the screen hoping to see themselves mythologized now stare into it in order to see themselves staring back as social observers.

But this in itself may be a symptom of our social condition. So many of the idols of postwar corporate culture have proved false, but so little has taken their place. We see the structures of our society cracking under their own weight—schools, streets, hospitals, courts, families— and we seem to lack even the terms to discuss what to do about it. We can no longer define who we are or what life we want. We look at ourselves in the acute perceptivity of paralysis, in denial or in fear or in ironic amusement, waiting for some movement to prove we are alive.

When national or international circumstances force us to move as a society again, we will have to invent new comic models of behavior to guide and comfort ourselves. The situation comedy, that most responsive product of the corporate entertainment factory, may again be used to tell us which way we are moving—or which way the managers of corporate culture wish we would move.

Further Reading

Mention should first be made of a few sources, included in the lists below, which were particularly valuable in the writing of this book. Both the Brooks-Marsh *Complete Directory to Prime Time Network TV Shows* and the McNeil *Total Television* are indispensable references for anyone needing information on the casts, schedules, premises, and ratings of television programs. Rick Mitz's *Great TV Sitcom Book* proved to be my most consulted source on the histories of many shows, and Castleman and Podrazik's *Watching TV* was an essential overview of the history of the medium. Much of the information in Chapter 4 was drawn from Thomas Cripps's superb essay "*Amos 'n' Andy* and the Debate over American Racial Integration." David Marc's astute and witty *Comic Visions* contributed much to my knowledge of and perspective on *Father Knows Best, The Dick Van Dyke Show*, and *All in the Family*, and Ella Taylor's *Primetime Families* did the same for my understanding of the MTM sitcoms and *One Day at a Time*.

Further Reading on Television

Andrews, Bart. *The I Love Lucy Book*. Garden City: Doubleday, 1985.

Applebaum, Irwin. *The World According to Beaver*. New York: Bantam, 1983.

Arlen, Michael. "The Media Dramas of Norman Lear." *The View from Highway One: Essays on Television*. New York: Farrar, Straus, and Giroux, 1976.

Barnouw, Erik. *The Sponsor: Notes on a Modern Potentate*. New York: Oxford, 1978.

_____. *Tube of Plenty: The Evolution of American Television*. New York: Oxford, 1975.

Bathwick, Serafina. "*The Mary Tyler Moore Show:* Women at Home and at Work." In *MTM "Quality Television,"* edited by Jane Feuer, Paul Kerr, and Tise Vahimagi. London: British Film Institute, 1984.

Beck, Ken, and Jim Clark. *The Andy Griffith Show Book*. New York: St. Martin's, 1984.

Bedell, Sally. *Up the Tube: Primetime TV in the Silverman Years*. New York: Viking, 1981.

Berle, Milton, and Haskel Frankel. *Milton Berle: An Autobiography*. New York: Dell, 1974.

Blythe, Cheryl, and Susan Sackett. *Say Goodnight, Gracie*. New York: E. P. Dutton, 1986.

Broadcasting (May 15, 1961).

Brooks, Tim, and Earle Marsh. *The Complete Directory to Prime Time Network TV Shows, 1946–Present*. New York: Ballantine, 1988.

Brown, Les. *The New York Times Encyclopedia of Television*. New York: Times Books, 1977.

_____. *Television: The Business Behind the Box*. New York: Harvest, 1971.

Bryars, Chris. *The Real Mary Tyler Moore Show*. New York: Pinnacle, 1977.

Burns, George. *Gracie: A Love Story*. New York: Putnam, 1988.

_____, and David Rich. *All My Best Friends*. New York: Putnam, 1989.

Castleman, Harry, and Walter J. Podrazik. *Watching TV: Four Decades of American Television*. New York: McGraw-Hill, 1982.

Committee on Nationwide Television Audience Measurements. *TV Ratings Revisited*. New York, 1976.

Crescenti, Peter, and Bob Columbe. *The Official Honeymooners Treasury*. New York: Perigee, 1990.

Cripps, Thomas. "*Amos 'n' Andy* and the Debate over American Racial Integration." In *American History/American Television: Interpreting the Video Past*, edited by John E. O'Connor. New York: Frederick Ungar Publishing, 1983.

Doan, Richard K. "The Ratings, How Can They Be True?" *TV Guide* (March 18, 1967).

Eisner, Joel, and David Krinsky. *Television Comedy Series*. Winston-Salem: McFarland, 1984.

Filice, Steven and Joseph. *The Chico Marx Syndrome: Pro-Social Reconstruction and Compromise of Anarchic Comic Figures in American Commercial Entertainment*. Gilroy: Qwert Uiop, 1971.

Friedan, Betty. "Television and the Feminine Mystique." *TV Guide* (February 1, 1964).

Gans, Herbert. "The Creator-Audience Relationship in the Mass Media." In *Mass Culture: The Popular Arts in America*, edited by Bernard Rosenberg and David Manning White. Glencoe: Free Press, 1957.

Gitlin, Todd. *Inside Prime Time*. New York: Pantheon, 1985.

_____. *The Whole World Is Watching: Mass Media in the Making and the Unmaking of the New Left*. Berkeley: University of California, 1980.

Hey, Kenneth. "*Marty*: Aesthetics vs. Medium in Early Television Drama." In *American History/American Television*, loc. cit.

Hobson, Dick. "Who Watches What?" *TV Guide* (July 27, 1968).

Jacobs, Will, and Gerard Jones. *The Beaver Papers: The Story of the Lost Season*. New York: Crown, 1983.

Javna, John. *The Best of TV Sitcoms*. New York: Harmony, 1988.

_____. *Cult TV: A Viewer's Guide to the Shows America Can't Live Without*. New York: St. Martin's, 1985.

Kagan, Norman. "Amos 'n' Andy: Twenty Years Late or Two Decades Early?" *Journal of Popular Culture* 6 (Summer 1972).

Leonard, Sheldon. "Why Do You Laugh?" *TV Guide* (February 11, 1961).

McCrohan, Donna. *Archie, Edith, Mike, and Gloria*. New York: Workman, 1984.

_____. *The Honeymooners Companion: The Kramdens and Nortons Revisited*. New York: Workman, 1978.

Macdonald, Dwight. "A Theory of Mass Culture." *Diogenes* 3 (1953).

Macdonald, J. Fred. *Television and the Red Menace: The Video Road to Vietnam*. New York: Praeger, 1985.

McNeil, Alex. *Total Television: A Comprehensive Guide to Programming from 1948 to the President*. New York: Penguin, 1980.

Marc, David. *Comic Visions: Television Comedy and American Culture*. Boston: Unwin Hyman, 1989.

————. *Demographic Vistas: Television in American Culture*. Philadelphia: University of Pennsylvania, 1984.

Marx, H. L. *Television and Radio in American Life*. New York: H. W. Wilson, 1953.

Mayer, Martin. *How Good Are Television Ratings?* New York: Committee on Nationwide Television Audience Measurements, 1966.

Meroney, John. "Dwayne Hickman Is Dobie Gillis." *TV Gold* 3 (July 1986).

Meyersohn, Rolf B. "Social Research in Television." In *Mass Culture*, loc. cit.

Mitz, Rick. *The Great TV Sitcom Book*. New York: Perigee, 1988.

Morgan, Robin. "I Remember Me." In *TV Book: The Ultimate Television Book*, edited by Judy Fireman. New York: Workman, 1977.

National Association for Better Radio and Television. *Children's Radio and Television Programs*. Los Angeles: 1953.

Nelson, Ozzie. *Ozzie*. New York: Prentice-Hall, 1973.

Newcomb, Horace S., and Robert S. Alley. *The Producer's Medium: Conversations with Creators of American Television*. New York: Oxford, 1983.

Nye, Russel. *The Unembarrassed Muse: The Popular Arts in America*. New York: Dial Press, 1970.

O'Connor, John E. "Television and the Historian." In *American History/American Television*, loc. cit.

Paley, William S. *As It Happened*. New York: Doubleday, 1979.

Peary, Danny. "Remembering *Father Knows Best*." In *TV Book*, loc. cit.

"Red Channels," *Sponsor* (October 1951).

Reiss, David. *M*A*S*H: The Exclusive Inside Story of TV's Most Popular Show*. New York: Bobbs-Merrill, 1980.

Seldes, Gilbert. *The Great Audience*. New York: Viking, 1950.

Shulman, Arthur, and Roger Youman. *How Sweet It Was: Television, a Pictorial Commentary*. New York: Bonanza, 1966.

Spector, Bert. "A Clash of Cultures: The Smothers Brothers vs. CBS Television." In *American History/American Television*, loc. cit.

Sturcker, Frank. *Live TV*. Jefferson: McFarland, 1990.

Taylor, Ella. *Primetime Families: Television Culture in Postwar America*. Berkeley: University of California, 1989.

Taylor, John P. "The History of TV Technology," in *TV Book*, loc. cit.

Variety (October 4, 1950, July 4, 1951, January 28, 1953): various news items and editorials on *Amos 'n' Andy*.

Waldron, Vince. *Classic Sitcoms*. New York: Collier, 1983.

Weissman, Ginnie, and Coyne Steven Sanders. *The Dick Van Dyke Show*. New York: St. Martin's, 1983.

Wertheim, Arthur Frank. "The Rise and Fall of Milton Berle." In *American History/ American Television*, loc. cit.

Wilk, Max. *The Golden Age of Television: Notes from the Survivors*. New York: Delacorte, 1975.

Wit and Wisdom of Archie Bunker, The. New York: Popular Library, 1971.

On Radio

Alexander, H. B. "Negro Opinion Regarding *Amos 'n' Andy*." In *Sociology and Social Research* 16 (March 1932).

Allen, Fred. *Treadmill to Oblivion*. Boston: Little, Brown, 1954.

Andrews, Raymond. *The Last Radio Baby*. Atlanta: Peachtree, 1990.

Archer, Gleason L. *Big Business and Radio*. New York: American Historical Society, 1939.

Arnheim, Rudolph. "The World of the Daytime Serial." In *Radio Research*, edited by Paul F. Lazarsfeld and Frank K. Stanton. New York: Duell, Sloan and Pearce, 1943.

Benny, Jack, and Joan Benny. *Sunday Nights at Seven: The Jack Benny Story*. New York: Warner Books, 1990.

Burns, George. *Gracie: A Love Story*. New York: Putnam, 1988.

————, and David Rich. *All My Best Friends*. New York: Putnam, 1989.

Buxton, Frank, and Bill Owen. *The Big Broadcast, 1920–1950*. New York: Viking Press, 1972.

Fein, Irving. *Jack Benny*. New York: Putnam, 1976.

Gosden, Freeman F., and Charles J. Correll. *All About Amos 'n' Andy*. New York: Rand McNally, 1929.

Harmon, Jim, *The Great Radio Comedians*. Garden City: Doubleday, 1970.

Lazarsfeld, Paul F. *Radio and the Printed Page*. New York: Duell, Sloan and Pearce, 1940.

MacDonald, J. Fred. *Don't Touch That Dial: Radio Programming in American Life from 1920 to 1960*. Chicago: Nelson-Hall, 1979.

————. "Radio's Black Heritage: *Destination Freedom*." In *Phylon* 39 (March 1978).

Marquis, Alice Goldfarb. *Hopes and Ashes: The Birth of Modern Times, 1929–1939*. New York: Free Press, 1986.

Nelson, Ozzie. *Ozzie*. New York: Prentice-Hall, 1973.

Nye, Russel. *The Unembarrassed Muse: The Popular Arts in America*. New York: Dial Press, 1970.

Paley, William S. *As It Happened*. New York: Doubleday, 1979.

Settel, Irving. *A Pictorial History of Radio*. New York: Citadel Press, 1960.

Smith, Ralph Lewis. *A Study of the Professional Criticism of Broadcasting in the United States, 1920–1955*. New York: Arno, 1979.

Stamps, Charles Henry. *The Concept of the Mass Audience in American Broadcasting*. New York: Arno, 1959.

Stedman, Raymond William. *The Serials*. Norman: University of Oklahoma, 1970.

Stumpf, Charles K. *Ma Perkins, Little Orphan Annie, and Heigh Ho Silver!* New York: Carlton Press, 1971.

Wertheim, Arthur Frank. *Radio Comedy*. New York: Oxford, 1979.

Works on Other Topics Cited in This Book

Allen, Frederick Lewis. *Only Yesterday: An Informal History of the 1920's*. New York: Harper & Row, 1931.

Aronowitz, Stanley. *False Promises: The Shaping of American Class Consciousness*. New York: McGraw-Hill, 1973.

Bell, Daniel. *The End of Ideology*. New York: Collier, 1961.

Bennett, Lerone, Jr. *Before the Mayflower: A History of the Negro in America*. New York: Penguin Books, 1966.

Biskind, Peter. *Seeing Is Believing: How Hollywood Taught Us to Stop Worrying and Love the Fifties*. New York: Pantheon, 1983.

Bogle, Donald. *Toms, Coons, Mulattoes, Mammies & Bucks: An Interpretive History of Blacks in American Films*. New York: Viking Press, 1973.

Boorstin, Daniel J. *The Americans: The Democratic Experience*. New York: Random House, 1973.

————. "Welcome to the Consumption Community." *Fortune* (September 1967).

Brooks, Elston. *I've Heard Those Songs Before: The Weekly Top Ten Tunes for the Last Fifty Years*. New York: Morrow, 1981.

Burns, James MacGregor. *The Crosswinds of Freedom*. Vol. III, *The American Experiment*. New York: Alfred A. Knopf, 1989.

Davis, Kenneth C. *Two-Bit Culture: The Paperbacking of America*. Boston: Houghton Mifflin, 1984.

Gottfried, Martin. *A Theater Divided: The Postwar American Stage*. Boston: Little, Brown, 1967.

Hendra, Tony. *Going Too Far: The Rise of Sick, Gross, Black, Sophomoric, Weirdo, Pinko, Anarchist, Underground, Anti-Establishment Humor*. New York: Dolphin, 1987.

Hine, Thomas. *Populuxe: The Look and Life of America in the '50s and '60s*. New York: Alfred A. Knopf, 1987.

Jackson, Kenneth T. *Crabgrass Frontier: The Suburbanization of the United States*. New York: Oxford, 1985.

Jones, Landon Y. *Great Expectations: America and the Baby Boom Generation*. New York: Coward, McCann & Geoghegan, 1980.

Katz, Ephraim. *The Film Encyclopedia*. New York: Perigee, 1979.

Lasch, Christopher. *Haven in a Heartless World: The Family Besieged*. New York: Basic Books, 1979.

Leff, Leonard J., and Jerold L. Simmons. *The Dame in the Kimono: Hollywood, Censorship, and the Production Code from the 1920s to the 1960s*. New York: Grove Weidenfeld, 1990.

Lenburg, Jeff. *The Encyclopedia of Animated Cartoon Series*. New York: Da Capo, 1981.

Leuchtenberg, William. *A Troubled Feast: American Society Since 1945*. Boston: Little, Brown, 1973.

"The Lush Suburban Market." *Fortune* (November 1953).

Manchester, William. *The Glory and the Dream: A Narrative History of America, 1932–1972.* Boston: Little, Brown, 1974.

Olson, Sidney. "The Boom." *Fortune*, June 1946.

Rieff, Philip. *The Triumph of the Therapeutic: Uses of Faith After Freud.* New York: Harper & Row, 1968.

Schlesinger, Arthur, Jr. *The Vital Center.* London: Andre Deutsch, 1970.

Simon, George T. *The Big Bands.* New York: Schirmer, 1981.

Smith, Page. *Redeeming the Time.* Vol. VIII, *A People's History of the United States.* New York: McGraw-Hill, 1987.

Sullivan, Mark. *The Twenties.* Vol. VI, *Our Times.* New York: Charles Scribner's Sons, 1935.

Ward, Ed; Geoffrey Stokes; and Ken Tucker. *Rock of Ages: The Rolling Stone History of Rock and Roll.* Englewood Cliffs: Prentice-Hall, 1986.

Whyte, William H. *The Organization Man.* Garden City: Doubleday, 1957.

Index

Index